CRIMINAL FINA
2017

A Guide to the New Law

Hugo Daniel Lodge

The Law Society

Crown copyright material is reproduced with the permission of the Controller of Her Majesty's Stationery Office

ISBN-13: 978-1-78446-091-4

Published in 2017 by the Law Society
113 Chancery Lane, London WC2A 1PL

Typeset by Columns XML Design Ltd, Reading
Printed by CPI Antony Rowe, Chippenham, Wilts

FSC
www.fsc.org
MIX
Paper from
responsible sources
FSC® C013604

The paper used for the text pages of this book is FSC® certified. FSC (the Forest Stewardship Council®) is an international network to promote responsible management of the world's forests.

Dedicated to Helen Watson and HMS Indefatigable

CONTENTS

FOREWORD

The UK government felt action was necessary following the Panama Papers scandal – a leak of more than 11 million files that exposed how the world's fourth largest offshore law firm had protected its wealthy clients' assets in tax havens (particularly the British Virgin Islands).

The legislative response comes in Part 3 of the Criminal Finances Act (CFA) 2017, in the form of new criminal offences for a 'failure to prevent facilitation of tax evasion', in relation to both UK and foreign tax laws. These mirror the offence of 'failure of commercial organisations to prevent bribery' in s.7 of the Bribery Act 2010.

Another parallel with the Bribery Act 2010 is the use of a reverse burden of proof in its statutory defence of taking 'reasonable prevention measures'. In a further reversal of the usual burden, Part 1 of CFA 2017 amends the Proceeds of Crime Act regime to include draconian unexplained wealth orders (UWOs). There is a nod again to the Panama Papers in CFA 2017's focus on 'politically exposed persons' (12 national leaders were implicated among 143 politicians).

No doubt this legislation will place yet more burdens on businesses, especially in terms of risk assessment and promulgating appropriate procedures. Compliance departments will bear the brunt.

The complexity inherent in the foreign tax evasion facilitation offence may deter prosecutions, not least because different prosecuting authorities are tasked with investigating the various stages of each alleged foreign tax evasion.

I commend this book to you; it reads as a punchy and practical work which will assist practitioners and those charged with taking 'reasonable prevention measures'. The emphasis on interpretation of HMRC guidance will be particularly helpful to those seeking to grapple with their new responsibilities.

Rupert Bowers QC
Doughty Street Chambers
May 2017

ACKNOWLEDGEMENTS

I am very grateful to Rupert Bowers QC, my erstwhile leader and co-author, for writing the Foreword. Collingwood Thompson QC, Head of Chambers at 7BR, provided an excellent structure for this Guide and indeed a template for analysis of the new offences. Andrew McKenna is to be thanked for his part in an inspirational seminar, and his experience and common sense from the coalface of corporate criminal defence.

I have borrowed heavily from the HMRC's guidance on tackling tax evasion (updated October 2016). It strikes me that careful consideration of the 44 pages from HMRC explaining what they understand by the crucial four pages of the Criminal Finances Act (CFA) 2017, and more than a hint or two as to how HMRC intends to interpret it, will repay prosecutors, advisers, compliance departments and defenders alike. Thanks to HMRC for allowing us to reproduce the examples at **Appendix B**.

Thank you to HMSO for allowing us to reproduce CFA 2017 at **Appendix A**.

Any apparent references to Rumpole of the Bailey are in homage and gratitude to the late great Sir John Mortimer.

Finally (and most importantly) thanks to my patient wife, Sophie.

H. D. Lodge
Barrister, 7BR
May 2017

TABLE OF CASES

TABLE OF STATUTES

TABLE OF INTERNATIONAL INSTRUMENTS

ABBREVIATIONS

AFI	accredited financial investigator
AFN	account forfeiture notice
AFO	account freezing order
AML/CTF	anti-money laundering and counter-terrorism financing
BA 2010	Bribery Act 2010
CFA 2017	Criminal Finances Act 2017
CTFI	counter-terrorism financial investigator
DPA	deferred prosecution agreement
ECHR	European Convention on Human Rights
EEA	European Economic Area
EFTA	European Free Trade Association
EU	European Union
FATF	Financial Action Task Force
FCA	Financial Conduct Authority
JMLSG	Joint Money Laundering Steering Group
NCA	National Crime Agency
OECD	Organisation for Economic Co-operation and Development
PACE 1984	Police and Criminal Evidence Act 1984
PEP	politically exposed person
POCA 2002	Proceeds of Crime Act 2002
SAR	suspicious activity report
SFO	Serious Fraud Office
UN	United Nations
UWO	unexplained wealth order

1 BACKGROUND AND OVERVIEW OF THE CRIMINAL FINANCES ACT 2017

1.1 BACKGROUND: THE PANAMA PAPERS

The Panama Papers scandal, which eventually led to the passing of the Criminal Finances Act (CFA) 2017, began with the leaking of 11.5 million files from the law firm Mossack Fonseca, reputed to be the world's fourth largest offshore law firm. An anonymous source sent the records to a German newspaper, which shared them via the International Consortium of Investigative Journalists.

According to the *Guardian*:[1]

> The documents show the myriad ways in which the rich can exploit secretive offshore tax regimes. Twelve national leaders are among 143 politicians, their families and close associates from around the world known to have been using offshore tax havens.

The Panamanian firm acted as registered agent for more than 200,000 companies, approximately half of which were registered in the British Virgin Islands.

From the *Guardian* again:[2]

> Rather than dealing directly with company owners, Mossack Fonseca mostly acted on instructions from intermediaries, usually accountants, lawyers, banks and trust companies. In Europe, these offshore facilitators are concentrated in Switzerland, Jersey, Luxembourg and the United Kingdom.

This explains the focus of CFA 2017 on intermediaries. The draft guidance published by HMRC[3] states (at section 1.1):

> The Government believes that relevant bodies should be criminally liable where they fail to prevent those who act for, or on their behalf from criminally facilitating tax evasion … The new offence, however, does not radically alter *what* is criminal, it simply focuses on *who* is held to account for acts contrary to the current criminal law. It does this by focusing on the failure to prevent the crimes of those who act for or on behalf of a corporation, rather than trying to attribute criminal acts to that corporation.

---

[1] 'What are the Panama Papers? A guide to history's biggest data leak', *Guardian*, 5 April 2016.

[2] Ibid.

[3] *Government guidance for the corporate offence of failure to prevent the criminal facilitation of tax evasion* (Draft Government Guidance, updated October 2016) ('the HMRC guidance') – see **Appendix B** for extracts.

1.2   POLICY BACKGROUND: RISK-BASED APPROACH

According to the Explanatory Notes to CFA 2017 (at notes 9–11):

> The Government's strategic response to money laundering is founded upon a risk-based approach. [We have] set out the Government's intention to introduce new measures to make the UK a more hostile place for those seeking to move, hide or use the proceeds of crime or corruption or to evade sanctions. [We have] focused on three priorities: a more robust law enforcement response; reforming the supervisory regime; and increasing our international reach. All three are underpinned by the Government's commitment to building a new and powerful partnership with the private sector.

1.3   CONTEXT: DEFERRED PROSECUTION AGREEMENTS AND OTHER CORPORATE OFFENCES

CFA 2017 adds 'failure to prevent the facilitation of tax evasion' to the list of financial crimes for which deferred prosecution agreements (DPAs) can be deployed. That list already includes conspiracy to defraud and cheating the public revenue at common law, as well as more than 20 statutory offences running from the Theft Act 1968 up to and including the Bribery Act (BA) 2010.

Though available in a multitude of cases, the use of DPAs has been restricted to a handful of high profile cases. Tesco Stores Ltd will pay £235 million to settle investigations by the Serious Fraud Office (SFO) and Financial Conduct Authority (FCA) into false accounting which led to over-stated profits. Rolls-Royce recently agreed to pay £671 million to settle bribery allegations.

Followers of the SFO are urged not to consider the use of DPAs as the 'new normal'. At time of publication, investigations are reported to be ongoing in respect of Barclays, GSK and Airbus. The SFO has emphasised that early co-operation will maximise the scope for any DPA.

As for legislative next steps, an offence of corporate failure to prevent fraud is a likely companion to the bribery and tax evasion offences.

1.4   NOT THE 'CONTROLLING WILL OR MIND' TEST

The aim of CFA 2017 is to make prosecution of corporate bodies easier – it will no longer be necessary to make a finding of 'controlling will or mind'.

The perceived 'problems' with the current law are, from a prosecutorial standpoint, that: first, multi-national corporations frequently have no controlling central board and therefore no 'controlling mind'; and, second, if there is a danger of becoming identified as the controlling mind of a company, there is an incentive *not* to ask questions.

1.5   THE IDENTIFICATION PRINCIPLE AND MULTI-NATIONALS

At its core, the 'identification principle' holds that only the acts and knowledge/ intention of those individuals who represent the directing mind and will of the company can be imputed to the company itself. This test must be satisfied to prove the *mens rea* or mental element of any offence against a company. Historically, it has proven a high hurdle that has often prevented companies from being held liable for the acts of individuals who work with or for them.

In the case of *Lennard's Carrying Co Ltd* v. *Asiatic PetroleumCo Ltd* [1915] AC 705 it was held that in considering corporate criminal liability the mental element of an offence must be attributed to 'the directing mind and will of the corporation'.

The more recent leading decision of *Tesco Supermarkets Ltd* v. *Nattrass* [1971] 2 WLR 1166 considered the identification principle further, affirming *Lennard* and specifically endorsing the notion of the 'directing mind and will'. The *Tesco* case further defined the directing mind and will of a company as extending to the 'board of directors, the managing director and perhaps other superior officers of the company who carry out functions of management and speak and act as the company'. Critics, especially on the prosecution side, argue that this approach is artificial and inflexible.

Something of a departure from this line of authorities was seen in the Privy Council case of *Meridian Global Funds Management Asia Ltd* v. *Securities Commission* [1995] 2 AC 500. The Court apparently adopted a novel approach to the question of corporate criminal responsibility, seeking to avoid the rigid application of the identification principle. Rather, it was suggested that normal principles of interpretation should be applied to the particular statute which created the offence, to determine which individual's acts, knowledge or state of mind could be imputed to the body corporate.

This nuanced diversion was short-lived. More recent cases such as *R* v. *St Regis Paper Co Ltd* [2011] EWCA Crim 2527 have preferred a stricter application of the identification principle as propounded in the *Tesco* case.

The identification principle is a serious impediment to prosecuting multi-national corporations, especially those without a controlling central board.

1.6   'ASK NO QUESTIONS' CULTURE

HMRC guidance, again, states (at section 1.1):

> The common law method of criminal attribution may have acted as an incentive for the most senior members of an organisation to turn a blind eye to the criminal acts of its representatives in order to shield the relevant body from criminal liability … [it] … may also have acted as a disincentive to internal reporting of suspected illegal tax activity to the most senior members, who would be required to act upon such reporting since otherwise the corporate entity might be criminally liable.

The guidance points out the resulting inequality (at section 1.1):

> This also created an un-level playing field in comparison to smaller businesses where the Board of Directors will be more actively involved in the day-to-day activities of a business ...

1.7   RELEVANCE OF THE ACT

Compliance departments, solicitors, accountants, trustees, agents and other intermediaries will need to understand CFA 2017 because:

- They may be at risk of prosecution for the offence of 'corporate failure to prevent the facilitation of tax evasion' in the UK and abroad.
- Their corporate clients may be at risk and need advice on statutory defences (especially accountants, estate agents and other regulated professionals).
- Their private clients may be at risk from a new 'unexplained wealth order' (UWO) and this is extended to a foreigner who is a 'politically exposed person' (PEP).
- The Proceeds of Crime Act (POCA) 2002 and the Money Laundering Regulations 2007 are amended by CFA 2017, in particular the duties of solicitors to submit 'suspicious activity reports' (SARs).

1.8   INVESTIGATIONS

The HMRC guidance states (at section 1.5):

> The UK tax offence will be investigated by HMRC, with prosecutions brought by the Crown Prosecution Service (CPS), whilst the foreign tax offence will be investigated by the Serious Fraud Office (SFO) or National Crime Agency (NCA) and prosecutions will be brought by either the SFO or CPS.

This has the potential for confusion, especially as in some cases different agencies will investigate different stages of the offending. See the discussion of 'double criminality' at 3.4 below.

1.9   SCHEME OF THE ACT

Part 1 of CFA 2017 deals with the proceeds of crime, money laundering, civil recovery, enforcement powers and related offences, and creates a range of new powers for law enforcement agencies to request information and seize monies stored in bank accounts and mobile stores of value.

Unexplained wealth orders (relating, *inter alia*, to PEPs) are found in CFA 2017, Chapter 1 along with disclosure orders; all amending the POCA regime.

Chapter 2 of Part 1 amends POCA 2002 in relation to the power to extend the moratorium period following a 'suspicious activity report'.

Part 2 extends relevant money laundering and asset recovery powers to apply to investigations under the Terrorism Act 2000 as well as POCA 2002, detailed consideration of which is beyond the scope of this Guide, but which is dealt with in outline.

Part 3 is the main part of the new Act, creating two new corporate offences of failure to prevent facilitation of tax evasion. This is the main focus of **Chapters 1–5** of this Guide. The key concepts of 'B', a relevant body corporate, and 'P', an associated person, are defined in CFA 2017, s.44. Failing to prevent the facilitation of UK tax evasion is dealt with in s.45, and its foreign tax evasion counterpart appears at s.46. A statutory defence of 'reasonable prevention procedures' is contained within each section, and this will be considered in detail. The HMRC guidance is particularly helpful in anticipating how the new offences will be prosecuted.

Part 4 includes minor and consequential amendments to POCA 2002 and other enactments, and is dealt with in summary only in this Guide.

1.10   OVERHAUL OF THE POCA REGIME

In October 2015, the government published the 'National Risk Assessment for Money Laundering and Terrorist Financing'.[4] This identified a number of risks and areas which 'required a strengthening of the response to criminal finances'.

Further, the 'Action plan for anti-money laundering and counter-terrorist finance',[5] published in April 2016, sets out the action needed to 'strengthen the UK's anti-money laundering and terrorist financing regime'. CFA 2017 gives effect to key elements of the action plan.

The passage of the CFA 2017 into law took place in the run up to the snap General Election called for June 2017. While the Lords' timetable was *not* curtailed up to Committee, one wonders whether more consideration at Report stage, or indeed a more thorough examination of the Lords' amendments by the Commons, would have been desirable. Otherwise there is the appearance of a tide of legislation, transferring ever more draconian powers to agents of the State without resistance.

One of the rough and ready compromises which was agreed in the rush to pass the Act was in relation to beneficial ownership, into which there will now be a detailed report, by virtue of CFA 2017, s.9. Sir Humphrey Appleby[6] would be proud.

---

[4]   www.gov.uk/government/uploads/system/uploads/attachment_data/file/468210/UK_NRA_October_2015_final_web.pdf.

[5]   www.gov.uk/government/uploads/system/uploads/attachment_data/file/517992/6-2118-Action_Plan_for_Anti-Money_Laundering__web_.pdf.

[6]   Fictional Cabinet Secretary in the classic BBC series *Yes, Prime Minister*.

2 NEW OFFENCE: FAILING TO PREVENT THE FACILITATION OF UK TAX EVASION

2.1 NEW OFFENCES: REMOTENESS FROM TAX EVASION

It is worth pausing to note how remote the offences created by CFA 2017 are from any crime of tax evasion. The new offences are not tax evasion. They are not the facilitation of tax evasion. They are the failure to prevent facilitation of tax evasion.

Take an example, with characters and chronology. Horace has had a lean year at the criminal bar; the Timpson clan are all in prison; and his wife Hilda recently insisted upon taking a cruise, alone. Meanwhile, the price of his favourite claret, Chateau Fleet Street, has spiked this year.

Horace sits at his computer on 30 January 2018 and, with a little help from his son Nick, sends off a self-assessment tax return which is a work of utter fiction. Horace deliberately and considerably over-states his chambers and accounting expenses, thus reducing his apparent taxable profit. Horace is a taxpayer who is guilty of tax evasion (the precise offences are explored below). He has truly become a *criminal* barrister. He is *not*, however, caught by CFA 2017.

In our narrative, a week earlier, Ms Bean-Countah had provided Horace with an invoice and fee receipt for £10,000 for 'ad hoc accountancy', on the headed paper of ABC Accountants, while sat at her desk engaged in the yearly task of belatedly compiling Horace's accounts – a task she has undertaken for 30 years, never charging more than £500 for the work. Ms Bean-Countah is guilty of facilitating tax evasion in providing a fraudulent fee receipt (precise offence explored below). She, like Horace, is *not* caught by CFA 2017.

Three months earlier, Ms Bean-Countah's employer, ABC Accountants, received an email from HMRC reminding the firm of the need to comply with CFA 2017, and promptly flagged it as 'something very important we should one day take the time to do something about'. ABC Accountants did not embark upon a training programme for staff nor advertise its disdain for tax evasion on its website and intranet. ABC Accountants did nothing at all. The firm is remote from Horace and his expensive claret.

ABC Accountants *is* caught by CFA 2017. The firm has failed to prevent the facilitation of tax evasion.

2.2   FOUR-STAGE TEST FOR NEW OFFENCE

There is a basic structure in considering whether an offence has been committed, in relation to the UK tax evasion offence:

- **Stage one**: is there a criminal tax evasion by a taxpayer (either an individual or a legal entity) under existing law?
- **Stage two**: is there a criminal facilitation of the tax evasion by an 'associated person' of the relevant body who is acting in that capacity?
- **Stage three**: has the relevant body therefore failed to prevent its representative from committing the criminal facilitation act?
- **Stage four**: is there a defence available, where the relevant body has put in place 'reasonable prevention procedures' to prevent its associated persons from committing tax evasion?

2.3   KEY CONCEPTS

Two key concepts are used by CFA 2017 to achieve its purpose, namely that of:

- a relevant body (B); and
- a person (P) acting in the capacity of a person associated with a relevant body (B), i.e. an associated person.

This approach broadly mirrors that of BA 2010.

2.3.1   Definition of relevant body ('B')

Definitions are set out at CFA 2017, s.44.

A 'relevant body' is defined as a 'body corporate, or partnership (wherever incorporated or formed)' and includes a limited partnership.

The definition in CFA 2017 extends by s.44(3) to a 'firm or entity of a similar character formed under the law of a foreign country'.

As the HMRC guidance has it (at section 3.1):

> The UK tax offence can be committed by any relevant body regardless of whether it is established under UK law or the law of a foreign jurisdiction. This reflects the fact that under the current law any person can be guilty of a UK tax evasion offence contrary to UK law, regardless of their location, if they assist somebody to evade UK tax with the requisite guilty state of mind. The fact that an offence is committed against the UK is sufficient to give the criminal courts of the UK jurisdiction over the offence. Thus companies incorporated under the law of France or partnerships formed under German law would be capable of committing the offence … in relation to taxes owed to the UK.

Note that it is the 'relevant body' that is criminally liable under the Act – an individual natural person (as opposed to legal person) cannot commit an offence under s.44.

There is a difference in the definition of 'B' (the relevant body) in respect of the foreign tax offence: see **Chapter 3**. The above definition holds for the UK tax evasion offence.

This approach broadly mirrors the structural definitions of 'partnerships' and 'relevant commercial organisations' in BA 2010, s.7, though in the anti-bribery regime there is an additional requirement of nexus to the UK.

2.3.2   Definition of 'a person acting in the capacity of a person associated with a relevant body' ('P')

The definition of 'P' is provided in CFA 2017, s.44(4) and (5). 'P' acts in the capacity of a person associated with 'B' (the relevant body) if P is:

- an employee of B who is acting in the capacity of an employee;
- an agent of B (other than an employee) who is acting in the capacity of an agent; or
- any other person who performs services for and on behalf of B who is acting in the capacity of a person performing such services.

To identify an employee or agent is not likely to be problematic, but the third category, of a person providing services for or on behalf of the company, requires elaboration. As in BA 2010, the label put on the relationship by the parties is not decisive; whether P is performing services for or on behalf of B is to be determined by reference to 'all relevant circumstances' (CFA 2017, s.44(5)). This will be a question of fact, with which prosecutors and juries will need to wrestle as case law develops.

On any view, this is a deliberately broad definition and similar to the 'associated person' provisions in BA 2010, s.8, which include an employee, agent, subsidiary and 'a person who performs services for or on behalf of' the company. A slightly more elegant restatement of the definition in BA 2010 is provided in CFA 2017.

The HMRC guidance elaborates (at section 3.2):

> The associated person must commit the tax evasion facilitation offence in the capacity of an associated person. Where an employee criminally facilitates his or her partner's tax evasion in the course of their private life and as a 'frolic of their own', they commit a tax evasion facilitation offence but NOT in the capacity of person associated with their employer. Therefore in this situation the employer does not commit the new offence.

That much is made plain by the 'acting in the capacity of' employee, agent, etc., in each part of s.44 above, which by definition excludes liability for them acting in a personal capacity.

What of those who act for multiple relevant bodies? An introducer or agent third party may work with multiple organisations and may be performing tasks for several relevant bodies, or even be acting in a personal capacity, at any given time.

The HMRC guidance states (at section 3.2):

> [T]he new offence is only committed where a tax evasion facilitation offence is committed by a person acting in the capacity of a person associated to the relevant body, that is undertaken 'for or on behalf of' the relevant body. Any activity of the associated person beyond that relationship, for example for other relevant bodies or carried out in their private capacity would not lead to liability for the relevant body.

This broad definition has the effect that contractors and subcontractors may be 'associated' persons to the extent that they are performing services for or on behalf of a particular commercial organisation.

The HMRC guidance indicates (at section 3.2):

> The decision will always necessitate looking past the contractual form and considering all the relevant factors including contractual proximity, control, and benefit. The Government recognises that the relevant body will be able to operate greater levels of control and supervision over some categories of representatives (for example those directly employed) than over others (for example those ordinarily employed by another entity but providing services on a temporary basis). We recognise that the reasonableness of procedures should take account of the level of control, proximity and supervision the organisation is able to exercise over a particular person acting on its behalf.

This, with respect, confuses the 'stage two' question (i.e. to ask whether there has been a criminal facilitation of tax evasion by an 'associated person') with the 'stage four' question (i.e. is the defence of having 'reasonable prevention procedures' in place made out?).

This defence of 'reasonable prevention procedures' is explored in **Chapter 4**.

For now, the practical effect of this confusion is to say to a corporate body: 'You have more liability for the actions of your direct employees because you can and should exercise more control over them.' The converse is also true: 'You are less liable for temporary employees, because you can exercise less control over them.'

It would be better to separate the two stages and say:

> There is a low threshold for part of the stage two test which requires the government to establish that an individual was an 'associated person': you are liable for permanent employees and temps alike. But when it comes to the fourth stage, of asking whether there is an effective defence, the answer will depend on what was reasonable – and it is obvious that a company has more control (and therefore more liability for) the actions of an employee, as opposed to a temp.

What of the case in which there is a supply chain, involving several corporates? Or the case where a construction project is to be executed by a prime contractor with a series of subcontractors (and even a chain of sub-subcontractors)? A business is likely to exercise control over only its relationship with its contractual counterparty. Moreover, the corporate body may not even know the identity of those further down the chain than its immediate contractual counter-party.

According to the HMRC guidance (at section 3.2), in an effort to secure a trickle-down effect of due diligence:

> The principal way in which commercial organisations may decide to approach tax fraud risks which arise as a result of a supply chain is by employing the types of

anti-tax evasion facilitation procedures referred to elsewhere in this guidance (e.g. risk-based due diligence or the use of contract terms and conditions) in the relationship with their contractual counterparty, and by requesting that counterparty to adopt a similar approach with the next party in the chain.

Again, this is to make the same confusion as identified earlier, between identifying who is an associated person (at stage two) and determining whether or not there is a defence (at stage four of 'reasonable prevention procedures'). It would be clearer to say that in a chain situation the threshold is low at stage two, and so a corporate is liable for subcontractors acting on its behalf. However, remoteness and lack of control will come in at the stage when any defence is considered.

Although this approach is clearer, it may be objectionable on the grounds that it will be for the prosecution to prove there is an 'associated person' at stage two, whereas the defence must discharge the burden at stage four. Doubtless the courts will need to grapple with this ambiguity.

In terms of the four-stage test, a domino analogy may assist. Stage one is a domino which falls easily and frequently: a taxpayer evades paying tax. Stage two is a heavier domino some distance from the first: it must be established that there was a *criminal* facilitation of that evasion by an associated person of the relevant body. Stage three is a feather-weight domino, standing perilously close to the second, which will fall the instant it is brushed: the relevant body has failed to prevent its representative from committing the criminal facilitation act. Finally, the fourth domino is the defence of reasonable prevention measures: this stands or falls based on the nature and quality of the measures in place.

Here, we are at stage three, and strict vicarious liability is a domino which tumbles automatically. The HMRC guidance (at section 1.3) is blunt:

> As the offence is a *strict liability* offence, if stages one and two offences are committed then the relevant body will have committed the new corporate offence unless it can show it has put in place reasonable preventative procedures.

2.4   OVERVIEW OF OFFENCES IN RELATION TO A 'RELEVANT BODY'

CFA 2017 creates offences of strict liability, subject to a statutory defence. The burden of proving the defence will lie on the relevant body, and case law suggests the standard will be the balance of probabilities.

There are two 'facilitation' offences:

■ Facilitation of UK tax evasion offences (s.45), which are the focus of this chapter.
■ Facilitation of foreign tax evasion offences (s.46), dealt with in **Chapter 3**.

The basic elements that the prosecution has to prove are similar for both offences. It is controversial that foreign offences are included as this undermines the convention that the UK does not help to enforce demands made by foreign tax authorities.

2.5   UK TAX EVASION OFFENCE: 'FAILURE TO PREVENT FACILITATION OF UK TAX EVASION OFFENCES'

By CFA 2017, s.45(1), where B is the relevant corporate body and P is the associated person, B is guilty of an offence if P commits a UK tax evasion facilitation offence when acting in the capacity of a person associated with B.

This offence therefore simply requires two elements:

- criminal evasion of tax by a taxpayer;
- criminal facilitation of that tax evasion offence by P when acting in the capacity of a person associated with B.

The Explanatory Notes to CFA 2017 make it plain that the conduct must be criminal, so negligent mistake would not suffice.

2.5.1   Definition of offence at stage one: the taxpayer

What must be proved in relation to the tax evasion by the legal or natural person at the first stage?

'UK tax evasion offence' means an offence of cheating the revenue or an offence under the law of any part of the UK, consisting of being knowingly concerned in, or taking steps with a view to, the fraudulent evasion of tax.

'Tax' means a tax imposed under any part of the law of the UK, including National Insurance contributions. This would also include VAT. The most likely offence will be cheating the revenue.

There are a range of statutory offences which consist of 'fraudulently evading' certain taxes, e.g. fraudulently evading VAT, contrary to the Value Added Tax Act 1994, s.72, or fraudulently evading income tax, contrary to the Taxes Management Act 1970, s.106A. These provisions make it an offence to dishonestly 'take steps with a view to' or 'be knowingly concerned in' the evasion of the particular tax. So, for these offences to be committed it is not necessary that any tax actually be successfully evaded.

It is not necessary that there be a *conviction* for a UK tax evasion offence – but such an offence would have to be proved to the criminal standard as a relevant fact in the case brought against 'B', the relevant corporate body.

The HMRC guidance explains (at section 1.3) why it may well be the case that there is no conviction at stage one:

> For example, a taxpayer may voluntarily come forward and make a full and honest disclosure to HMRC of their actions and it may not be in the interests of justice to criminally prosecute that individual.

As to the *mens rea* or mental element required at stage one, the HMRC guidance (at section 1.3) again provides a useful context to the statute:

> For the corporate offence to be committed there must first be a *criminal offence* at the *taxpayer level* (stage one). Non-compliance, falling short of fraud, at the taxpayer level will not result in the corporate offence being committed. This offence only relates to the failure to prevent the facilitation of fraud. Any fraudulent activity that intends to divert funds from the public revenue constitutes the common law offence of cheating the public revenue.

This is a useful indication for those defending: plainly it is a defence to any crime to assert that the prosecution is not able to prove a fact in issue to the requisite standard. In the example at the start of this chapter, if Horace had merely been negligent, perhaps after a good lunch, in under-reporting his income (rather than deliberately relying upon a false expense document), and Ms Bean-Countah then relied upon this in drafting his tax return, then her employer ABC Accountants would not be liable under CFA 2017. There is non-compliance short of fraud at stage one.

2.5.2   Definition of offence at stage two: the 'associated person'

What must be proved in relation to the *facilitation* of the tax evasion at the second stage?

The UK tax evasion facilitation offence is also defined, at CFA 2017, s.45(5) (committed by 'P'), and consists of different activities:

■ being knowingly concerned in, or taking steps with a view to, the fraudulent evasion of tax by another person;
■ aiding, abetting, counselling or procuring the commission of a UK tax evasion offence.

It is a crime, notwithstanding CFA 2017, to deliberately and dishonestly facilitate the commission of revenue fraud by another person. It is also an offence for a person to be knowingly concerned in, or take steps with a view to, another person fraudulently evading tax that they owe. It is also a crime, under the usual principles of accessorial liability, to aid and abet another person in committing any revenue fraud.

The rationale of CFA 2017 is that if a professional intermediary, such as a banker, accountant or lawyer, deliberately and dishonestly facilitates the commission of revenue fraud by a client, then that professional also commits a crime. The fact that the crime is committed during the course of his or her work is obviously no defence for that person.

Again, the HMRC guidance (at section 1.3) is helpful in clarifying the *mens rea* required:

> For the corporate offence to be committed there must be *criminal facilitation* of the taxpayer evasion *by an associated person* (stage two). The associated person must deliberately and dishonestly take action to facilitate the taxpayer-level evasion. If the associated person is only proved to have accidentally, ignorantly or even negligently facilitated the tax evasion offence then the new offence is not committed by the relevant body.

In contrast to the bribery scheme of BA 2010, where there is a UK tax evasion facilitation offence (the stage two test) it does not make a difference whether 'B', the relevant corporate body, is based in the UK or established under the law of another country, nor whether 'P', the associated person who performs the criminal act of facilitation, is in the UK or abroad. In such cases the new offence will have been committed and can be tried by the courts of the UK.

2.5.3   Definition of offence at stage three

As discussed above, CFA 2017, s.45(1) creates a strict vicarious liability offence, subject to a statutory defence at stage four.

2.5.4   The defence of 'prevention procedures' at stage four: an outline

If elements (1) and (2) are proved, B is guilty unless B can prove that at the time the UK tax facilitation offence was committed:

- B had such prevention procedures in place as it was reasonable in all the circumstances to expect B to have; or
- it was not reasonable in all the circumstances to expect B to have any prevention procedures in place.

The defences are considered in detail in **Chapter 4**. It is not a 'one size fits all' approach and so what is reasonable will depend on many factors, e.g. the size of the corporate body.

The defences mirror those of BA 2010, s.7(2), where, in relation to the offence of failure of commercial organisations to prevent bribery, it is a 'defence for [B] to prove that [B] had in place adequate procedures designed to prevent persons associated with [B] from undertaking such conduct'.

As Lord Woolf said in response to that corporate bribery offence:

> The Act is also unusual for criminal legislation … it reverses the burden of proof (which usually constitutes a contravention of Article 6 of the ECHR, though here it is justifiable because the facts are usually peculiarly within the knowledge of the proposed defendants).

2.6   EXTRA-TERRITORIALITY

2.6.1   The test

Extra-territoriality applies to both the UK and foreign offences in CFA 2017, as per s.48 which provides that it is 'immaterial' for the purposes of ss.45 or 46 (save to the extent that the nexus for the foreign tax evasion facilitator offence is set out in s.46(2)) whether:

- any relevant conduct of a relevant body; or
- any conduct which constitutes part of a relevant UK tax evasion offence, or foreign tax evasion facilitation; or
- any conduct which constitutes part of a relevant UK tax evasion offence or foreign tax evasion offence

took place in the UK or elsewhere.

2.6.2   Example of extra-territoriality

The above test casts the net very wide. It certainly covers the situation of a foreign company with a taxpayer filing in Germany, evading tax in the UK.

An inevitable consequence is that a foreign relevant body with no connection to the UK other than using an agent in the UK can commit the s.45 UK tax evasion offence. Even if it gives advice entirely outside the UK to facilitate a taxpayer evading tax within the UK, it can still be liable.

Extra-territoriality stretches to include the situation where an agent flies into the Channel Islands for a meeting, talks to a trustee based there and facilitates an offence. In this situation, the relevant corporate body could be liable.

2.7   BRANCHES

Branches of an organisation are discussed in more detail in the next chapter on foreign tax evasion, but may also be relevant to the UK tax evasion offence. For now, the HMRC guidance (at section 3.3) is clear enough: 'The law does not view branches as separate legal entities (in the way that subsidiaries are): all the branches of a relevant body comprise a single legal entity.'

A short example involving branches follows at the end of this chapter.

2.8   JOINT VENTURES

Joint ventures vary in their structures, sometimes operating through a separate legal entity, but at other times through contractual arrangements.

In the case of a joint venture operating through a separate legal entity, where a tax fraud has been facilitated by the entity this may lead to liability for a participant in the joint venture if the entity is performing services on behalf of that participant.

However, the existence of a joint venture entity will not of itself mean that it is automatically 'associated' with any of the participants at stage two. The facilitation of tax evasion by an employee or associated person of the joint venture entity will therefore not always trigger liability for participants in the joint venture simply by virtue of them being connected through their investment in or ownership of the joint venture. The question will always remain whether or not the joint venture entity is acting for or on behalf of the participant.

According to the HMRC guidance (at section 3.4):

> The degree of control that a participant has over the arrangement (for example where the joint venture is conducted through a contractual arrangement) is likely to be one of the 'relevant circumstances' that would be taken into account in deciding whether a person who facilitated tax evasion in the conduct of the joint venture business was 'performing services for or on behalf of' a participant in that arrangement.

The question is always whether the person performing the facilitating act is providing a service for or on behalf of the relevant body. A corporate entity set up to deliver a joint venture may perform services for or on behalf of the participants in that venture and when it does, it will be an associated person

2.9   REFERRALS

Where a relevant body makes an introduction in good faith and believes that the external service provider is unlikely to be involved in facilitating tax evasion, and also steps away from the transaction entirely, the company which makes the referral is unlikely to fall within the scope of the new offence.

The HMRC guidance (at section 3.5) explains:

> This is because in this instance the company to which the referral is made does not provide services for or on behalf of the referrer, it [is] a 'vanilla' referral, not a case of sub-contracting.

However, this would not be the case where the introducing party is aware that either the motive of the client involved is to evade tax or that the external provider to whom a client has been introduced is likely to be involved in facilitating tax evasion. This dishonest referral would itself constitute a deliberate action to facilitate tax evasion at the taxpayer level.

2.10   EXAMPLE OF THE FOUR-STAGE TEST APPLIED TO UK TAX EVASION

Inevitably this example requires some consideration of the prevention procedures defence set out in **Chapter 4**, but appears here to show an application of the four-stage approach, with detailed reference to CFA 2017 and substantive tax evasion offences included.

■   **Stage one: taxpayer**
    Gordon has deliberately and dishonestly failed to declare his taxable income (as an independent arms dealer) and assets to HMRC. He intends not paying the tax that he legally owes, consoling himself that his vast personal expenditure may yet kick-start the economy. He has committed the offence of being

knowingly concerned in the fraudulent evasion of income tax contrary to the Taxes Management Act 1970, s.106A.

- **Stage two: employees at a bank in Panama**
Gordon needed help concealing from HMRC his ownership of an ocean-going yacht, and a multi-million pound stream of income (from his other work as an independent estate agent). To this end, employees working at Brown Bank's Panamanian Head Office have deliberately and dishonestly provided services to Gordon to help him conceal his taxable income and assets, with the purpose of assisting him evade his UK income tax liability. The *employees* at Brown Bank are therefore guilty of being knowingly concerned in the fraudulent evasion of income tax, an offence contrary to the Taxes Management Act 1970, s.106A.

- **Stage three: the bank**
Brown Bank is *not* guilty of the Taxes Management Act 1970, s.106A offence. It is not possible for prosecutors to attribute the requisite *mens rea*/mental element to Brown Bank in respect of the criminal act committed by staff at its head office, because none of the individuals considered to be the bank's directing mind and will, typically the board of directors, were involved in the offence.

    Applying the CFA 2017, s.44 test, the associated person (an employee at head office in Panama) was providing services (advice to a client) for or on behalf of Brown Bank when it committed the tax evasion facilitation offence.

    Brown Bank is liable under s.45 for having failed to prevent its associated persons operating in its Panamanian head office from criminally facilitating Gordon's UK income tax liability, unless it is able to establish the reasonable prevention procedures defence.

- **Stage four: is there a defence?**
Assume that Brown Bank has implemented training in relation to preventing the facilitation of tax evasion but only for a small number of London-based staff.

    Brown Bank cannot successfully run a reasonable prevention procedures defence. It is plainly *no* defence for Brown Bank to claim that it should not be expected to put in place prevention procedures designed to prevent its head office staff from being complicit in fraud resulting in a tax loss outside of Panama.

3 FOREIGN TAX EVASION

3.1 'FAILURE TO PREVENT FACILITATION OF FOREIGN TAX EVASION'

The previous chapter dealt with the first new offence, failing to prevent the facilitation of *UK* tax evasion.

This chapter deals with the second new offence, failing to prevent the facilitation of *foreign* tax evasion, created by CFA 2017, s.46.

The basic definitions as to the 'meaning of the relevant body and acting in the capacity of an associated person' hold good from s.44, just as they did in relation to UK tax evasion.

The foreign tax evasion offence requires the same basic elements as before but with important variations in relation to nexus to the UK and 'double criminality'. So, B is guilty of the foreign tax offence if P commits a foreign tax evasion facilitation offence when acting in the capacity of a person associated with B *and* any of the conditions in s.46(2) are satisfied – which relate to nexus to the UK.

There are requirements of 'double criminality' imposed by s.46(6) in relation to both the evasion and the facilitation, discussed at 3.4 below.

3.2 FOUR-STAGE TEST FOR FOREIGN TAX OFFENCE

Therefore, as with the UK tax offence, the same basic structure applies to consideration of whether an offence has been committed, with modifications.

- **Stage one**: has there been a criminal *evasion* of a foreign tax by a taxpayer? With the additional requirement of 'double criminality', i.e. would the evasion be criminal in the UK?
- **Stage two**: has there been a criminal *facilitation* of that tax evasion by an associated person 'P' of a relevant corporate body 'B'? Stage two is modified because the relevant corporate body must have a nexus to the UK in order to be liable for the foreign tax offence. Also, the requirement for 'double criminality' applies at this facilitation stage, i.e. would the facilitation of the evasion have been criminal in the UK?

- **Stage three**: no modifications to the previous test; as with the UK offence this part is straightforward. If stages one and two are satisfied, liability of the corporate body is strict and vicarious. It is automatically guilty unless there is a defence under stage four.
- **Stage four**: no modifications; as with the UK offence, can the relevant corporate body rely on the reasonable prevention procedures defence?

3.3   REQUIREMENTS OF FOREIGN TAX EVASION AND FACILITATION

Again, as with the UK offence, a *conviction* in the foreign jurisdiction is not necessary.

Consent of the Director of Public Prosecutions or the Director of the SFO is needed to institute proceedings for this offence.

Foreign tax *evasion* (at our stage one) is defined at s.46(5) as amounting to an offence and being a 'breach of a duty relating to a tax imposed under the law of that country'.

Foreign tax *facilitation* (at our stage two) is defined at s.46(6) as conduct amounting to an offence which 'relates to the commission by another person of a foreign tax evasion offence under that law'.

3.4   DOUBLE CRIMINALITY

3.4.1   Overview

Another important requirement for this offence is dual criminality; both the actions of the taxpayer and the facilitator ('P') must be an offence in the UK of tax evasion as well as equivalent offences in the jurisdiction concerned.

This will create complexities and a requirement for evidence of foreign law, which is a question of fact before UK criminal courts.

3.4.2   Both at stage one and stage two

At stage one, the foreign jurisdiction must have an equivalent tax evasion offence at the taxpayer level. It must be proved that the actions carried out by the taxpayer would constitute a crime if they took place in the UK. This equivalent crime is specified in CFA 2017 as being the UK offence of being knowingly concerned in or taking steps with a view to the fraudulent evasion of the tax.

Therefore, the corporate offence cannot be committed where the acts of the associated person would not be criminal if committed in the UK, regardless of the position under the overseas criminal law.

At stage two, the foreign jurisdiction must also have an equivalent offence covering the associated person's criminal act of facilitation, and it must be proven that the actions of the associated person would constitute a crime had they taken place in the UK.

Section 46(6)(c) refers back to s.45(5) and (6) for definitions of equivalent offences.

On a positive note, the HMRC guidance (at section 1.3) gives a helpful distinction as to what will not satisfy the double criminality test at both stages one and two:

> Even where the foreign criminal law renders inadvertent or negligent facilitation of tax evasion criminal, the corporate offence will not be committed because the requirement for dual criminality will not be met – UK law renders only deliberate and dishonest acts of facilitation criminal.

To give a new example: Horace makes the rash decision to set up a chambers' annex in the Basque-country enclave of Vin-et-pud, thinking 'Portia told me two years ago that EU law is a boom area'. After too much sun and refreshment one day, Horace *negligently* fails to declare his local income to the local authorities in a tax return, which is a crime in Vin-et-pud. His accountant Ms Bean-Countah and her firm ABC Accountants in London need not fear any consequences under CFA 2017, as the requirement of dual criminality at stage one is not met.

3.4.3   Criticism and challenge

There is scope for confusion here, as different agencies will investigate distinct parts of the alleged offending behaviour.

The HMRC guidance (at section 1.5) states:

> The UK tax offence will be investigated by HMRC, with prosecutions brought by the Crown Prosecution Service (CPS), whilst the foreign tax offence will be investigated by the Serious Fraud Office (SFO) or National Crime Agency (NCA) and prosecutions will be brought by either the SFO or CPS.

Further, this part of the legislation undermines the international convention that the courts of one nation will not sit in judgment on the laws of another (although there have long been exceptions to this general rule in the extradition regimes).

Recent statute has made clear that in extradition cases under the Extradition Act 2003, Part 1, in all cases where part of the conduct took place in the UK, that conduct must be criminalised in the UK for extradition to be possible. There will be much scope for arguing accessorial liability, which will vary from country to country and will not have obvious equivalence. As foreign law will be a question of fact to be decided on the basis of expert evidence, this will lead to further dispute and litigation.

There is a body of extradition case law, a detailed consideration of which is beyond the scope of this Guide. Suffice it to say that double criminality becomes more complex, and therefore arguable, when the conduct relied upon takes place partly within the UK and partly without. An obvious example is a company based in the

UK using an email server abroad to send a fraudulent invoice. Another is a customer in the UK concealing funds via an online betting site in the Republic of Ireland.

There is further case law on the extent to which the foreign offence must be analogous with the UK offence.

Norris v. *United States* [2010] UKSC 9 holds that it is unnecessary for there to be exact correspondence between the ingredients of the foreign offence and those of the UK offence which would be disclosed had the conduct occurred here. As for the doctrine of 'transposition', the UK court is concerned with the essentials of the conduct relied upon. It does not need to be concerned with:

■   the peculiarities of the foreign offence;
■   the position of victims or other players in the requesting country; or
■   institutional settings in the requesting country.

So, in our example in **3.4.2** above, if Horace has *deliberately and fraudulently* misrepresented his income to the local tax authority in Vin-et-pud and he was criminally facilitated in that by Ms Bean-Countah, on prosecution of her employer ABC Accountants it would not be open to the firm to argue that the system in Vin-et-pud was not precisely the same as the tax regime in the UK administered by HMRC. So it would not matter if it was a town council abroad enforcing a local income tax, the equivalent of which would be applied nationally by HMRC in the UK.

It may be that the courts will not need to follow the extradition authorities on this point, given the flexibility afforded by CFA 2017, s.46(6)(c).

A fully worked through example involving the question of 'dual criminality' is set out at **Appendix B**.

3.5   NEXUS TO THE UK

For the foreign tax offence to be committed, consideration must be given at stage two to whether or not the relevant corporate body 'B' has a sufficient connection to the UK.

Those UK nexus conditions are:

■   that B is a body incorporated, or a partnership formed, under the law of any part of the UK; or
■   that B carried on business or part of a business in the UK (which includes 'undertakings'); or
■   that any conduct constituting part of the foreign tax evasion facilitation offence took place in the UK.

Plainly the statute here demands a sufficient nexus to the UK. The alarming part of this provision is for a foreign bank with a single branch in the UK. This is still a very wide definition.

The HMRC guidance (at section 3.1) confirms the ambit of the definition of corporate 'B' with some useful examples.

> However, the foreign tax offence can only be committed:
>
> ■ by a relevant body incorporated under UK law, for example a limited company incorporated under UK law;
> ■ by a relevant body carrying on a business or other undertaking from within the UK, for example a company incorporated under the law of France but operating from an office in Manchester; or
> ■ by a relevant body whose associated person is located within the UK at the time of the act that facilitates the evasion of the overseas tax, for example a company incorporated under German law whose employee helps another person to commit a foreign tax evasion offence whilst in London.
>
> These bodies, described above, are considered to be sufficiently connected to the UK and therefore should be subject to the new foreign tax offence.

This definition would appear to cover any foreign bank with even a single London branch. This would also apply to the situation where the bank itself does not conduct business in the UK but where 'P' acting on behalf of the bank facilitates the foreign tax evasion offence from the UK.

3.6 EXTRA-TERRITORIALITY: THE TEST FOR FOREIGN TAX EVASION

It is worth re-iterating briefly: the principle of extra-territoriality applies to both the UK and foreign offences in CFA 2017, as per s.48, which provides that it is 'immaterial' for the purposes of ss.45 or 46 (save to the extent that the nexus for the foreign tax evasion facilitator offence is set out in s.46(2)) whether:

■ any relevant conduct of a relevant body; or
■ any conduct which constitutes part of a relevant UK tax evasion offence, or foreign tax evasion facilitation; or
■ any conduct which constitutes part of a relevant UK tax evasion offence or foreign tax evasion offence

took place in the UK or elsewhere.

3.7 BRANCHES AS DISTINCT FROM SUBSIDIARIES

These principles apply to both the UK tax offence considered in the previous chapter, and the foreign tax offence under review here. The sections in the previous chapter on referrals and joint ventures similarly apply to both offences.

The law does not view branches as separate legal entities, by marked contrast to subsidiaries. All the branches of a relevant body comprise a single legal entity. Any relevant corporate body with a number of branches, including just one in the UK, would be subject to these new CFA 2017 offences. The HMRC guidance (at section

3.3) is clear on the point: 'For the UK branch to say "But a different branch did this" is akin to a person's left arm protesting that an assault was committed by the right arm.'

Not only are subsidiaries not part of the same relevant corporate body, neither are subsidiaries automatically presumed to be associated persons of UK relevant corporate bodies, at stage two.

An examination of the relevant circumstances will be needed in each case to determine whether a subsidiary is an 'associated person' or not, in the same way as is required for entirely unrelated legal entities or sister companies that share a parent company.

Note also that in each case it is the relevant corporate body itself, not its UK branch, that would commit the offence.

4 DEFENCES

4.1 OVERVIEW

It is trite to say that it is a defence to any criminal allegation if one or more of the key elements (either external/*actus reus* or mental/*mens rea*) of the offence is not proved.

Such absence of a key element may be pointed out in correspondence with the prosecution, in which case it may decide to not embark upon (or withdraw from) bringing a case. It may be argued before a judge that there should be dismissal of a count (prior to arraignment) or that there is no case to answer at 'half time', i.e. close of the Crown's case. Failing all that, an address may be made at the conclusion of the case to the jury (or bench in the magistrates' court) that the tribunal of fact cannot be sure that one of the essential ingredients of the offence is not missing.

As has been discussed, there may be fruitful arguments to be had in, absent convictions which easily prove themselves (via certificate of conviction from the relevant court), challenging whether stage one and stage two are made out. Specifically, on a trial against the relevant corporate body under CFA 2017, whether it has been proven to the criminal standard that both the tax evader (stage one) and tax evasion facilitator (stage two) had the dishonest/fraudulent/deliberate intent and were not merely negligent.

Failing all that, and running in parallel, will be the final line of statutory defence (at stage four).

4.2 STATUTORY DEFENCE: REASONABLE PREVENTION PROCEDURES

The same statutory defence of 'reasonable preventative measures' applies to both the UK tax evasion offence and the foreign counterpart.

As the HMRC guidance (at section 1.3) succinctly confirms:

> *Defence*: where the relevant corporate body has put in place *reasonable prevention* procedures to prevent the criminal facilitation of tax evasion by an associated person (or where it is unreasonable to expect such procedures) the relevant body shall have

a defence. This guidance provides suggestions of the types of processes and procedures that can be put in place to prevent associated persons from criminally facilitating tax evasion.

4.3   COMMENTARY ON REASONABLE PREVENTATIVE MEASURES

The scheme of CFA 2017 codifies the principle that 'one size does not fit all' in terms of the statutory defences available to relevant bodies. As with any test of 'reasonableness' this creates scope for uncertainty, litigation and inconsistency in application. It will be demonstrated that the test here is an impure mixture of the objective (e.g. what is reasonable in the industry?) with the subjective (e.g. is the board engaged with the problems of tax evasion?).

As with the BA 2010, the government (in the form of the Chancellor of the Exchequer) must prepare and publish guidance about the procedures that relevant bodies can put in place to prevent their appropriate persons from committing UK tax or foreign tax facilitation offences at stage two: see CFA 2017, s.47.

That guidance will not come into operation until a statutory instrument containing the regulations is laid before Parliament and approved.

As at the time of writing (July 2017) draft guidance has been issued by the HMRC and this is relied upon heavily in this Guide. Extracts are reproduced with kind permission at **Appendix B**.

4.4   DEFENCE MIRRORS THAT OF THE BRIBERY ACT 2010

There is a mirroring here of the 'adequate procedures' defence to the BA 2010, s.7 offence of 'failure of a commercial organisation to prevent bribery'.

This bribery offence is one of strict vicarious liability, but it is a defence for the corporate entity to prove, on a balance of probabilities, that it had in place adequate procedures designed to prevent the associated person from paying bribes. Again, the defence is available in spite of the fact that there will by definition have been the commission of an offence of bribery, which the procedures have as a matter of fact failed to prevent.

During the passage of BA 2010 there was much parliamentary debate as to what would constitute adequate preventative procedures. The government made plain that this was not a 'one size fits all' approach, as it has with CFA 2017.

The Secretary of State is compelled by BA 2010, s.9(1) to publish guidance. This is said to be generic and non-prescriptive and is available at: **www.gov.uk/ government/publications/bribery-act-2010-guidance**.

The government has promised it will not embroil corporate bodies in excess expenditure or seek to micromanage their internal policy. These assurances look hollow. There is a commitment that the guidance will be interpreted in a flexible and proportionate way, taking into account the relative size of the business entity and the broader context of the risks in the particular sector in which it operates. Presumably, however, it will not be a defence that 'everyone else is at it'.

Lord Henley, at the second reading of the Bribery Bill, asked the questions which will occur to anyone contemplating a reasoned response to that legislation or CFA 2017:

> Who is to judge what is adequate and what is not? If a company has stringent rules in place, checks on its employees, has transparent accounting and so on, but a determined associate of that company still manages to bribe another, were those procedures adequate? They did not, after all, prevent the offence of bribery taking place. What about a company with weak procedures in place which nevertheless manage, perhaps more by chance than anything else, to stop an embryonic plan to commit bribery? Which of those cases should be prosecuted? What about the commercial organisations themselves? How will they know if they have put in place adequate procedures?
>
> Official Report, House of Lords, 7 January 2010; Vol. 716, c. GC45

If these are the correct questions to ask, where are the answers?

4.5   PRACTICAL GENERAL ADVICE ON 'REASONABLE PREVENTION' UNDER CFA 2017

By way of general suggestion, applicable to every business entity, a prudent starting point may begin with the following:

- Install a very public banner/notice on the corporate's external website affirming a commitment not to allow the facilitation of tax evasion at home or abroad.
- Internally, make the same emphatic statements on the intranet, at meetings, on notice boards, in staff training (routine and bespoke).
- Keep abreast of HMRC guidance as it is re-issued, and sector-specific best practice from your trade association or equivalent. Unsurprisingly, banking has led the way.
- Change contracts of employment – explicitly refer to CFA 2017.
- Risk assess – not just your own employees (so, for example, if advising on setting up a tax structure in Jersey, this requires a risk assessment of the clients who set up that tax structure).
- Take independent advice and consider going outside the organisation for a more robust risk assessment, and thus be in a position to say 'it's not our fault'.
- Have an effective 'whistle-blower' policy in place in relation to tax evasion.

4.6   A QUICK COMPARATIVE APPROACH: THE UNITED STATES

Also by way of general guidance, those who seek to provide expert advice on what amounts to 'reasonable prevention' may gain insight from the approach adopted in the US Sentencing Guidelines at para 8B2.1.

The following elements are held to be key to compliance, though some seem circular and nebulous:

- due diligence to prevent and detect criminal conduct;
- promoting a culture that encourages ethical conduct and a commitment to compliance with the law;
- establishing standards and procedures to prevent and detect criminal conduct;
- corporate governance oversight with respect to implementation and effectiveness of the compliance and ethics programme;
- high-level involvement with a specific individual assigned overall responsibility;
- conducting effective training programmes and otherwise disseminating information appropriately;
- monitoring, auditing and evaluation of any compliance programme;
- having and publicising a system, which may include mechanisms that allow for anonymity or confidentiality, whereby the organisation's employees and agents may report or seek guidance regarding potential or actual criminal conduct without fear of retaliation;
- disciplinary measures.

4.7   REASONABLE PREVENTION FOR LOW RISK SMALL AND MEDIUM SIZED COMPANIES

Section 4 of the HMRC guidance on 'Suggested reasonable prevention procedures for lower risk SMEs' is worth quoting in full here as it provides an essential structure:

> An SME should first undertake a risk assessment of the products and services it offers, as well as internal systems and client data that might be used to facilitate tax evasion, including by 'sitting at the desk' of employees and other associated persons, considering the motive, means and opportunity for facilitating tax evasion.
>
> Consider some of the hallmarks of fraud or fraud 'red flags' when undertaking the risk assessment, for example:
>
> - Are there staff who refuse to take leave and do not allow anyone else to review their files, or are overtly defensive over client relationships?
> - Do existing processes ensure that for higher risk activity at least a sample of files are routinely reviewed by a second pair of eyes?
>
> Then consider tailoring existing processes and procedures accordingly to prevent and detect potential tax evasion facilitation – this could include:
>
> - Having a commitment to preventing the involvement of those acting on the relevant body's behalf in the criminal facilitation of tax evasion, which might be demonstrated by issuing a prominent message from the board of directors (or the leadership team) against all forms of tax evasion
> - An overview of its strategy and timeframe to implement its preventative policies
> - Having terms in contracts (with employees and contractors) requiring them not to engage in facilitating tax evasion and to report any concerns immediately
> - Providing regular training for staff on financial crime detection and prevention

- Having clear reporting procedures for whistle-blowing of suspected facilitation
- Ensure their pay and bonus policy/structure encourages reporting and discourages pursuing profit to the point of condoning tax evasion
- Monitoring and enforcing compliance with prevention procedures
- Having regular reviews of the effectiveness of prevention procedures and refining them where necessary

4.8   REASONABLE PREVENTION PROCEDURES: SIX PILLARS

While the above represents common-sense first steps, there will be no substitute for fully considering the current guidance, which encompasses six core principles (with headline comments in brackets):

1. Risk assessment (usually, the likelihood of an agent or employee having the opportunity to facilitate).
2. Proportionality of risk-based prevention procedures (especially compared to the size and sophistication of the relevant corporate body).
3. Top-level commitment (from the corporate body's leaders to procedures which prevent the facilitation of tax evasion).
4. Due diligence (of the corporate body in respect of the agents, but also of the agents in respect of their clients. What if the agents lie to the corporate body?).
5. Communications (and training, for staff and associated persons).
6. Monitoring and review (this is based on actual experience).

4.9   HOW MUCH TO INVEST IN THE STATUTORY DEFENCE

Before the detailed work is done, it will be for others to determine how a cost-benefit analysis works out here: how much is it worth investing in (yet more) compliance procedures and policies to avoid a potentially unlimited fine and reputational damage?

Such an analysis will be informed by keeping track of prosecution and conviction rates, the length and disruption of investigations, the use of DPAs and the level of financial penalties and regulatory sanctions imposed.

4.10   STEP-BY-STEP APPROACH FOR ALL: UNDER THE HMRC GUIDANCE

The Chancellor of the Exchequer is mandated by CFA 2017, s.47 to publish guidance about the procedures that relevant bodies might put in place. This requirement is similar to the requirement in BA 2010 to publish guidance on how to prevent bribery.

Under CFA 2017, s.47(7) the Chancellor is enabled to endorse guidance prepared and published by others. It will thus be possible for guidance prepared by, e.g., a professional or trade association addressing the particular risks arising within that sector of industry, to be endorsed by the government. This would result in the overarching guidance under s.47(1) being supported by consistent guidance more closely tailored to the sector of industry at hand, e.g. banking, estate agency, etc.

The quotations are direct from Section 2 of the HMRC guidance, with commentary from the author following each principle. No apology is made for borrowing heavily from the guidance in this section. The new offences themselves are relatively easy to understand, but how the defence will be interpreted is more complex. The discussion which follows is by far the most detailed section of this Guide, and is aimed at providing assistance for practitioners.

Principle 1 will be dealt with in the body of this chapter, as it is of universal application. The remaining five principles are more nuanced and are dealt with at **Appendix B**.

4.11   RISK ASSESSMENT

Principle 1 – Risk assessment

The relevant body assesses the nature and extent of its exposure to the risk of those who act for or on its behalf engaging in activity during the course of business …

4.11.1   Commentary on risk assessment

The HMRC guidance states:

Those relevant bodies most affected by the new offence, for example those in the financial services, legal and accounting sectors, may already undertake a range of risk assessments relating to their business activities. The purpose of this principle is to promote the inclusion of tax evasion risk within the relevant body's wider financial crime risk assessment.

These risk assessments should not take place in a vacuum, but in the context of publicly available guidance from the major agencies, including:

■   the FCA's guide for firms on preventing financial crime;
■   the Law Society's Anti-Money Laundering Guidance, particularly Chapter 2 which considers a risk-based approach;
■   the Joint Money Laundering Steering Group (JMLSG) guidance.

Any relevant corporate body operating in a regulated sector will want to look to its own regulator's guidance, including:

■   HMRC as part of its anti-money laundering supervision;
■   money services businesses;
■   estate agency businesses.

Also, in terms of useful sources of publicly available comparative information:

- BA 2010 guidance, which is considered from a tax fraud perspective;
- more information from the Organisation for Economic Co-operation and Development (OECD) generally, and on common reporting standards.

When all of this is considered, the HMRC guidance re-states the basic test that must be kept in mind:

> Ultimately, relevant bodies need to 'sit at the desk' of their employees, agents and those who provide services for them or on their behalf and ask whether they have a motive, the opportunity and the means to criminally facilitate tax evasion offences, and if so how this risk might be managed.

Thus, the first step is to be thoroughly well informed of the benchmarks against which to weigh the risk to the corporate body.

4.11.2   Fundamentals of any risk assessment

The following points would appear essential:

- oversight of, and engagement with, the risk assessment process by the board or senior management, so that they weigh the risk;
- demonstrably appropriate allocation of time and funding resources to the detection and monitoring of risk; any subsequent questioning of this will have an eye to proportionality and reflect the size and nature of the relevant corporate body;
- identification of both the internal and external information sources that will enable the risk to be assessed and reviewed, as well as any gaps in the information available to the relevant body and how these gaps might be filled;
- due diligence enquiries (see Principle 4 for more details);
- risk assessments should be reviewed and updated in line with changing circumstances, e.g. taking on of new staff or business streams, especially if they appear high risk (e.g. where 'B' begins to provide services in jurisdictions not reporting taxpayer information under the Common Reporting Standard).

4.11.3   Particular types of risk to weigh in the balance

- **Country risk**: this is evidenced by perceived high levels of secrecy or use as a tax shelter. Such countries are also unlikely to subscribe to the Common Reporting Standard and will be given a low tax transparency score by the OECD. (Tax transparency ratings and lists of high risk tax jurisdictions published by organisations like the OECD may also be relevant for tax purposes.)
- **Sectoral risk**: some business sectors pose a higher risk of facilitating tax evasion than others, e.g. the financial services, tax advisory and legal sectors.
- **Transaction risk**: certain types of transaction give rise to higher risks, e.g. complex tax planning structures involving high levels of secrecy, overly complex supply chains or transactions involving PEPs.
- **Business opportunity risk**: such risks might arise in high value projects or with projects involving many parties, jurisdictions or intermediaries.

- **Business partnership risk**: certain relationships may involve higher risk, e.g. the use of intermediaries in transactions, where those intermediaries are based in jurisdictions operating lower levels of transparency and disclosure. Entering into a business partnership with an organisation that either has no fraud prevention procedures or has known deficiencies in its fraud procedures may involve higher risk.

In addition, the following risks may also be considered for tax fraud:

- **Product risk**: certain products and services may have a higher risk of misuse by either clients or associated persons.
- **Customer risk**: the identification that a business unit has particular risks related to customers or products is highly likely to indicate that there is a greater risk of the criminal facilitation of tax evasion by an associated person.

4.11.4   JMLSG guidance on high and low risk

In conducting an assessment of risk it would be prudent to consider the general JMLSG guidance on high and low risk factors, though re-considered specifically from a tax evasion perspective.

High risk factors (4.34–4.36)

CUSTOMER RISK FACTORS

- The business relationship is conducted in unusual circumstances.
- Non-resident customers.
- Legal persons or arrangements that are personal asset holding vehicles.
- Companies that have nominee shareholders or shares in bearer form.
- Business that are cash intensive.
- The ownership structure of the company appears unusual or excessively complex.

COUNTRY OR GEOGRAPHIC RISK FACTORS

- Countries identified by credible sources as not having adequate anti-money laundering and counter-terrorism financing (AML/CTF) approaches.
- Countries subject to sanctions, embargoes or similar measures issued by, e.g. the United Nations (UN).
- Countries identified by credible sources as providing support for terrorist activities or that have designated terrorist organisations operating within the country.

PRODUCT, SERVICE, TRANSACTION OR DELIVERY CHANNEL RISK FACTORS

- Private banking.
- Anonymous transactions (which may include cash).
- Non-face-to-face business relationships or transactions.
- Payment received from unknown or un-associated third parties.

Firms should examine, as far as reasonably possible, the background and purpose of all complex, unusually large transactions and all unusual patterns of transactions which have no apparent economic or lawful purpose.

Low risk factors (4.37–4.41)

CUSTOMER RISK FACTORS

■ Other regulated firms and other bodies where: they are subject to requirements to combat money laundering and terrorist financing consistent with the Financial Action Task Force (FATF) Recommendations; they have effectively implemented these requirements; and they are effectively supervised or monitored to ensure compliance with those requirements.
■ Public companies listed on a stock exchange and subject to disclosure requirements which impose requirements to ensure adequate transparency of beneficial ownership.
■ Public administrations or enterprises.

COUNTRY OR GEOGRAPHIC RISK FACTORS

■ Countries identified by credible sources as having effective AML/CTF systems.
■ Countries identified by credible sources as having a low level of corruption or criminal activity.
■ Product, service, transaction or delivery channel risk factors.
■ Life assurance policies where the premium is low.
■ Insurance policies for pension schemes if there is no early surrender option and the policy cannot be used as collateral.
■ A pension, superannuation or similar scheme that provides retirement benefits to employees, where contributions are made by way of deduction from wages, and the scheme rules do not permit the assignment of a member's interest under the scheme.
■ Financial products or services that provide appropriately defined and limited services to certain types of customers, so as to increase access for financial inclusion purposes.

4.11.5   Internal structures

A risk assessment should also consider the extent to which internal structures or procedures may themselves add to the level of risk. Commonly encountered internal factors may include:

■ deficiencies in employee training, skills and knowledge;
■ a bonus culture that rewards excessive risk taking;
■ lack of clarity on the organisation's policies on, and procedures for, the provision of high risk services and products;
■ deficiencies in the organisation's submission of suspicious activity reports (SARs);
■ lack of clear financial controls or whistle-blowing procedures;

- lack of clear messaging from top-level management on refusing to engage in tax fraud.

Note: There are a further five principles which have been given detailed guidance from HMRC and can be found at **Appendix B**.

5 PENALTIES AND SENTENCING FOR CORPORATE OFFENCES

5.1 OVERVIEW

This chapter deals with the penalties and sanctions available in respect of 'B' (the relevant corporate body) in the event of conviction of either UK or foreign failure to prevent the facilitation of tax evasion. B must be a legal entity and cannot be a natural person, therefore imprisonment is an impossibility.

In summary, the sentence will be a fine. Deferred prosecution agreements (DPAs) are available; there will be regulatory consequences and POCA 2002 applies; and serious crime prevention orders will be available.

5.2 PENALTIES: UNLIMITED FINE

Both offences are 'triable either way' (i.e. triable both in the magistrates' (or equivalent) or Crown Court, following a venue procedure). After conviction on indictment, the sentence for either offence is a potentially unlimited fine (s.45(8) for the UK offence and s.46(7) for the foreign offence). On summary conviction in England and Wales, the same financial penalty applies; in Scotland and Northern Ireland the penalty is restricted to a statutory maximum (s.45(8) or s.46(7)).

5.3 DEFERRED PROSECUTION AGREEMENTS

Deferred prosecution agreements are available: see discussion in **Chapter 1** for commentary and recent examples of high profile DPAs.

At its heart, a DPA is an agreement reached between a prosecutor and an organisation which is liable to be prosecuted, made with the supervision of a judge. In the same way that DPAs can be used for fraud, bribery and other economic crimes, they can also be used for these offences.

Any DPA suspends the criminal prosecution for a set period on condition that the relevant corporate body complies with certain specified conditions. The key features of DPAs, according to the HMRC guidance (at section 1.5), are:

■   They enable a corporate body to make full reparation for criminal behaviour without the collateral damage of a conviction (for example sanctions or reputational damage that could put the company out of business and destroy the jobs and investments of innocent people)

- They are concluded under the supervision of a judge, who must be convinced that the DPA is 'in the interests of justice' and that the terms are 'fair, reasonable and proportionate'
- They avoid lengthy and costly trials
- They are transparent, public events.

As ever, there are direct analogies with the bribery offences: a corporate convicted of a BA 2010, s.7 offence will also face an unlimited fine, and confiscation under POCA 2002, Part 2.

5.4   MITIGATION WHEN THE REGIME IS NEW

As this is a new regime there will be slack in the system at the outset. First, the defence of reasonable prevention measures (discussed in **Chapter 4**) will be more liberally interpreted while the offences are still relatively new. By extension, the very first cases to come through the system will be able to point to earlier toleration.

As the HMRC guidance (at section 1.4) has it:

      The prevention procedures that are considered reasonable will change as time passes. What is reasonable on the day that the new offences come into force will not be the same as what is reasonable when the offence has been in effect for a number of years. The Government accepts that some procedures (such as training programmes and new IT systems) will take time to roll out, especially for large multi-national organisations.

This seems like an unfortunate nod to the double standard where larger corporations enjoy an easier regulatory ride, and is flatly contradicted by the following from the same guidance (at section 1.4):

      At the same time the Government expects there to be rapid implementation, focusing on the major risks and priorities, with a clear timeframe and implementation plan on entry into force. In addition, HMRC expects reasonable procedures to be kept under regular review and to evolve as a relevant body discovers more about the risks that it faces and lessons are learnt.

5.5   REGULATORY CONSEQUENCES

No doubt the fact of a serious criminal conviction will have profound consequences for any relevant corporate body. A regulated body may well be required to disclose the conviction (and sanctions) to its professional regulators and insurers both in the UK and abroad. Such notoriety may prevent the body being awarded public contracts – at least that is the hope of those behind the legislation. On another view, it is difficult to foresee Rolls-Royce and Tesco Stores Group being fatally damaged by their recent DPAs in a similar context, with large financial settlements being paid by them.

5.6   SENTENCING GUIDELINES

There is no definitive sentencing guideline for these two new offences.

However, existing sentencing guidelines[1] on fraud, money laundering, etc. help in two respects. First, they demonstrate the way in which different tax evasion offending is categorised and, second, they set out general principles for sentencing corporate bodies for financial crime. Plainly, the actual table of sentencing guidelines for natural persons is irrelevant, with its focus on custody versus community rehabilitation.

First, the tax categorisations will be considered, then the approach to sentencing corporate bodies.

The following content is produced here with the kind permission of the Sentencing Council, and is based on its existing guidelines.

PART A: HOW WOULD AN INDIVIDUAL BE CATEGORISED FOR TAX EVASION/FACILITATION?

Which category would the tax evasion offence at stage one be in?

Step one: Determining the offence category

The level of culpability is determined by weighing up all the factors of the case to determine the offender's role and the extent to which the offending was planned and the sophistication with which it was carried out.

Culpability demonstrated by one or more of the following:

A: High Culpability

- A leading role where offending is part of a group activity
- Involvement of others through pressure, influence
- Abuse of position of power or trust or responsibility
- Sophisticated nature of offence/significant planning
- Fraudulent activity conducted over sustained period of time

B: Medium Culpability

- Other cases where characteristics for categories A or C are not present
- A significant role where offending is part of a group activity

---

[1]   www.sentencingcouncil.org.uk/wp-content/uploads/Fraud_bribery_and_money_laundering_offences_-_Definitive_guideline.pdf.

C: Low Culpability

■ Performed limited function under direction
■ Involved through coercion, intimidation or exploitation
■ Not motivated by personal gain
■ Opportunistic 'one-off' offence; very little or no planning
■ Limited awareness or understanding of extent of fraudulent activity

Where there are characteristics present which fall under different levels of culpability, the court should balance these characteristics to reach a fair assessment of the offender's culpability.

Harm – Gain/intended gain to offender or loss/intended loss to HMRC

Category 1
£50 million or more
Starting point based on £80 million

Category 2
£10 million–£50 million
Starting point based on £30 million

Category 3
£2 million–£10 million
Starting point based on £5 million

Category 4
£500,000–£2 million
Starting point based on £1 million

Category 5
£100,000–£500,000
Starting point based on £300,000

Category 6
£20,000–£100,000
Starting point based on £50,000

Category 7
Less than £20,000
Starting point based on £12,500

Step two: Category range

[Note: The precise ranges of sentences (custody versus unpaid work orders, etc.) available are irrelevant as they apply to natural persons, but the principles may assist.]

AGGRAVATING FACTORS

[The following are aggravating factors relating to a natural person under the guidelines which could apply to the relevant corporate body.]

- Previous convictions, having regard to a) the nature of the offence to which the conviction relates and its relevance to the current offence; and b) the time that has elapsed since the conviction
- Involves multiple frauds
- Number of false declarations
- Attempts to conceal/dispose of evidence
- Failure to comply with current court orders
- Failure to respond to warnings about behaviour
- Blame wrongly placed on others
- Damage to third party (for example as a result of identity theft)
- Dealing with goods with an additional health risk
- Disposing of goods to under age purchasers

MITIGATING FACTORS

[Listed in reference to natural persons but possibly also relevant to companies by analogy. For main mitigation, see Part B below.]

- No previous convictions or no relevant/recent convictions
- Good character and/or exemplary conduct
- Little or no prospect of success
- Lapse of time since apprehension where this does not arise from the conduct of the offender
- Offender co-operated with investigation, made early admissions and/or voluntarily reported offending
- Determination and/or demonstration of steps having been taken to address addiction or offending behaviour
- Activity originally legitimate

Step three: Consider any factors which indicate a reduction, such as assistance to the prosecution

The court should take into account sections 73 and 74 of the Serious Organised Crime and Police Act 2005 (assistance by defendants: reduction or review of sentence) and any other rule of law by virtue of which an offender may receive a discounted sentence in consequence of assistance given (or offered) to the prosecutor or investigator.

Step four: Reduction for guilty pleas

The court should take account of any potential reduction for a guilty plea in accordance with section 144 of the Criminal Justice Act 2003 and the Guilty Plea guideline.

Step five: Totality principle

If sentencing an offender for more than one offence, or where the offender is already serving a sentence, consider whether the total sentence is just and proportionate to the overall offending behaviour.

Step six: Confiscation, compensation and ancillary orders

The court must proceed with a view to making a confiscation order if it is asked to do so by the prosecutor or if the court believes it is appropriate for it to do so.

Where the offence has resulted in loss or damage the court must consider whether to make a compensation order.

If the court makes both a confiscation order and an order for compensation and the court believes the offender will not have sufficient means to satisfy both orders in full, the court must direct that the compensation be paid out of sums recovered under the confiscation order (section 13 of the Proceeds of Crime Act 2002).

The court may also consider whether to make ancillary orders. These may include a deprivation order, a financial reporting order, a serious crime prevention order and disqualification from acting as a company director.

Step seven: Reasons

Section 174 of the Criminal Justice Act 2003 imposes a duty to give reasons for, and explain the effect of, the sentence.

PART B: HOW WOULD A COMPANY BE DEALT WITH FOR SIMILAR FINANCIAL OFFENDING?

Step one: Compensation

The court must consider making a compensation order requiring the offender to pay compensation for any personal injury, loss or damage resulting from the offence in such an amount as the court considers appropriate, having regard to the evidence and to the means of the offender.

Where the means of the offender are limited, priority should be given to the payment of compensation over payment of any other financial penalty.

Reasons should be given if a compensation order is not made.

(See section 130 Powers of Criminal Courts (Sentencing) Act 2000)

Step two: Confiscation

Confiscation must be considered if either the Crown asks for it or the court thinks that it may be appropriate.

Confiscation must be dealt with before, and taken into account when assessing, any other fine or financial order (except compensation).

(See Proceeds of Crime Act 2002 sections 6 and 13)

Step three: Determining the offence category

The court should determine the offence category with reference to culpability and harm.

CULPABILITY

The sentencer should weigh up all the factors of the case to determine culpability. Where there are characteristics present which fall under different categories, the court should balance these characteristics to reach a fair assessment of the offender's culpability.

Culpability demonstrated by the offending corporation's role and motivation. May be demonstrated by one or more of the following **non-exhaustive** characteristics.

A: High culpability

■ Corporation plays a leading role in organised, planned unlawful activity (whether acting alone or with others)
■ Wilful obstruction of detection (for example destruction of evidence, misleading investigators, suborning employees)
■ Involving others through pressure or coercion (for example employees or suppliers)
■ Targeting of vulnerable victims or a large number of victims
■ Corruption of local or national government officials or ministers
■ Corruption of officials performing a law enforcement role
■ Abuse of dominant market position or position of trust or responsibility
■ Offending committed over a sustained period of time
■ Culture of wilful disregard of commission of offences by employees or agents with no effort to put effective systems in place (section 7 Bribery Act only)

B: Medium culpability

■ Corporation plays a significant role in unlawful activity organised by others
■ Activity not unlawful from the outset
■ Corporation reckless in making false statement (section 72 VAT Act 1994)
■ All other cases where characteristics for categories A or C are not present

---

C: Lesser culpability

■ Corporation plays a minor, peripheral role in unlawful activity organised by others
■ Some effort made to put bribery prevention measures in place but insufficient to amount to a defence (section 7 Bribery Act only)
■ Involvement through coercion, intimidation or exploitation

HARM

Harm is represented by a financial sum calculated by reference to the table below.

Amount obtained or intended to be obtained (or loss avoided or intended to be avoided)	
Fraud	For offences of fraud, conspiracy to defraud, cheating the Revenue and fraudulent evasion of duty or VAT, harm will normally be the actual or intended gross gain to the offender.

Step four: Starting point and category range

Having determined the culpability level at step three, the court should use the table below to determine the starting point within the category range below. The starting point applies to all offenders irrespective of plea or previous convictions.

The harm figure at step three is multiplied by the relevant percentage figure representing culpability.

	Culpability Level		
	A	**B**	**C**
Harm figure multiplier	*Starting point* 300%	*Starting point* 200%	*Starting point* 100%
	Category range 250% to 400%	*Category range* 100% to 300%	*Category range* 20% to 150%

Having determined the appropriate starting point, the court should then consider adjustment within the category range for aggravating or mitigating features. In some cases, having considered these factors, it may be appropriate to move outside the identified category range. (See below for a non-exhaustive list of aggravating and mitigating factors.)

Factors increasing seriousness

- Previous relevant convictions or subject to previous relevant civil or regulatory enforcement action
- Corporation or subsidiary set up to commit fraudulent activity
- Fraudulent activity endemic within corporation
- Attempts made to conceal misconduct
- Substantial harm (whether financial or otherwise) suffered by victims of offending or by third parties affected by offending
- Risk of harm greater than actual or intended harm (for example in banking/credit fraud)
- Substantial harm caused to integrity or confidence of markets
- Substantial harm caused to integrity of local or national governments
- Serious nature of underlying criminal activity (money laundering offences)
- Offence committed across borders or jurisdictions

Factors reducing seriousness or reflecting mitigation

- No previous relevant convictions or previous relevant civil or regulatory enforcement action
- Victims voluntarily reimbursed/compensated
- No actual loss to victims
- Corporation co-operated with investigation, made early admissions and/or voluntarily reported offending
- Offending committed under previous director(s)/manager(s)
- Little or no actual gain to corporation from offending

GENERAL PRINCIPLES TO FOLLOW IN SETTING A FINE

The court should determine the appropriate level of fine in accordance with section 164 of the Criminal Justice Act 2003, which requires that the fine must reflect the seriousness of the offence and requires the court to take into account the financial circumstances of the offender.

Obtaining financial information – Companies and bodies delivering public or charitable services

Where the offender is a company or a body which delivers a public or charitable service, it is expected to provide comprehensive accounts for the last three years, to enable the court to make an accurate assessment of its financial status. In the absence of such disclosure, or where the court is not satisfied that it has been given sufficient reliable information, the court will be entitled to draw reasonable inferences as to the offender's means from evidence it has heard and from all the circumstances of the case.

1. *For companies*: annual accounts. Particular attention should be paid to turnover; profit before tax; directors' remuneration, loan accounts and pension provision; and assets as disclosed by the balance sheet. Most companies are required to file audited accounts at Companies House. Failure to produce relevant recent accounts on request may properly lead to the conclusion that the company can pay any appropriate fine.
2. *For partnerships*: annual accounts. Particular attention should be paid to turnover; profit before tax; partners' drawings, loan accounts and pension provision; assets as above. Limited liability partnerships (LLPs) may be required to file audited accounts with Companies House. If adequate accounts are not produced on request, see paragraph 1.
    ...
5. *For charities*: it will be appropriate to inspect annual audited accounts. Detailed analysis of expenditure or reserves is unlikely to be called for unless there is a suggestion of unusual or unnecessary expenditure.

Step five: Adjustment of fine

Having arrived at a fine level, the court should consider whether there are any further factors which indicate an adjustment in the level of the fine. The court should 'step back' and consider the overall effect of its orders. The combination of orders made, compensation, confiscation and fine ought to achieve:

- the removal of all gain
- appropriate additional punishment, and
- deterrence

The fine may be adjusted to ensure that these objectives are met in a fair way. The court should consider any further factors relevant to the setting of the level of the fine to ensure that the fine is proportionate, having regard to the size and financial position of the offending organisation and the seriousness of the offence.

The fine must be substantial enough to have a real economic impact which will bring home to both management and shareholders the need to operate within the law. Whether the fine will have the effect of putting the offender out of business will be relevant; in some bad cases this may be an acceptable consequence.

In considering the ability of the offending organisation to pay any financial penalty the court can take into account the power to allow time for payment or to order that the amount be paid in instalments.

The court should consider whether the level of fine would otherwise cause unacceptable harm to third parties. In doing so the court should bear in mind that the payment of any compensation determined at step one should take priority over the payment of any fine.

The table below contains a **non-exhaustive** list of additional factual elements for the court to consider. The court should identify whether any combination of these, or other relevant factors, should result in a proportionate increase or reduction in the level of fine.

Factors to consider in adjusting the level of fine

- Fine fulfils the objectives of punishment, deterrence and removal of gain
- The value, worth or available means of the offender
- Fine impairs offender's ability to make restitution to victims
- Impact of fine on offender's ability to implement effective compliance programmes
- Impact of fine on employment of staff, service users, customers and local economy (but not shareholders)
- Impact of fine on performance of public or charitable function

---

Step six: Consider any factors which would indicate a reduction, such as assistance to the prosecution

The court should take into account sections 73 and 74 of the Serious Organised Crime and Police Act 2005 (assistance by defendants: reduction or review of sentence) and any other rule of law by virtue of which an offender may receive a discounted sentence in consequence of assistance given (or offered) to the prosecutor or investigator.

Step seven: Reduction for guilty pleas

The court should take into account any potential reduction for a guilty plea in accordance with section 144 of the Criminal Justice Act 2003 and the Guilty Plea guideline.

Step eight: Ancillary Orders

In all cases the court must consider whether to make any ancillary orders.

Step nine: Totality principle

If sentencing an offender for more than one offence, consider whether the total sentence is just and proportionate to the offending behaviour.

Step ten: Reasons

Section 174 of the Criminal Justice Act 2003 imposes a duty to give reasons for, and explain the effect of, the sentence.

6 UNEXPLAINED WEALTH ORDERS AND POLITICALLY EXPOSED PERSONS

6.1 OVERVIEW OF UNEXPLAINED WEALTH ORDERS AND THEIR TARGETS

A UWO compels a person to explain the source of his or her wealth; while that happens the funds are frozen. If the person refuses to respond, there is a presumption that the funds are 'recoverable' by the State through civil means. If a person gives a false statement under compulsion, that person commits a new criminal offence.

However, nothing said under compulsion is admissible in criminal proceedings against the maker of the statement.

One target following the Panama Papers scandal is the corrupt foreign politician and their family; after all, 12 'national leaders' were implicated in the scandal, out of 143 of their political colleagues.

As an Explanatory Note to CFA 2017 (at note 13) makes plain (emphasis added):

> A UWO made in relation to an overseas PEP would *not* require suspicion of serious criminality. This measure reflects the concern about those involved in corruption overseas laundering the proceeds of crime in the UK …

Anecdotally, investigators in the UK have been frustrated since at least the mid 1990s by the existence of a handful of crime families who successfully evade prosecution. They hide in plain sight with enormous wealth, but with no legitimate employment and receiving no welfare benefits.

An Explanatory Note (at note 12) again explains frankly:

> Law enforcement agencies often have reasonable grounds to suspect that identified assets of such persons are the proceeds of serious crime. However, they are unable to freeze or recover the assets under the current provisions in POCA due to an inability to obtain evidence (often due to the inability to rely on full cooperation from other jurisdictions to obtain evidence).

6.2 CRITIQUE OF UNEXPLAINED WEALTH ORDERS

There is something Kafka-esque about the term 'unexplained wealth' – perhaps 'disproportionate wealth' sounds less alarming, and reveals the underlying test. In

2014 secondary legislation was issued to ban individuals from management roles in education if they sought to 'undermine British values'.

There is an unfortunate coupling here of politics with organised crime which does nothing to dispel cynicism in the democratic process. Respect for that process and the rule of law are fundamental British values.

Arguably, this is a draconian measure that crosses an important threshold of reverse burden, blurring the line between criminal and civil recovery as it goes. The rule of law is undermined through the extension of these far reaching powers at a time of crisis.

6.3   REQUIREMENTS FOR UNEXPLAINED WEALTH ORDERS

The mechanism chosen is to add UWOs to the existing POCA regime (detailed consideration of which is beyond the scope of this Guide) by amending POCA 2002 with the insertion of new sections after s.362. All references in the discussion below are to the new sections inserted into POCA 2002 by CFA 2017, ss.1–6.

No notice is required for the substantive application for a UWO. A respondent will have to apply to vary or discharge a UWO *post facto* (see practical objections below). It may be that rules or practice directions will be issued in respect of the procedure for UWOs as it is unusual for a substantive order to be issued entirely *ex parte* without notice.

Application is made by an enforcement agency to the High Court, not lower courts. There is a fear at the criminal bar that Crown Court judges, who will often find themselves part-heard in a trial or dealing with a long list of preliminary matters, are accustomed to dealing with *ex parte* matters such as warrants and production orders in a manner which is reminiscent of summary justice.

It appears that the High Court has a discretion in that it 'may' not 'must' make a UWO if each requirement is satisfied.

The applicant enforcement agency must 'specify or describe' the property in respect of which the order is sought (s.362A(2)(a)) and 'specify' the person against whom the order is sought, whether that person is in the UK or abroad. These measures appear to relate to natural persons rather than legal corporate entities, as a 'person' failing to comply may be imprisoned for up to two years.

The High Court must be *satisfied* that the respondent holds the property and also that the value of the property is over £50k.[1] If the property comprises more than one item, the total value applies.

---

[1]   See POCA 2002, s.362B(2)(b). The original figure in the Commons Bill of £100,000 was reduced by the House of Lords.

'Satisfied' presumably means to a civil standard (balance of probabilities). This is the default position in the POCA regime. In the case of money in a bank account held in an unusual name, these matters are obvious. But what of 'Mr John Smith' who holds funds in a dollar account when the exchange rate fluctuates such that the value is on or around £50k sterling? What of a vintage bottle of Chateau Fleet Street, purchased for £30k ten years ago, and insured for £60k last week?

6.4   THE CENTRAL TEST: 'UNEXPLAINED'

6.4.1   The definition of the test

Though the word 'unexplained' does not feature in the definition of the test, this is the central test, with a surprisingly low evidential threshold, lying at the heart of a UWO. Section 362B(3) states (emphasis added):

> The High Court must be satisfied that there are reasonable grounds for *suspecting* that the *known* sources of the respondent's lawfully obtained income would have been *insufficient* for the purpose of *enabling* the respondent to *obtain* the property.

The bar is set very low with 'reasonable grounds for suspecting', especially at an *ex parte* hearing without notice nor any opportunity to challenge the evidence at this substantive stage.

The same test has long applied to powers of arrest and search. Code A to the Police and Criminal Evidence Act (PACE) 1984 provides some guidance (see paras A:2.2 to A:2.11, *Archbold: Criminal Pleading, Evidence and Practice 2017* (Sweet & Maxwell), Appendix A-5). The test is described as being an objective one. There must be an objective basis for suspicion based on facts, information or intelligence which are relevant.

There is an amplification of the test in the case of *O'Hara* v. *Chief Constable of the RUC* [1997] AC 286 (HL), where it was held that such grounds could arise from the information received from another (even if it subsequently proves to be false), provided that a reasonable man, having regard to all of the circumstances, would regard them as reasonable grounds for suspicion; however, a mere order from a superior officer to arrest a particular individual could not constitute reasonable grounds for suspicion.

By contrast, if the arresting officer knows at the time of the arrest that there is no possibility of a charge being made, the arrest would be unlawful as they must have acted on an irrelevant consideration or for some improper motive: *Plange* v. *Chief Constable of South Humberside Police*, *The Times*, 23 March 1992 (CA). This may assist in defeating a spurious application for a UWO, although presumably only on appeal.

6.4.2   Deciding whether income is lawful or unlawful

What are 'known sources' of lawful income: known to whom? There is a perverse incentive here for the enforcement authority not to seek out potential explanations for lawful wealth.

The definition at s.362B(6)(d) says that the sources from employment, assets or otherwise are those that are 'reasonably ascertainable from available information at the time'. Ascertainable by whom? A High Court judge has no investigative function and the respondent will be absent at this stage. The applicant authority will probably satisfy itself with a simple 'investigator online' check from a credit reference agency. This approach is criticised below and may be challenged.

There is no fully developed disclosure regime here, so will the public law duty of candour suffice? No doubt counsel for the applicant will apply utmost good faith? Will the applicant behave as a minister of justice, as would prosecution counsel? None of these questions are answered in the statute, and all will have to be litigated unless secondary regulations are issued.

At what stage must funds be judged lawful or unlawful? Are they unlawful if someone has earned them lawfully but failed to pay tax on them? At least no one can be convicted under Part 3 of this Act for failing to prevent the facilitation of tax evasion, and as a result of that conviction be subject to a Part 1 UWO: the former applies only to corporate bodies, and the latter only to natural persons.

The definition at s.362B(6)(c) does not assist much: 'income is "lawfully obtained" if it is obtained lawfully under the laws of the country from where the income arises'.

So the Act is silent as to the meaning of 'lawfully obtained' but indicates that the test to be applied is whether or not the income is lawful by the local rules where it 'arises'. On a narrow interpretation, the judgment is to be made at the stage when the income is first received. There is no explicit concept here of unlawfully 'retained' income, e.g. in breach of a tax regime.

It would be much fairer to ask the person concerned at this initial hearing stage to explain, in person or via an advocate, in general terms, the source of the wealth. That person is best placed to 'know' the answer.

If a person can demonstrate a recent win at the poker World Series, the National Lottery or by betting on the Grand National (each of which may be possible with a single document or a gleeful photograph from the local newspaper) many resources would be spared. If that person does not wish to put forward any explanation, then let the draconian presumptions apply.

Granted, an initial freezing order must be without notice or there is a risk of disposal of the property. However, it is objectionable for a final order to be made without the chance to test the evidence at all, albeit variation and discharge can be sought of the consequent interim freezing. The first remedy available on the substantive order is an appeal against it.

How will a judge determine whether or not the lawfully obtained income would have been *insufficient* to *enable* the respondent to *obtain* the property? The judge may need expert assistance from accountants.

6.4.3   Lawful or unlawful income: an example

To give an example, Horace makes a snap decision to withdraw £3k from his bank account and fly to Nevada with the cash. If later faced with a UWO he could show, on a single page of his bank statement, a brief fee going in and a cash withdrawal for an identical amount the same day.

At the nearest casino to the airport in Las Vegas he puts all his cash on number 7 at a roulette table, which comes in at a return of 35:1. Horace has just sailed past the £50,000 UWO threshold. He uses his winnings to buy an original painting at the Venetian, tucks it under his arm and flies back to Heathrow in search of a proper steak and kidney pudding.

If the High Court judge knew any of this information, the judge would apply s.362B in the following way:

■   As a matter of fact, Horace's £3k was not *insufficient* to obtain a gain of more than £250k, yet Horace did not request a receipt from the croupier.
■   He was *enabled* by whim and good fortune.
■   He *obtained* the painting lawfully by purchasing it with money he had won.

This simple example demonstrates how the High Court judge may have to make decisions while deprived of basic explanations, and how impossible it will be to apply any rigour to the test at this hearing stage. In effect, the applicant authority will be saying to the court: 'We are suspicious, trust us.'

6.5   THE SECOND LIMB: PEP OR INVOLVED IN SERIOUS CRIME

6.5.1   Politically exposed persons

In the previous example, Horace would not fall foul of a UWO unless he was also in the category of people caught by the second limb.

By s.362B(4), the High Court must also be 'satisfied' that the respondent is either a PEP or that there are reasonable grounds for suspecting that:

■   the respondent is, or has been, involved in serious crime (whether in a part of the UK or elsewhere); or
■   a person connected with the respondent is, or has been, so involved.

Third party rights to the property and retro-activity both are dealt with by the phrase 'does not matter' according to Parliament (see below for suggested challenges).

6.5.2   Definition of politically exposed person

A PEP is (s.326B(7)):

[A]n individual who is, or has been, entrusted with prominent public functions by an international organisation or by a State other than the United Kingdom or another EEA State ...

To clarify, the European Economic Area (EEA) provides for the free movement of persons, goods, services and capital within the single market of the European Union (EU) between its 28 Member States, as well as three of the four Member States of the European Free Trade Association (EFTA): Iceland, Liechtenstein and Norway.

So, in drafting the definition Parliament is not saying that EEA countries are less risky than non-EEA countries. Indeed, Liechtenstein has been regarded in the past as a tax haven. Rather, there is a competing international obligation to allow free movement of capital, for the moment. This is one of the many aspects to the negotiations as the UK moves towards withdrawing from the EU (Brexit).

There is more EU legislation on the definitions of PEPs applied by s.362B(8), which may or may not be included in UK law post-Brexit. For now, it is helpful in providing a list of people who are PEPs by Directive 2015/849/EU, Art.3:

(9)   'politically exposed person' means a natural person who is or who has been entrusted with prominent public functions and includes the following:

   (a)   heads of State, heads of government, ministers and deputy or assistant ministers;
   (b)   members of parliament or of similar legislative bodies;
   (c)   members of the governing bodies of political parties;
   (d)   members of supreme courts, of constitutional courts or of other high-level judicial bodies, the decisions of which are not subject to further appeal, except in exceptional circumstances;
   (e)   members of courts of auditors or of the boards of central banks;
   (f)   ambassadors, chargés d'affaires and high-ranking officers in the armed forces;
   (g)   members of the administrative, management or supervisory bodies of State-owned enterprises;
   (h)   directors, deputy directors and members of the board or equivalent function of an international organisation.

   No public function referred to in points (a) to (h) shall be understood as covering middle-ranking or more junior officials.

The same Directive also helps define family members and close associates:

(10) 'family members' includes the following:

   (a)   the spouse, or a person considered to be equivalent to a spouse, of a politically exposed person;
   (b)   the children and their spouses, or persons considered to be equivalent to a spouse, of a politically exposed person;
   (c)   the parents of a politically exposed person;

(11) 'persons known to be close associates' means:

   (a)   natural persons who are known to have joint beneficial ownership of legal entities or legal arrangements, or any other close business relations, with a politically exposed person;
   (b)   natural persons who have sole beneficial ownership of a legal entity or

legal arrangement which is known to have been set up for the de facto benefit of a politically exposed person.

These are detailed definitions. Spouses of children, and parents of the individuals will not necessarily be their dependants or have a close connection with them at all, yet they will be caught by the definition.

There is scope for mischief in considering the relatively junior people (e.g. a sole director) who may be caught by the measure as they are involved in peripheral 'international' organisations.

If a future pope took personal possession of a very small fraction of the wealth (e.g. a priceless gold seal) in the Vatican and came to the UK on a Papal Visit, he would certainly qualify as a politically exposed person (spiritual leader to 1.1 billion people), with almost untold unexplained wealth (CNN puts a figure of $8 billion on assets in the Vatican Bank, which has frequently been accused of corruption since its inception in 1942).

Or what if the director of Greenpeace registered personal ownership of the *Rainbow Warrior* ship? Would the director have to account for all of the donations that went into the purchase of the vessel?

This is a problem inherent in having no threshold of criminal wrongdoing for PEPs: we are asked to trust the enforcement authorities not to seek UWOs against the 'wrong' targets.

6.5.3   Definition of 'involved in serious crime'

The second alternative within the second limb is that there are reasonable grounds for suspecting that the 'person is involved in serious crime'.

The danger revealed in the previous discussion of the low threshold for 'reasonable grounds for suspecting' is even more stark here. This is using a criminal justification for a draconian measure without any of the criminal safeguards.

In its amendment of POCA at the new s.362B(9)(a) and (b), CFA 2017 refers back to a definition in the Serious Crime Act 2007 and another in the Corporation Tax Act 2010.

Note the extra-territoriality of this: the person may have been involved in crime abroad. A test of double criminality is imputed by s.362B(9)(a) (see **Chapter 3** for discussion of double criminality).

The list of serious crimes

The SCA 2007 list of serious crimes is, in summary, as follows:

- drug trafficking;
- slavery;
- people trafficking;
- firearms offences;

- armed robbery;
- prostitution (brothel keeping);
- child sex offences, including pornography;
- serious organised crime;
- money laundering:
  an offence under any of the following provisions of POCA 2002:

  – s.327 (concealing etc. criminal property);
  – s.328 (facilitating the acquisition etc. of criminal property by or on behalf of another);
  – s.329 (acquisition, use and possession of criminal property);
- fraud:
  – an offence under s.17 of the Theft Act 1968 (false accounting);
  – an offence under any of the following provisions of the Fraud Act 2006:
    - s.1 (fraud by false representation, failing to disclose information or abuse of position);
    - s.6 (possession etc. of articles for use in frauds);
    - s.7 (making or supplying articles for use in frauds);
    - s.9 (participating in fraudulent business carried on by sole trader);
    - s.11 (obtaining services dishonestly);
  – an offence at common law of conspiracy to defraud;
- offences in relation to the public revenue:
  – an offence under the Customs and Excise Management Act 1979. s.170 (fraudulent evasion of duty etc.);
  – an offence under the Value Added Tax Act 1994, s.72 (fraudulent evasion of VAT etc.);
  – an offence under the Taxes Management Act 1970, s.106A (fraudulent evasion of income tax);
  – an offence under the Tax Credits Act 2002, s.35 (tax credit fraud);
  – an offence at common law of cheating in relation to the public revenue;
- bribery:
  an offence under any of the following provisions of BA 2010:
  – s.1 (offences of bribing another person);
  – s.2 (offences relating to being bribed);
  – s.6 (bribery of foreign public officials);
- counterfeiting:
  an offence under any of the following provisions of the Forgery and Counterfeiting Act 1981:
  – s.14 (making counterfeit notes or coins);
  – s.15 (passing etc. counterfeit notes or coins);
  – s.16 (having custody or control of counterfeit notes or coins);
  – s.17 (making or having custody or control of counterfeiting materials or implements).

The list of 'connected persons'

Note that the EU Directive above defines 'family member' and 'close associate' for the purposes of PEPs, but a different test applies to the third part of the second limb at s.362B(4), i.e. the court may grant a UWO in respect of a person of whom there are reasonable grounds for suspecting that a 'person connected with the respondent is, or has been, so involved [in serious crime].'

The list is incorporated from the Corporation Tax Act 2010, s.1122:

> (5) An individual ('A') is connected with another individual ('B') if –
>
>> (a) A is B's spouse or civil partner,
>> (b) A is a relative of B,
>> (c) A is the spouse or civil partner of a relative of B,
>> (d) A is a relative of B's spouse or civil partner, or
>> (e) A is the spouse or civil partner of a relative of B's spouse or civil partner.
>
> (6) A person, in the capacity as trustee of a settlement, is connected with –
>
>> (a) any individual who is a settlor in relation to the settlement,
>> (b) any person connected with such an individual,
>> (c) any close company whose participators include the trustees of the settlement,
>> (d) any non-UK resident company which, if it were UK resident, would be a close company whose participators include the trustees of the settlement,
>> (e) any body corporate controlled (within the meaning of section 1124) by a company within paragraph (c) or (d),
>> (f) if the settlement is the principal settlement in relation to one or more sub-fund settlements, a person in the capacity as trustee of such a sub-fund settlement, and
>> (g) if the settlement is a sub-fund settlement in relation to a principal settlement, a person in the capacity as trustee of any other sub-fund settlements in relation to the principal settlement.
>
> (7) A person who is a partner in a partnership is connected with –
>
>> (a) any partner in the partnership,
>> (b) the spouse or civil partner of any individual who is a partner in the partnership, and
>> (c) a relative of any individual who is a partner in the partnership.

6.6   THE TERMS OF THE UNEXPLAINED WEALTH ORDER

UWOs require a person who is either a PEP or is suspected of involvement in, or association with, serious criminality to explain the origin of assets that appear to be disproportionate to that person's known income.

That explanation is required in the form of a statement from the respondent as ordered by the court.

Under CFA 2017, s.362A:

> (3) An unexplained wealth order is an order requiring the respondent to provide a statement –
>
>> (a) setting out the nature and extent of the respondent's interest in the property in respect of which the order is made,

(b) explaining how the respondent obtained the property (including, in particular, how any costs incurred in obtaining it were met),

(c) where the property is held by the trustees of a settlement, setting out such details of the settlement as may be specified in the order, and

(d) setting out such other information in connection with the property as may be so specified.

(4) The order must specify –

(a) the form and manner in which the statement is to be given,

(b) the person to whom it is to be given, and

(c) the place at which it is to be given or, if it is to be given in writing, the address to which it is to be sent.

The court sets time limits for a response which may vary with each part of the order.

A failure to provide a response would give rise to a presumption that the property was recoverable (for the purposes of Part 5, i.e. that the government can keep the property), unless the contrary is shown in order to assist any subsequent civil recovery action.

It would seem this section applies only to a total failure to respond; any sort of response at all counts as 'purported compliance' if not 'compliance'. There is a tactical choice here. A respondent who simply does not reply faces the worst case, i.e. that the property is presumed recoverable. Someone who does reply risks going to prison and a fine (see new offence below).

6.7   COMPLIANCE AND NON-COMPLIANCE: NEW OFFENCE

This will be an 'either way' offence, per s.362E (i.e. it can be heard in the magistrates' court or the Crown Court, following a procedure to determine venue and/or election by the accused).

A person could also be convicted of a criminal offence if that person makes false or misleading statements in response to a UWO.

362E   Offence

(1) A person commits an offence if, in purported compliance with a requirement imposed by an unexplained wealth order, the person –

(a) makes a statement that the person knows to be false or misleading in a material particular, or

(b) recklessly makes a statement that is false or misleading in a material particular.

(2) A person guilty of an offence under this section is liable –

(a) on conviction on indictment, to imprisonment for a term not exceeding 2 years, or to a fine, or to both;

(b) on summary conviction in England and Wales, to imprisonment for a term not exceeding 12 months, or to a fine, or to both;

    (c)   on summary conviction in Northern Ireland, to imprisonment for a term not exceeding 6 months, or to a fine not exceeding the statutory maximum, or to both.

6.8   INTERIM FREEZING ORDERS

As with a UWO, an interim freezing order may be made without notice. The interim freezing order and UWO may be combined in one document if it is in the same proceedings as the UWO.

The test is whether the court 'considers it necessary to do so for the purposes of avoiding the risk of any recovery order that might subsequently be obtained being frustrated'.

Note that under s.362 you *may* apply to discharge and vary an interim freezing order, and it will lapse, which is fairer than a UWO.

There is a discretion inherent in the variation and discharge of the interim freezing order. By s.362K(1): 'The High Court may at any time vary or discharge an interim freezing order.'

There is no discretion in the following circumstances, where by s.362(3)–(5) the High Court *must* discharge in three particular circumstances:

    (3)   The first case is where –

        (a)   the applicable 48 hour period has ended, and
        (b)   a relevant application has not been made before the end of that period in relation to the property concerned.

    (4)   The second case is where –

        (a)   a relevant application has been made before the end of the applicable 48 hour period in relation to the property concerned, and
        (b)   proceedings on the application (including any on appeal) have been determined or otherwise disposed of.

    (5)   The third case is where the court has received a notification in relation to the property concerned under section 362D(4) (notification from enforcement authority of no further proceedings).

Note, by s.362K(9), there is, finally, a hearing *inter partes* (emphasis added):

    (9)   Before exercising power under this section to vary or discharge an interim freezing order, the court *must (as well as giving the parties to the proceedings an opportunity to be heard)* give such an opportunity to any person who may be affected by its decision.

6.9   SAFEGUARDS

Under POCA 2002, s.360, statements made under compulsion cannot be used in evidence in criminal proceedings against the maker of the statement.

    (3)   A statement may not be used by [...] against a person unless –

(a)   evidence relating to it is adduced, or

(b)   a question relating to it is asked,

by him or on his behalf in proceedings arising out of the prosecution.

6.10   PRACTICAL OBJECTIONS

The following points may in due course be litigated:

- No notice is required of the substantive application for a UWO: a respondent will have to apply to vary or discharge the interim freezing order *post facto*. This is extraordinary.
- Possible infringement of Article 6 of the European Convention on Human Rights (ECHR) (notwithstanding Baroness Williams of Trafford, sponsoring the Bill, making the standard statement of compatibility with the ECHR). It appears that the State as applicant has much more access to the court than the individual as respondent.
- It is extraterritorial: the applicant must specify against whom the order is sought, whether that person is in the UK or abroad.
- The measure is retro-active.
- It represents a serious reversal burden of proof.
- Is this the thin end of the wedge? The House of Lords reduced the threshold in the Commons Bill from £100,000 to £50,000. Inflation will erode this threshold.
- The scheme relies on inertia; in many cases the respondent will not contest so the State will keep assets by default.
- On the test of *'income ascertainable'* – by whom? The High Court judge has no investigative function and the respondent will be absent at this stage. This may infringe Articles 6 and 8 ECHR.

7 SUSPICIOUS ACTIVITY REPORTS, DISCLOSURE AND INFORMATION SHARING

7.1 OVERVIEW

Under existing provisions, regulated companies[1] are under a duty to inform the National Crime Agency (NCA) of client activity which the reporter suspects may amount to money laundering, without 'tipping off' those clients. This is a fraught area of responsibility: a solicitor must 'grass' on a client and not reveal this to the client, or commit a criminal offence (POCA 2002, s.330).

The number of reports is high. In excess of 381,000 SARs were received by the NCA between September 2014 and October 2015 (per the Explanatory Note to CFA 2017).

By POCA 2002, s.335, some 14,672 of the SARs received in 2014/15 were given 'consent' by the NCA.

As practitioners will know, in the event that the NCA refuses consent, the regulated company loses its statutory defence (POCA 2002, ss.327–329) 31 days from the date of refusal.

The Explanatory Note to CFA 2017 (note 18) states:

> This has the effect of preventing the activity from going ahead during that period. This is known as the 'moratorium period'. The purpose of the moratorium period is to allow investigators time to gather evidence to determine whether further action, such as restraint of the funds, should take place. This period, which is not currently renewable, often does not allow sufficient time to develop the evidence, particularly where it must be sought from overseas through mutual legal assistance.

7.2 EXTENSION OF THE MORATORIUM PERIOD

CFA 2017, s.10 inserts new sections into POCA 2002. All references in this section are to the amended POCA statute.

By s.336A(7), the Crown Court will have the power to grant extensions of the moratorium period, up to a maximum of 186 days in total, beginning with the end

---

[1] I.e. one subject to the Money Laundering Regulations 2007 (MLRs), such as a bank, accountancy firm, legal firm or estate agent.

of the first 31-day period. At each extension the court must be satisfied that there is an ongoing investigation, being conducted 'diligently and expeditiously' (s.336A(1)), that further time is needed and that 'it is reasonable in all the circumstances'. Application must be made by a senior officer (s.336A(2) for the requirement and s.336D(7) for definition of 'senior officer', e.g. police inspector), and the court must determine the proceedings 'as soon as reasonably practicable' (s.336B(2)).

Further, the moratorium period may be extended 'from the time when it would otherwise end until the court determines the application or it is otherwise disposed of' (s.336C(2)), but subject to a 31-day maximum (s.336C(5)). The effect of this is that short term problems in court listing will not frustrate the continuation of the moratorium period. Moreover, there is a five-day period of grace following refusal of the court to grant an extension of the moratorium period (s.336C(8)).

7.3   WITHHOLDING INFORMATION FROM INTERESTED PERSONS

By s.336B(4), the applicant may ask the court for an order to withhold information from an 'interested person' (defined at s.336D(3)) or anyone representing that person if the court is satisfied there are 'reasonable grounds to believe' (s.336B(5)) that disclosure would lead to interference with: evidence, information gathering about an offence, a person (or that that person would be injured) or the recovery of property. Disclosure may also be withheld if national security would be put at risk. Moreover the court 'must' (s.336B(6)) direct that the interested person and that person's representatives are excluded from the hearing.

Appeals lie from the Crown Courts (s.336B(8)–(11)) and by the Senior Courts Act 1981, s.28.

7.4   INFORMATION SHARING AND 'SUPER-SARS': AN OVERVIEW

A legal shield for the sharing of information between entities within the regulated sector (e.g. banks) is provided by CFA 2017, driving a coach and horses through the existing Data Protection Act and PACE regimes (PACE 1984, s.9, and see 7.6 below).

The Explanatory Notes (at note 22) describe the government's policy objective:

> The private sector holds data on financial transactions and related personal data; the law enforcement agencies hold details of criminals, and intelligence on crime. When this data has been shared, such as under the Joint Money Laundering Intelligence Taskforce (JMLIT) pilot, there have been positive outcomes for both sectors. Although existing data protection legislation allows for the sharing of information for the prevention and detection of crime, regulated companies are concerned that

there should be express legal cover that is directly related to the anti-money laundering regime, in order to reduce the risk of civil litigation for breach of confidentiality.

There is no mention in this equation of the individual's right to privacy (Art.8 ECHR); the Data Protection Act is merely acknowledged in passing; and the undermining of the protection of 'special procedure material' under the existing production order regime is ignored (PACE 1984, s.9, and see 7.6 below).

Here, the policy justification is to the effect that the law enforcement agencies know who the criminals are, so the banks and credit reference agencies should provide data on their financial dealings.

The one part of the process being entirely circumvented is the judicial scrutiny currently required.

7.5   SUPER-SARS: PROCESS

Regulated bodies are allowed by CFA 2017 to share information with each other, where they have notified the NCA that they suspect that certain activity is related to money laundering (s.339ZB(4) regarding disclosure to an NCA officer; see also the section generally for other conditions, which are easily met).

The Explanatory Notes say (at note 23):

> This measure enables the submission of joint disclosure reports, which bring together information from multiple reporters into a single SAR that provides the whole picture to law enforcement agencies. To begin with, this measure will be applied to financial sector organisations – some of which are already part of the JMLIT – but it can be extended to all of the regulated sector in due course.

Provision is made for the information which must appear in such a disclosure request (s.339ZC), identifying the person and the information sought.

The first legal cover or shield granted by the new provisions is that a 'joint disclosure report' (i.e. super-SAR) made in good faith is to be treated as a SAR and satisfies each party's requirements to disclose (s.339ZD(3)).

The second legal cover, at the heart of the new provisions, is that (s.339ZF):

   (1)   A relevant disclosure made in good faith does not breach –

       (a)   an obligation of confidence owed by the person making the disclosure, or,
       (b)   any other restriction on the disclosure of information

       however imposed.

It is quite extraordinary that such a fundamental shift in the relationship between the State and the individual – a measure entirely circumventing long-established judicial scrutiny – should be concealed under the heading '339ZF Section 339ZB: supplementary'.

By contrast, the privacy of the law enforcement agencies is preserved; by s.339ZF(2) information obtained by them cannot be shared without their consent.

7.6   CHALLENGE TO INFORMATION SHARING AND SUPER-SARS

Rather than go to a Crown Court judge to apply for this information, the NCA will now look to the regulated sector to do the legwork, and in doing so circumvent judicial scrutiny.

The pre-existing law on data protection of such information is as follows.

Disclosure of 'personal data' by a data controller as defined by the Data Protection Act 1998, s.1 is permitted in certain circumstances. 'Personal data' is 'information' processed by automatic equipment relating to a living individual identifiable from such data.

The Data Protection Act 1998, s.29 reads (with emphasis added):

Crime and taxation

(1)   Personal data processed for any of the following purposes –

   (a)   the *prevention or detection of crime*,
   (b)   the apprehension or prosecution of offenders, or
   (c)   the assessment or *collection of any tax* or duty or of any imposition of a similar nature,

   are exempt from the first data protection principle (except to the extent to which it requires compliance with the conditions in Schedules 2 and 3) and section 7 in any case to the extent to which the application of those provisions to the data would be likely to prejudice any of the matters mentioned in this subsection.

(2)   Personal data which –

   (a)   are processed for the purpose of discharging statutory functions, and
   (b)   consist of information obtained for such a purpose from a person who had it in his possession for any of the purposes mentioned in subsection (1),

   are exempt from the subject information provisions to the same extent as personal data processed for any of the purposes mentioned in that subsection.

(3)   Personal data are exempt from the non-disclosure provisions in any case in which –

   (a)   the disclosure is for any of the purposes mentioned in subsection (1), and
   (b)   the application of those provisions in relation to the disclosure would be likely to prejudice any of the matters mentioned in that subsection.

(4)   Personal data in respect of which the data controller is a relevant authority and which –

   (a)   consist of a classification applied to the data subject as part of a system of

> risk assessment which is operated by that authority for either of the
> following purposes –
>
> (i)   the assessment or collection of any tax or duty or any imposition
>   of a similar nature, or
>
> (ii)   the prevention or detection of crime, or apprehension or prosecu-
>   tion of offenders, where the offence concerned involves any
>   unlawful claim for any payment out of, or any unlawful applica-
>   tion of, public funds, and
>
> (b)   are processed for either of those purposes,
>
> are exempt from section 7 to the extent to which the exemption is required
> in the interests of the operation of the system.

So, there is an adequate safeguard in place for those regulated companies who, via their data controllers, provide information to the NCA.

The contents of bank statements or credit reports or account details unquestionably constitute more than 'information'; they are 'material' within the meaning of PACE 1984 relating to warrants and production orders, as defined by the High Court (see e.g. *R (Faisaltex Ltd)* v. *Preston Crown Court* [2009] 1 WLR 1687, paras.76–79).

The material is 'special procedure material' within the meaning of the Data Protection Act 1998, s.14, being held by banks etc. subject to a duty of confidence. It is only obtainable if the conditions of Sched.1 to PACE 1984 are satisfied and a circuit judge grants either a warrant or a production order.

The opportunity to challenge this new information-sharing regime and super-SARs will only come after an investigation is based upon them and a criminal case comes to court.

It could then be argued that evidence obtained via the new regime is to be excluded from PACE 1984, s.78, or that the proceedings amount to an abuse of process, or that any subsequent conviction is unsafe.

Given that the statute is clear and widely drawn (i.e. that disclosure under the new regime does not breach any restriction however imposed, by previous statute or common law) it may be that Art.8 ECHR is the only remedy.

7.7   FURTHER COMPULSORY DISCLOSURES TO THE NCA

7.7.1   The notice

As per the Explanatory Note (at note 19):

> In order to enhance the effectiveness of this regime, the Act also creates a power for
> the NCA to seek an order compelling further information from any person in the
> regulated sector (as defined by Schedule 9 of POCA), following receipt of a SAR; or
> where they have received a request from a Financial Intelligence Unit (FIU) in
> another country.

No doubt this makes the NCA's job easier, but it is a further re-balancing of power towards the State, against individual privacy. The Extradition Act 2003 can scarcely be said to jealously guard UK citizens against requests from foreign countries, but at least there are two clear schemes available. There will be no judicial oversight at all of the initial requests for financial information from overseas Financial Intelligence Units which the NCA decides to act upon. Granted, a magistrates' court will supervise any *order* sought (see below) if there is non-compliance with the *notice*. It is to be hoped that these applications will be placed before specialist extradition (or at least stipendiary) magistrates.

Part 7 of POCA 2002 is amended by CFA 2017 to allow the NCA to direct the reporter, or another regulated sector entity, to answer a 'further information notice' relating to the SAR (CFA 2017, s.12 amends POCA 2002 by inserting s.339ZH).

7.7.2   Order and sanction

The sanction (and therefore compulsion) is that if the information requested is not provided, the NCA can apply to a magistrates' court (or sheriff's court in Scotland) for an order compelling the person to provide it; and failure to comply would result in a fine of up to £5,000 (s.339ZH(8)).

The Explanatory Note (at note 19) baldly asserts: 'This power is required to allow the NCA to perform its analytical functions. The decision of the court would be appealable in the normal way.'

7.8   SAFEGUARDS AND RESTRICTIONS

Any information provided would be given immunity from any restriction on the disclosure of information, such as confidentiality clauses in contracts or the law of confidence, per s.339ZM(3). It is a major shift away from having a circuit judge consider special procedure material (s.9 and PACE 1984, Sched. 1) to placing powers into the hands of investigators and magistrates.

The information provided under compulsion could not be used in criminal proceedings against the person who made the statement (s.339ZI(1)), except in the case of perjury.

8 THE POCA REGIME OVERHAULED

8.1 BRIEF OVERVIEW OF EXISTING POCA REGIME

Unexplained wealth orders, which are a radical change to the POCA regime, are considered in detail at **Chapter 6**. Here we turn to the other amendments to POCA, apart from those which overlap with terrorism (dealt with in the following chapter).

A detailed analysis of the POCA regime is beyond the scope of this Guide. For further analysis see *Blackstone's Guide to the Proceeds of Crime Act 2002* (OUP, 5th edn, 2015) and *Archbold: Criminal Pleading, Evidence and Practice 2017* (Sweet & Maxwell), at 5-734 et seq.

The Proceeds of Crime Act 2002 was introduced to consolidate the two previous regimes under the Drug Trafficking Act 1994 and the Criminal Justice Act 1998. New, far reaching and draconian powers to trace and recover criminal assets are provided by POCA 2002.

Four main heads for the recovery of assets are provided by POCA 2002:

- criminal confiscation (post-conviction, either guilty plea or trial);
- civil recovery (anomalously, given the name of the Act, used where there has been no criminal conviction);
- cash seizure and forfeiture; and
- taxation.

Powers to restrain assets which are merely suspected to derive from criminal conduct are also provided.

8.1.1 Criminal confiscation orders

Confiscation orders are made by a court following conviction after trial or by plea, for a criminal offence. Confiscation orders do not provide for the confiscation of identified property, but orders the defendant to pay a sum of money, calculated by determining, first, 'the criminal benefit' and, second, the 'available amount', i.e. whatever resources are deemed by the court to be available to the defendant. Defendants fear a finding of 'hidden assets' which may be used by the court to find an 'available amount' far in excess of anything demonstrable, which must be paid on pain of default sentence.

The defendant is given a period to pay the order, after which the defendant is liable for interest and may be subject to a default sentence of imprisonment for failing to pay. Gone are the days when experienced villains would elect to do the time in order to retain their ill-gotten proceeds, as sentences in default will often double the period in custody in relation to the original substantive sentence.

8.1.2   Restraint

Restraint orders prevent a person subject to mere criminal investigation or actual criminal proceedings dealing with any realisable property (e.g. by freezing funds in a bank account) on the face of it to prevent the removal of assets which may later be subject to a confiscation order. Restrained assets may be used to satisfy a confiscation order or returned to the individual(s) if the POCA order is in an amount less than the funds restrained. Restraint orders based on mere suspicion are arguably objectionable: if the funds are alleged to be criminal there should be a prosecution. This Kafka-esque reversal of the burden of proof is taken to a new level by UWOs (see **Chapter 6**).

8.1.3   Civil recovery

This part of the POCA regime allows recovery of 'criminal' assets where no conviction has in fact occurred, e.g. because individuals were remote from the crimes committed (but nonetheless benefited financially, as in the example of a drug baron who was never 'hands-on' or physically near the narcotics) or fled the jurisdiction pre-trial.

8.1.4   Cash forfeiture

Provisions allow for cash in sums above £1,000 to be seized, if it is *suspected* (that low hurdle again) to be unlawful in origin, or to be intended for use in unlawful conduct. These are civil proceedings, and it is not therefore necessary to arrest the person physically in possession of the cash. The seized cash may be detained for up to two years while its origin and purpose are investigated. Ultimately, the cash is either given back or forfeited at a magistrates' court or (if certain conditions are met) administratively. Once forfeited the cash is transferred into a central fund, held by the government.

8.1.5   Revenue functions under the POCA regime

The NCA has certain revenue functions under POCA 2002 which enables it to make a tax assessment where the source of income cannot be identified but are *suspected* (our familiar test) to be criminal assets. These powers are in addition to those exercised by HMRC. Investigative powers are also provided by POCA 2002 to NCA officers, such as search and seizure, and powers to apply for production orders and disclosure orders.

8.2   SEIZURE AND FORFEITURE POWERS

8.2.1   Overview

New civil powers are provided by CFA 2017, similar to the existing cash seizure and forfeiture scheme in POCA 2002, Part 5, Chapter 3, to enable the forfeiture of monies stored in bank accounts and items of personal property, like precious metals and jewels.

The Home Office asserts that there is evidence that these items are being used to move value, both domestically and across international borders. A list of items is specified which can be amended by affirmative order as required. The power will be exercisable where there is reasonable *suspicion* (low hurdle) that the property is the proceeds of crime or that it will be used in unlawful conduct, in a manner similar to cash.

8.2.2   Forfeiture

Section 14: Forfeiture of casino chips and betting slips

The current position is as per POCA 2002, Part 5, Chapter 3 by s.289(6) of that Act, which contains seizure provisions that allow law enforcement agencies to seize items including cash, cheques and bearer bonds, where they believe that they are recoverable property or intended for use in unlawful conduct.

To these powers, the new CFA 2017, s.14, adds three new items to the list of items that may be seized under these provisions. Section 289(6) of POCA 2002 will be amended to include gaming vouchers, fixed value casino tokens and betting receipts.

Gaming vouchers are defined as a voucher in physical form issued by a gaming machine, such as a fixed odds betting terminal, that represents a right to be paid the amount stated on it. They are usually thin pieces of paper which resemble a till receipt, with a bar code which can be scanned at the casino cash desk in return for cash.

Fixed value casino tokens means a token issued by a casino that represents a right to be paid the value stated on it. Presumably these would include classic round 'chips' and rectangular 'bars'. The fact that they are 'fixed value' would preclude poker tournament chips, and it would seem this is a (small) loophole in the legislation.

Forfeiture of certain personal (or moveable) property: jewellery, art, vouchers and stamps

The new CFA 2017, s.15 inserts, into Part 5 of POCA 2002, a new Chapter 3A, which makes provision for the seizure and recovery of listed types of personal or moveable property ('listed assets') that are the proceeds of unlawful conduct or intended for use in such conduct. The provisions build on existing powers in

Chapter 3 to seize and recover cash that is the proceeds of unlawful conduct or intended for use in such conduct. All section references are to the amended POCA 2002. The definition of 'unlawful conduct' can be found in s.241.

Listed assets are defined in POCA 2002, s.303B. The current list is:

(a) precious metals (gold, silver or platinum);
(b) precious stones (not defined here);
(c) watches;
(d) artistic works (defined at s.4(1)(a) of the Copyright, Designs and Patents Act 1988);
(e) face-value vouchers (in physical form);
(f) postage stamps.

This section also provides that the Secretary of State, following consultation with Scottish Ministers, may proscribe by order additional assets by regulations. The new powers may only be exercised where the suspected listed asset or assets exceed the threshold set under s.303Y.

Section 303C also provides that the search powers will only be exercisable on private premises where the relevant officer has lawful authority to be present. Sub-sections (5) and (6) include the power to search vehicles and persons. Section 303C(9) provides that police constables, HMRC officers, SFO officers and AFIs are 'relevant officers' for the purpose of these provisions.

Section 303D sets out the conditions under which the powers of search may be used. There is a low threshold of 'reasonable ground to suspect', though this is consistent with standard police powers.

The search powers may only be used where prior judicial authority has been obtained or, if that is not practicable, with the approval of a senior officer (s.303E). 'Senior officer' is defined for all of the agencies permitted to use these powers.

Section 303E(6) provides that where the search powers are not approved by a judicial authority prior to the search, and any listed asset is either not seized or is released before the matter comes before a court, the officer exercising the power must prepare a written report and submit it to an independent person, appointed by the Secretary of State in relation to England and Wales, by Scottish Ministers in relation to Scotland, or by the Department of Justice in relation to Northern Ireland ('the appointed person'). This is a nod towards judicial supervision of investigative powers.

Section 303F provides that the appointed person must provide a yearly (at the end of each financial year) report, to be laid before Parliament, the Scottish Parliament and the Northern Ireland Assembly as appropriate. This report must give the appointed person's opinion as to the circumstances in which the search powers were exercised in cases where the relevant officer was required to make a report under s.306E(6). Though this is, again, a nod towards legislative scrutiny of investigative powers, it would be better to have proper judicial supervision.

Section 303G provides that a code of practice must be published by the Secretary of State in connection with the exercise of the search powers in s.303C. The provisions require consultation on the draft code with the Attorney General in relation to the use of the powers by the SFO. There are parallel provisions for Scotland and Northern Ireland. No doubt the authors of this code of practice will look to the PACE codes as a starting point.

As for an officer seizing personal property, s.303J provides that a relevant officer may seize any listed asset or assets found, if the office has (our low threshold again) reasonable grounds for *suspecting* that the listed asset or assets are recoverable property or intended for use in unlawful conduct. The value of the listed asset or aggregate value of listed assets must exceed the minimum threshold currently set at £1,000, under s.303Y. Under subsection (2) a relevant officer may seize a listed asset where that asset cannot reasonably be divided and only part of that asset is under suspicion (provided that part meets the minimum threshold). So this would plainly extend to a casino chip (or more likely a casino 'bar') for £5,000 or a single betting receipt for the same value.

As for initial detention, s.303K provides that any listed asset seized by a relevant officer may only be detained for an initial period of six hours. It may be further detained for a period of 42 hours with the approval of a senior officer; presumably with modern technology and modes of communication this is not a difficult test to satisfy, especially given that the clock does not run at all at the weekend, bank holidays, Christmas Day or Good Friday. It is to be hoped that a junior officer seizing a casino chip on the Thursday before Easter would not yield to temptation in the following four days.

Section 303L provides that the detention of any listed asset may be extended by a judicial authority up to a maximum of two years, and time runs from the first order. To make such an order, the judicial authority must be satisfied that there are (which should come as no surprise) reasonable grounds for *suspecting* that the continued detention is justified, for the purposes of investigating the property's origin or the property's intended use, or that continued detention is justified because consideration is being given to the bringing of criminal proceedings or such proceedings have been commenced and not concluded. Again, this is a very low threshold for interference with personal property rights. The rationale is a debatable one: effectively that law enforcement agencies know who the criminals are and so should be trusted to take their property.

Section 303M provides for the testing of the listed property to determine whether it is a listed asset, presumably not by biting into a gold coin (though the statute does not preclude it, as officers may 'carry out' the test themselves), and that the property must be safely stored while this is done – though there is no sanction whatsoever if this is breached. A mere nod here to personal property rights.

Section 303N provides that the listed assets may be released by a magistrates' court (or equivalent in Scotland) to the person from whom they were seized where a judicial authority is satisfied, on application by the person from whom the property was seized, that it is not recoverable property or is not intended for use in unlawful conduct. There is no express reference to the burden or standard of proof here (unremarkable, given the POCA regime). Given that the property is seized on mere suspicion, the defence may argue, it would be fair that the State authority bear the burden and this should be to a criminal standard. At very least, the balance of probabilities should be on the State to prove.

As for an application for forfeiture, s.303O provides that a judicial authority may order the forfeiture of property or any part of it if 'satisfied' (again, no mention here of a burden or standard) that it is recoverable property or is intended for use in unlawful conduct, and defines who may apply for forfeiture: a police constable, commissioner for HMRC, SFO officer or accredited financial investigator (AFI).

Sections 303P–303R explain how associated property and joint property are to be dealt with when forfeiture is ordered. The most draconian part of this is that the magistrates' court may 'make an order requiring the person who holds the associated property or who is the excepted joint owner to make a payment to a person identified in the order' (s.303Q(1)(b)).

'Associated property' is defined by s.303P and defines an 'excepted joint owner' for the purpose of considering forfeitable property of a joint tenant.

By s.303Q, a judicial authority may order that a person who holds associated property or who is an excepted joint owner may retain the property but must pay the law enforcement agency a sum equivalent to the value of the recoverable share. Happily, this section applies where there is agreement among the parties as to the extent of the recoverable portion of the property.

However, s.303R describes how a judicial authority can deal with a person who holds associated property or who is an excepted joint owner but where there is *no* agreement under s.303Q. If an order for forfeiture of part of the property is made, and the court considers it is 'just and equitable' to do so, it may also order that the excepted joint owner's interest will be extinguished, or that the excepted joint owner's interest will be severed, and it may order that a payment be made to that individual. There is a robust element of compulsion here, in relation to private property rights of a person who may have no criminal involvement at all.

There is a right of appeal by s.303S, which provides for appeal against a forfeiture decision made under ss.303O and 303R, to the Crown Court in England and Wales, the Sheriff Appeal Court in Scotland and the county court in Northern Ireland.

Where forfeiture is ordered, s.303T provides that the relevant agency must realise the property or make arrangements for its realisation, subject to any appeal rights against the forfeiture being exhausted. There is a duty to maximise the value obtained for the property, though no benchmark or sanction is in place to enforce this 'duty'.

Section 303U sets out the order in which the proceeds realised should be applied, first paying costs incurred in the process, finally vesting in the relevant Consolidated Fund.

By s.303V, the true owner of the property may apply for its release, in whole or in part. The magistrates (or equivalent) will determine (again, no express burden and standard of proof) whether (s.303V(6):

(a) the applicant is not the person from whom the property to which the application relates was seized,
(b) it appears to the court or sheriff that that property belongs to the applicant,
(c) the court or sheriff is satisfied that the release condition is met in relation to that property, and
(d) no objection to the making of an order … has been made by the person from whom that property was seized.

In terms of compensation, s.303W states that, where no forfeiture is made, following seizure the person from whom the property was seized, or the person to whom the cash belongs, may apply to the court for compensation where the circumstances are exceptional.

Changes to POCA regime introduced by ss.303X–303Z

The remaining new sections (i.e. ss.303X–303Z19) make further procedural changes to the POCA regime, a detailed consideration of which is beyond the scope of this Guide. The following is, of necessity, a bald summary, taken from the Explanatory Note.

Section 303X provides that the CPS or the Director of Public Prosecutions for Northern Ireland may appear in proceedings on behalf of a police constable or an AFI, if asked to do so and if it is considered appropriate for them to do so.

Section 303Y sets the minimum value threshold below which these powers do not apply. It also provides a power for the Secretary of State to amend this figure by Regulations.

Section 303Z specifies that where an AFI makes an application under this section, subsequent steps in any proceedings can be taken by a different AFI of the same description.

Forfeiture of money held in bank and building society accounts

New ss.303Z1–303Z19 make provision for the freezing and forfeiture of bank and building society accounts, where those accounts contain the proceeds of unlawful conduct (i.e. criminality).

Section 303Z1 provides that the powers can be exercised by police constables, HMRC officers, SFO officers or AFIs. It allows a senior officer (as defined in s.303Z2(7)) to apply for an account freezing order (AFO) on bank and building society accounts, where there are reasonable grounds to suspect that the money in them is recoverable property or is intended by any person for use in unlawful conduct. The AFO can be made without notice, if notice of application would prejudice the taking of any steps to later forfeit monies under this section.

The AFO prohibits any person from dealing with the account to which the order applies. The AFO must be applied for at a magistrates' court in England, Wales and

Northern Ireland, or to the Sheriff in Scotland. The funds within the account remain with the bank or building society.

Section 303Z2 sets out a number of restrictions on applications for the AFO, including where an account is excluded, or where the amount is below the minimum amount set by the Secretary of State, as defined in s.303Z8.

Section 303Z3 provides that the court may make the order, if is satisfied that the funds in the account (whether all or in part), are either recoverable property or are intended for use in unlawful conduct. The court sets the timeframe for the freezing order, which must be no more than two years.

Section 303Z4 allows a court to vary or set aside an AFO at any time, and can also do so upon application by any person affected by such an order. This is at the discretion of the court.

Section 303Z5 allows the court to make exclusions from the restriction on activity on the account for the purpose of meeting living expenses or to allow a person to carry on a business or trade. It also permits exclusions for legal expenses.

Section 303Z6 provides that a court in which proceedings relating to a frozen account are proceeding can stay those proceedings, if it is satisfied that an AFO has been applied for or obtained. That court may also order that the proceedings can continue on any terms it thinks are appropriate.

Section 303Z7 defines the term 'bank'.

Section 303Z8 defines that the minimum amount of funds that an account must contain will be specified in regulations made by the Secretary of State, after consultation with the Scottish Ministers and with the Department of Justice in Northern Ireland.

Section 303Z9 allows a senior officer to issue an 'account forfeiture notice' (AFN), which is a notice for the purposes of forfeiting the funds in an account. The funds must be subject to an AFO order for an AFN to be served. This is an administrative procedure.

The senior officer may give a notice that forfeiture of the balance of the account will be sought, provided that the officer is satisfied that the contents are either recoverable property, or are intended to be used in unlawful conduct. The AFN must set out the amount to be forfeited, the period for objecting to the forfeiture, and the address to which any objections must be sent. The period for objecting must be at least 30 days. An objection may be made by anyone, in writing. If no objection is received, at the end of the period the amount of money stated in the AFN will be forfeited, and the bank or building society must transfer that money into the interest-bearing account nominated by the senior officer. An objection does not prevent forfeiture of the money by court order under s.303Z14. It is not necessary for an AFN to be sought if the senior officer wishes to seek forfeiture of the money by order of a court under s.303Z14.

Section 303Z10 requires the Secretary of State to make regulations about how an AFN is to be given to the interested parties.

Section 303Z11 sets out the conditions under which an AFN lapses. The AFN lapses if an objection is received; an application for forfeiture is made; or if the AFO is recalled or set aside. The section provides for a senior officer to either extend the period of the AFO, or to seek forfeiture of the money under s.303Z14.

Section 303Z12 sets out the procedure for applying for an administrative forfeiture to be set aside. The application must be made before the end of the objection period. It can be made after a longer period if the court is satisfied there are exceptional circumstances. The court must consider whether the forfeiture should be set aside, and if it determines that this is the case, it must consider whether the money should be forfeited through a forfeiture order under s.303Z14. If the court determines that the funds should not be forfeited, it must order the release of that money.

Section 303Z13 provides that any money forfeited under an AFN is paid into the Consolidated Fund.

Section 303Z14 defines the procedure for the relevant court to order the forfeiture of the money in an account if the court is satisfied that the money is recoverable property or that it is intended for use in unlawful conduct. If the court determines that the money meets the criteria, the bank or building society must transfer the funds to an interest-bearing account nominated by the enforcement officer.

Section 303Z15 provides that, where a court declines to order the forfeiture of an asset, and the law enforcement agency appeals, it may also apply for an extension of the AFO pending the appeal.

Section 303Z16 provides for an appeal to be made against the forfeiture order. The time period for the lodging of an appeal is 30 days from the day that the court makes the order. If the appeal is upheld, it may order the release of the whole or part of the funds. If a forfeiture order is successfully appealed, and the funds are returned to the individual, any interest which accrued during the time that the funds were held by the police must also be returned to the individual.

Section 303Z17 provides that any funds forfeited under a forfeiture order should be paid into the Consolidated Fund.

Section 303Z18 provides that if an AFO is made and none of that money is later forfeited, the person by or for whom the account is operated may make an application to court for compensation. The amount of compensation is the amount the relevant court thinks reasonable, having regard to the loss suffered and any other relevant circumstances.

Section 303Z19 provides for prosecutors to appear in proceedings on behalf of a police constable or an AFI, if this is requested and they consider it appropriate.

8.3   CIVIL RECOVERY OF THE PROCEEDS OF 'GROSS HUMAN RIGHTS ABUSES'

This can be seen as a corollary of the PEP provisions explored in **Chapter 6**, allowing the assets of PEPs to be frozen based on reasonable suspicion. Here, public officials are stripped of wealth derived from human rights abuses. There is an element of hyperbole and symbolism in this section: why should only 'gross' human rights abuses be caught?

The following passages explain the provisions, and are taken from the Explanatory Notes to CFA 2017.

25   This provision expands the definition of 'unlawful conduct' within Part 5 of POCA to include conduct by a public official that constitutes gross human rights abuse (defined as torture or inhuman, cruel or degrading treatment) of a person on the grounds that they have been obtaining, exercising, defending or promoting human rights, or have sought to expose gross human rights abuse conducted by a public official. Activity by any person that is connected with such conduct is also caught within the expanded definition. As a result, any property obtained through this conduct will be subject to the existing civil recovery powers within Part 5.

. . .

113   Section 13 provides for an expansion to the existing civil recovery provisions in POCA. This is so they can be relied upon to seek recovery of property obtained as a result of the conduct, outside the UK, of a public official which constitutes gross human rights abuses or violations (or conduct by any person that is connected with that abuse) of a person because they have whistle-blown in relation to conduct of a public official, or sought to obtain, exercise, defend or promote human rights where such conduct would be an offence (triable either way or on indictment) if it took place in the UK.

114   Sub-section (3) inserts a new section into POCA. New section 241A defines the nature of the 'gross human rights abuse or violations' as torture or cruel, inhuman or degrading treatment or punishment by a public official (or a person acting in an official capacity or with the consent or acquiescence of a public official) of a person because they have sought to expose illegal activity of a public official or obtain, exercise, defend or promote human rights. Conduct connected with this is also captured, including a range of activity connected with such abuse or violations such as directing it, assisting or supporting anyone conducting it or anyone who profits from this activity is also subject to these provisions.

115   Sub-section (3) also outlines that torture is defined by intentional infliction of severe pain or suffering, can include both mental and physical pain, and can be caused by either act or omission.

116   Sub-sections (4) and (5) specify that this provision can apply to conduct constituting torture (or that connected with it) – an offence for which the UK applies universal jurisdiction – where it occurred prior to this enactment. Conduct constituting cruel, inhuman and degrading treatment will be caught only where it occurs after the coming into force of these provisions. The time period during which civil recovery claims must be brought is expressly limited so that a claim may not be brought in respect of any conduct occurring more than twenty years earlier (as per sub-section (5) and paragraphs 1, 2 and 5 of Schedule 5).

117   Sub-sections (6) and (7) set out the legal procedures for these measures within England, Wales, Northern Ireland and Scotland.

9 COUNTER-TERRORISM

Detailed consideration of the counter-terrorism regime is beyond the scope of this Guide, and so this chapter is inevitably somewhat brief. Practitioners are advised to read the relevant Explanatory Notes (see **9.2**) for a more detailed overview. See also A. Jones, R. Bowers and H.D. Lodge, *Blackstone's Guide to the Terrorism Act 2006* (OUP, 2006) and C. Walker, *Blackstone's Guide to the Anti-Terrorism Legislation* (OUP, 2009).

9.1 TERRORIST FINANCE

The Explanatory Note to CFA 2017 (at note 39) states:

> Countering terrorist finance is an important part of the Government's response to terrorism and financial investigation is a key tool in the investigation of a number of terrorism offences. The vulnerabilities in the financial sector which are at risk of being exploited are broadly the same as those for the proceeds of crime.

Thus, the following powers in CFA 2017 are extended to apply to investigations in relation to suspected terrorist property and terrorist financing, as well as under the POCA regime:

- the powers to enhance the SARs regime;
- information sharing;
- seizure and forfeiture powers – for bank accounts and mobile stores of value; and
- disclosure orders.

Each of these areas is dealt with more generally in **Chapter 7**.

A number of powers under Terrorism Act 2000 and the Anti-Terrorism, Crime and Security Act 2001, which are currently only available to police constables, are extended by CFA 2017 to civilian counter-terrorism financial investigators (CTFIs) employed by the police.

According to the Explanatory Note to CFA 2017 (at note 40), 'Counter-terrorism policing indicate that the extension of these powers to CTFIs will increase the capacity of the police to apply for the orders in question by over 50%'.

9.2   THE EXPLANATORY NOTES

HMRC's Explanatory Notes for Part 2 of CFA 2017 ('Terrorist Property') are provided in **Appendix C** and can be read in conjunction with the analysis provided in **Chapter 7** in respect of SARs and information sharing, generally.

Appendix A
CRIMINAL FINANCES ACT 2017[1]

[2017 c.22]

An Act to amend the Proceeds of Crime Act 2002; make provision in connection with terrorist property; create corporate offences for cases where a person associated with a body corporate or partnership facilitates the commission by another person of a tax evasion offence; and for connected purposes.

[27th April 2017]

BE IT ENACTED by the Queen's most Excellent Majesty, by and with the advice and consent of the Lords Spiritual and Temporal, and Commons, in this present Parliament assembled, and by the authority of the same, as follows:

PART 1   PROCEEDS OF CRIME

CHAPTER 1   INVESTIGATIONS

Unexplained wealth orders: England and Wales and Northern Ireland

1   Unexplained wealth orders: England and Wales and Northern Ireland

In Chapter 2 of Part 8 of the Proceeds of Crime Act 2002 (investigations: England and Wales and Northern Ireland), after section 362 insert –

'Unexplained wealth orders

362A   Unexplained wealth orders

(1)   The High Court may, on an application made by an enforcement authority, make an unexplained wealth order in respect of any property if the court is satisfied that each of the requirements for the making of the order is fulfilled.

(2)   An application for an order must –

(a)   specify or describe the property in respect of which the order is sought, and

(b)   specify the person whom the enforcement authority thinks holds the property ("the respondent") (and the person specified may include a person outside the United Kingdom).

(3)   An unexplained wealth order is an order requiring the respondent to provide a statement –

(a)   setting out the nature and extent of the respondent's interest in the property in respect of which the order is made,

---

[1]   *Note on commencement:* general provisions in ss.51–54 and any other necessary provisions to come into force on Royal Assent; provisions in s.39 ('Extension of powers of financial investigators') to come into force two months after Royal Assent; all other provisions will be brought into force by commencement regulations made by the Treasury (in relation to Part 3), or devolved ministers as appropriate. (See CFA 2017, s.58.)

(b) explaining how the respondent obtained the property (including, in particular, how any costs incurred in obtaining it were met),

(c) where the property is held by the trustees of a settlement, setting out such details of the settlement as may be specified in the order, and

(d) setting out such other information in connection with the property as may be so specified.

(4) The order must specify –

(a) the form and manner in which the statement is to be given,

(b) the person to whom it is to be given, and

(c) the place at which it is to be given or, if it is to be given in writing, the address to which it is to be sent.

(5) The order may, in connection with requiring the respondent to provide the statement mentioned in subsection (3), also require the respondent to produce documents of a kind specified or described in the order.

(6) The respondent must comply with the requirements imposed by an unexplained wealth order within whatever period the court may specify (and different periods may be specified in relation to different requirements).

(7) In this Chapter "enforcement authority" means –

(a) the National Crime Agency,

(b) Her Majesty's Revenue and Customs,

(c) the Financial Conduct Authority,

(d) the Director of the Serious Fraud Office, or

(e) the Director of Public Prosecutions (in relation to England and Wales) or the Director of Public Prosecutions for Northern Ireland (in relation to Northern Ireland).

362B Requirements for making of unexplained wealth order

(1) These are the requirements for the making of an unexplained wealth order in respect of any property.

(2) The High Court must be satisfied that there is reasonable cause to believe that –

(a) the respondent holds the property, and

(b) the value of the property is greater than £50,000.

(3) The High Court must be satisfied that there are reasonable grounds for suspecting that the known sources of the respondent's lawfully obtained income would have been insufficient for the purposes of enabling the respondent to obtain the property.

(4) The High Court must be satisfied that –

(a) the respondent is a politically exposed person, or

(b) there are reasonable grounds for suspecting that –

(i) the respondent is, or has been, involved in serious crime (whether in a part of the United Kingdom or elsewhere), or

(ii) a person connected with the respondent is, or has been, so involved.

(5) It does not matter for the purposes of subsection (2)(a) –

(a) whether or not there are other persons who also hold the property;

(b) whether the property was obtained by the respondent before or after the coming into force of this section.

(6) For the purposes of subsection (3) –

(a)   regard is to be had to any mortgage, charge or other kind of security that it is reasonable to assume was or may have been available to the respondent for the purposes of obtaining the property;

(b)   it is to be assumed that the respondent obtained the property for a price equivalent to its market value;

(c)   income is "lawfully obtained" if it is obtained lawfully under the laws of the country from where the income arises;

(d)   "known" sources of the respondent's income are the sources of income (whether arising from employment, assets or otherwise) that are reasonably ascertainable from available information at the time of the making of the application for the order;

(e)   where the property is an interest in other property comprised in a settlement, the reference to the respondent obtaining the property is to be taken as if it were a reference to the respondent obtaining direct ownership of such share in the settled property as relates to, or is fairly represented by, that interest.

(7)   In subsection (4)(a), "politically exposed person" means a person who is –

(a)   an individual who is, or has been, entrusted with prominent public functions by an international organisation or by a State other than the United Kingdom or another EEA State,

(b)   a family member of a person within paragraph (a),

(c)   known to be a close associate of a person within that paragraph, or

(d)   otherwise connected with a person within that paragraph.

(8)   Article 3 of Directive 2015/849/EU of the European Parliament and of the Council of 20 May 2015 applies for the purposes of determining –

(a)   whether a person has been entrusted with prominent public functions (see point (9) of that Article),

(b)   whether a person is a family member (see point (10) of that Article), and

(c)   whether a person is known to be a close associate of another (see point (11) of that Article).

(9)   For the purposes of this section –

(a)   a person is involved in serious crime in a part of the United Kingdom or elsewhere if the person would be so involved for the purposes of Part 1 of the Serious Crime Act 2007 (see in particular sections 2, 2A and 3 of that Act);

(b)   section 1122 of the Corporation Tax Act 2010 ("connected" persons) applies in determining whether a person is connected with another.

(10)   Where the property in respect of which the order is sought comprises more than one item of property, the reference in subsection (2)(b) to the value of the property is to the total value of those items.

362C   Effect of order: cases of non-compliance

(1)   This section applies in a case where the respondent fails, without reasonable excuse, to comply with the requirements imposed by an unexplained wealth order in respect of any property before the end of the response period.

(2)   The property is to be presumed to be recoverable property for the purposes of any proceedings taken in respect of the property under Part 5, unless the contrary is shown.

(3)   The presumption in subsection (2) applies in relation to property –

(a)   only so far as relating to the respondent's interest in the property, and

(b)   only if the value of that interest is greater than the sum specified in section 362B(2)(b).

It is for the court hearing the proceedings under Part 5 in relation to which reliance is placed on the presumption to determine the matters in this subsection.

(4)   The "response period" is whatever period the court specifies under section 362A(6) as the period within which the requirements imposed by the order are to be complied with (or the period ending the latest, if more than one is specified in respect of different requirements).

(5)   For the purposes of subsection (1) –

(a)   a respondent who purports to comply with the requirements imposed by an unexplained wealth order is not to be taken to have failed to comply with the order (see instead section 362D);

(b)   where an unexplained wealth order imposes more than one requirement on the respondent, the respondent is to be taken to have failed to comply with the requirements imposed by the order unless each of the requirements is complied with or is purported to be complied with.

(6)   Subsections (7) and (8) apply in determining the respondent's interest for the purposes of subsection (3) in a case where the respondent to the unexplained wealth order –

(a)   is connected with another person who is, or has been, involved in serious crime (see subsection (4)(b)(ii) of section 362B), or

(b)   is a politically exposed person of a kind mentioned in paragraph (b), (c) or (d) of subsection (7) of that section (family member, known close associates etc of individual entrusted with prominent public functions).

(7)   In a case within subsection (6)(a), the respondent's interest is to be taken to include any interest in the property of the person involved in serious crime with whom the respondent is connected.

(8)   In a case within subsection (6)(b), the respondent's interest is to be taken to include any interest in the property of the person mentioned in subsection (7)(a) of section 362B.

(9)   Where an unexplained wealth order is made in respect of property comprising more than one item of property, the reference in subsection (3)(b) to the value of the respondent's interest in the property is to the total value of the respondent's interest in those items.

362D   Effect of order: cases of compliance or purported compliance

(1)   This section applies in a case where, before the end of the response period (as defined by section 362C(4)), the respondent complies, or purports to comply, with the requirements imposed by an unexplained wealth order in respect of any property in relation to which the order is made.

(2)   If an interim freezing order has effect in relation to the property (see section 362J), the enforcement authority must determine what enforcement or investigatory proceedings, if any, it considers ought to be taken in relation to the property.

(3)   A determination under subsection (2) must be made within the period of 60 days starting with the day of compliance.

(4)   If the determination under subsection (2) is that no further enforcement or investigatory proceedings ought to be taken in relation to the property, the enforcement authority must notify the High Court of that fact as soon as

reasonably practicable (and in any event before the end of the 60 day period mentioned in subsection (3)).

(5)   If there is no interim freezing order in effect in relation to the property, the enforcement authority may (at any time) determine what, if any, enforcement or investigatory proceedings it considers ought to be taken in relation to the property.

(6)   A determination under this section to take no further enforcement or investigatory proceedings in relation to any property does not prevent such proceedings being taken subsequently (whether as a result of new information or otherwise, and whether or not by the same enforcement authority) in relation to the property.

(7)   For the purposes of this section –

(a)   the respondent complies with the requirements imposed by an unexplained wealth order only if all of the requirements are complied with,

(b)   references to the day of compliance are to the day on which the requirements imposed by the order are complied with (or, if the requirements are complied with over more than one day, the last of those days), and

(c)   where an order requires the sending of information in writing to, or the production of documents at, an address specified in the order, compliance with the order (so far as relating to that requirement) occurs when the written information is received, or the documents are produced, at that address,

and in paragraphs (a) to (c) references to compliance include purported compliance.

(8)   In this section "enforcement or investigatory proceedings" means any proceedings in relation to property taken under –

(a)   Part 2 or 4 (confiscation proceedings in England and Wales or Northern Ireland) (in relation to cases where the enforcement authority is also a prosecuting authority for the purposes of that Part),

(b)   Part 5 (civil recovery of the proceeds of unlawful conduct), or

(c)   this Chapter.

362E   Offence

(1)   A person commits an offence if, in purported compliance with a requirement imposed by an unexplained wealth order, the person –

(a)   makes a statement that the person knows to be false or misleading in a material particular, or

(b)   recklessly makes a statement that is false or misleading in a material particular.

(2)   A person guilty of an offence under this section is liable –

(a)   on conviction on indictment, to imprisonment for a term not exceeding 2 years, or to a fine, or to both;

(b)   on summary conviction in England and Wales, to imprisonment for a term not exceeding 12 months, or to a fine, or to both;

(c)   on summary conviction in Northern Ireland, to imprisonment for a term not exceeding 6 months, or to a fine not exceeding the statutory maximum, or to both.

(3)   In relation to an offence committed before the coming into force of section 282 of the Criminal Justice Act 2003 (increase in maximum sentence on

summary conviction of offence triable either way), the reference in subsection (2)(b) to 12 months is to be read as a reference to 6 months.

362F   Statements

(1)   A statement made by a person in response to a requirement imposed by an unexplained wealth order may not be used in evidence against that person in criminal proceedings.

(2)   Subsection (1) does not apply –

    (a)   in the case of proceedings under Part 2 or 4,

    (b)   on a prosecution for an offence under section 362E,

    (c)   on a prosecution for an offence under section 5 of the Perjury Act 1911 or Article 10 of the Perjury (Northern Ireland) Order 1979 (S.I. 1979/1714 (N.I. 19)) (false statements), or

    (d)   on a prosecution for some other offence where, in giving evidence, the person makes a statement inconsistent with the statement mentioned in subsection (1).

(3)   A statement may not be used by virtue of subsection (2)(d) against a person unless –

    (a)   evidence relating to it is adduced, or

    (b)   a question relating to it is asked,

by the person or on the person's behalf in proceedings arising out of the prosecution.

362G   Disclosure of information, copying of documents, etc

(1)   An unexplained wealth order has effect in spite of any restriction on the disclosure of information (however imposed).

(2)   But subsections (1) to (5) of section 361 (rights in connection with privileged information, questions and material) apply in relation to requirements imposed by an unexplained wealth order as they apply in relation to requirements imposed under a disclosure order.

(3)   The enforcement authority may take copies of any documents produced by the respondent in connection with complying with the requirements imposed by an unexplained wealth order.

(4)   Documents so produced may also be retained for so long as it is necessary to retain them (as opposed to a copy of them) in connection with an investigation of a kind mentioned in section 341 in relation to the property in respect of which the unexplained wealth order is made.

(5)   But if the enforcement authority has reasonable grounds to believe that the documents –

    (a)   may need to be produced for the purposes of any legal proceedings, and

    (b)   might otherwise be unavailable for those purposes,

they may be retained until the proceedings are concluded.

362H   Holding of property: trusts and company arrangements etc

(1)   This section applies for the purposes of sections 362A and 362B.

(2)   The cases in which a person (P) is to be taken to "hold" property include those where –

    (a)   P has effective control over the property;

    (b)   P is the trustee of a settlement in which the property is comprised;

(c)   P is a beneficiary (whether actual or potential) in relation to such a settlement.

(3)   A person is to be taken to have "effective control" over property if, from all the circumstances, it is reasonable to conclude that the person –

(a)   exercises,
(b)   is able to exercise, or
(c)   is entitled to acquire, direct or indirect control over the property.

(4)   Where a person holds property by virtue of subsection (2) references to the person obtaining the property are to be read accordingly.

(5)   References to a person who holds or obtains property include any body corporate, whether incorporated or formed under the law of a part of the United Kingdom or in a country or territory outside the United Kingdom.

(6)   For further provision about how to construe references to the holding of property, see section 414.

362I   Supplementary

(1)   An application for an unexplained wealth order may be made without notice.

(2)   Rules of court may make provision as to the practice and procedure to be followed in connection with proceedings relating to unexplained wealth orders before the High Court in Northern Ireland.

(3)   An application to the High Court in Northern Ireland to discharge or vary an unexplained wealth order may be made by –

(a)   the enforcement authority, or
(b)   the respondent.

(4)   The High Court in Northern Ireland –

(a)   may discharge the order;
(b)   may vary the order.'

2   Interim freezing orders

After section 362I of the Proceeds of Crime Act 2002 (inserted by section 1 above) insert –

'Unexplained wealth orders: interim freezing of property

362J   Application for interim freezing order

(1)   This section applies where the High Court makes an unexplained wealth order in respect of any property.

(2)   The court may make an interim freezing order in respect of the property if the court considers it necessary to do so for the purposes of avoiding the risk of any recovery order that might subsequently be obtained being frustrated.

(3)   An interim freezing order is an order that prohibits the respondent to the unexplained wealth order, and any other person with an interest in the property, from in any way dealing with the property (subject to any exclusions under section 362L).

(4)   An interim freezing order –

(a)   may be made only on the application of the enforcement authority that applied for the unexplained wealth order to which the interim freezing order relates,
(b)   must be made in the same proceedings as those in which the unexplained wealth order is made, and

(c)   may be combined in one document with the unexplained wealth order.

(5)   If an application for an unexplained wealth order in respect of any property is made without notice, an application for an interim freezing order in respect of the property must also be made without notice.

362K   Variation and discharge of interim freezing order

(1)   The High Court may at any time vary or discharge an interim freezing order.

(2)   The High Court must discharge an interim freezing order, so far as it has effect in relation to any property, in each of the following three cases.

(3)   The first case is where –

(a)   the applicable 48 hour period has ended, and
(b)   a relevant application has not been made before the end of that period in relation to the property concerned.

(4)   The second case is where –

(a)   a relevant application has been made before the end of the applicable 48 hour period in relation to the property concerned, and
(b)   proceedings on the application (including any on appeal) have been determined or otherwise disposed of.

(5)   The third case is where the court has received a notification in relation to the property concerned under section 362D(4) (notification from enforcement authority of no further proceedings).

(6)   The "applicable 48 hour period" is to be read as follows –

(a)   in a case where the respondent complies, or purports to comply, with the requirements imposed by an unexplained wealth order before the end of the response period, it is the period of 48 hours beginning with the day after the day with which the 60 day period mentioned in section 362D(3) ends;
(b)   in any other case, it is the period of 48 hours beginning with the day after the day with which the response period ends.

(7)   In calculating a period of 48 hours for the purposes of subsection (6), no account is to be taken of –

(a)   any Saturday or Sunday,
(b)   Christmas Day,
(c)   Good Friday, or
(d)   any day that is a bank holiday under the Banking and Financial Dealings Act 1971 in the part of the United Kingdom in which the interim freezing order concerned is made.

(8)   Section 362D(7) applies for the purposes of subsection (6) in determining whether a person complies, or purports to comply, with the requirements imposed by an unexplained wealth order and when such compliance, or purported compliance, takes place.

(9)   Before exercising power under this section to vary or discharge an interim freezing order, the court must (as well as giving the parties to the proceedings an opportunity to be heard) give such an opportunity to any person who may be affected by its decision.

(10)   Subsection (9) does not apply where the court is acting as required by subsection (2).

(11)   In this section –

"relevant application" means an application for –

(a) a restraint order under section 41 or 190,

(b) a property freezing order, or

(c) an interim receiving order; "response period" has the meaning given by section 362C(4).

362L Exclusions

(1) The power to vary an interim freezing order includes (amongst other things) power to make exclusions as follows –

(a) power to exclude property from the order, and

(b) power, otherwise than by excluding property from the order, to make exclusions from the prohibition on dealing with the property to which the order applies.

(2) Exclusions from the prohibition on dealing with the property to which the order applies (other than exclusions of property from the order) may also be made when the order is made.

(3) An exclusion may (amongst other things) make provision for the purpose of enabling any person –

(a) to meet the person's reasonable living expenses, or

(b) to carry on any trade, business, profession or occupation.

(4) An exclusion may be made subject to conditions.

(5) Where the court exercises the power to make an exclusion for the purpose of enabling a person to meet legal expenses that the person has incurred, or may incur, in respect of proceedings under this Chapter, it must ensure that the exclusion –

(a) is limited to reasonable legal expenses that the person has reasonably incurred or reasonably incurs,

(b) specifies the total amount that may be released for legal expenses in pursuance of the exclusion, and

(c) is made subject to the same conditions as would be the required conditions (see section 286A) if the order had been made under section 245A (in addition to any conditions under subsection (4)).

(6) The court, in deciding whether to make an exclusion for the purpose of enabling a person to meet legal expenses in respect of proceedings under this Chapter –

(a) must have regard to the desirability of the person being represented in any proceedings under this Chapter in which the person is a participant, and

(b) must disregard the possibility that legal representation of the person in any such proceedings might, were an exclusion not made, be made available under arrangements made for the purposes of Part 1 of the Legal Aid, Sentencing and Punishment of Offenders Act 2012 or funded by the Northern Ireland Legal Services Commission.

(7) If excluded property is not specified in the order it must be described in the order in general terms.

362M Restrictions on proceedings and remedies

(1) While an interim freezing order has effect –

(a) the High Court may stay any action, execution or other legal process in respect of the property to which the order applies, and

(b) no distress may be levied, and no power to use the procedure in

Schedule 12 to the Tribunals, Courts and Enforcement Act 2007 (taking control of goods) may be exercised, against the property to which the order applies except with the leave of the High Court and subject to any terms the court may impose.

(2)   If a court (whether the High Court or any other court) in which proceedings are pending in respect of any property is satisfied that an interim freezing order has been applied for or made in respect of the property, it may –

(a)   stay the proceedings, or
(b)   allow them to continue on any terms it thinks fit.

(3)   If an interim freezing order applies to a tenancy of any premises, a right of forfeiture in relation to the premises is exercisable –

(a)   only with the leave of the High Court, and
(b)   subject to any terms that the court may impose.

(4)   The reference in subsection (3) to a "right of forfeiture" in relation to premises is to the right of a landlord or other person to whom rent is payable to exercise a right of forfeiture by peaceable re-entry to the premises in respect of any failure by the tenant to comply with a term or condition of the tenancy.

(5)   Before exercising a power conferred by this section, the court must (as well as giving the parties to any proceedings concerned an opportunity to be heard) give such an opportunity to any person who may be affected by the court's decision.

362N   Receivers in connection with interim freezing orders

(1)   This section applies where the High Court makes an interim freezing order on an application by an enforcement authority.

(2)   The court may, on an application by the enforcement authority, by order appoint a receiver in respect of any property to which the interim freezing order applies.

(3)   An application under subsection (2) may be made at the same time as the application for the interim freezing order or at any time afterwards.

(4)   The application may be made without notice if the circumstances of the case are such that notice of the application would prejudice the right of the enforcement authority to obtain a recovery order in respect of any property.

(5)   In its application the enforcement authority must nominate a suitably qualified person for appointment as a receiver.

(6)   The person nominated may be a member of staff of the enforcement authority.

(7)   The enforcement authority may apply a sum received by it under section 280(2) in making payment of the remuneration and expenses of a receiver appointed under this section.

(8)   Subsection (7) does not apply in relation to the remuneration of the receiver if that person is a member of staff of the enforcement authority (but it does apply in relation to such remuneration if the receiver is a person providing services under arrangements made by the enforcement authority).

362O   Powers of receivers appointed under section 362N

(1)   If the High Court appoints a receiver under section 362N on an application by an enforcement authority, the court may act under this section on the application of the authority.

(2)   The court may by order authorise or require the receiver –

(a)   to exercise any of the powers mentioned in paragraph 5 of Schedule 6 (management powers) in relation to any property in respect of which the receiver is appointed;

(b) to take any other steps the court thinks appropriate in connection with the management of any such property (including securing the detention, custody or preservation of the property in order to manage it).

(3) The court may by order require any person in respect of whose property the receiver is appointed –

(a) to bring the property to a place (in England and Wales or, as the case may be, Northern Ireland) specified by the receiver or to place it in the custody of the receiver (if in either case the person is able to do so);

(b) to do anything the person is reasonably required to do by the receiver for the preservation of the property.

(4) The court may by order require any person in respect of whose property the receiver is appointed to bring any documents relating to the property which are in that person's possession or control to a place (in England and Wales or, as the case may be, Northern Ireland) specified by the receiver or to place them in the custody of the receiver.

(5) Any prohibition on dealing with property imposed by an interim freezing order does not prevent a person from complying with any requirements imposed by virtue of this section.

(6) Subsection (7) applies in a case where –

(a) the receiver deals with property that is not property in respect of which the receiver was appointed under section 362N, but

(b) at the time of dealing with the property the receiver believed on reasonable grounds that he or she was entitled to do so by virtue of the appointment.

(7) The receiver is not liable to any person in respect of any loss or damage resulting from the receiver's dealing with the property.

(8) But subsection (7) does not apply to the extent that the loss or damage is caused by the receiver's negligence.

362P Supervision of section 362N receiver and variations

(1) Any of the following persons may at any time apply to the High Court for directions as to the exercise of the functions of a receiver appointed under section 362N –

(a) the receiver;

(b) a party to the proceedings for the appointment of the receiver or the interim freezing order concerned;

(c) a person affected by an action taken by the receiver;

(d) a person who may be affected by an action proposed to be taken by the receiver.

(2) Before it gives directions under subsection (1) the court must give an opportunity to be heard to –

(a) the receiver;

(b) the parties to the proceedings for the appointment of the receiver and for the interim freezing order concerned;

(c) a person who may be interested in the application under subsection (1).

(3) The court may at any time vary or discharge –

(a)   the appointment of a receiver under section 362N,

(b)   an order under section 362O, or

(c)   directions under this section.

(4)   Before exercising a power under subsection (3) the court must give an opportunity to be heard to –

(a)   the receiver;

(b)   the parties to the proceedings for the appointment of the receiver, for the order under section 362O or (as the case may be) for the directions under this section;

(c)   the parties to the proceedings for the interim freezing order concerned;

(d)   any person who may be affected by the court's decision.

362Q   Registration

Sections 248 (registration: England and Wales) and 249 (registration: Northern Ireland) apply in relation to interim freezing orders as they apply in relation to property freezing orders under section 245A.

362R   Compensation

(1)   Where an interim freezing order in respect of any property is discharged, the person to whom the property belongs may make an application to the High Court for the payment of compensation.

(2)   The application must be made within the period of three months beginning with the discharge of the interim freezing order.

(3)   The court may order compensation to be paid to the applicant only if satisfied that –

(a)   the applicant has suffered loss as a result of the making of the interim freezing order,

(b)   there has been a serious default on the part of the enforcement authority that applied for the order, and

(c)   the order would not have been made had the default not occurred.

(4)   Where the court orders the payment of compensation –

(a)   the compensation is payable by the enforcement authority that applied for the interim freezing order, and

(b)   the amount of compensation to be paid is the amount that the court thinks reasonable, having regard to the loss suffered and any other relevant circumstances.'

3   External assistance

After section 362R of the Proceeds of Crime Act 2002 (inserted by section 2 above) insert –

'*Unexplained wealth orders: enforcement abroad*

362S   Enforcement abroad: enforcement authority

(1)   This section applies if –

(a)   the High Court makes an unexplained wealth order in respect of any property,

(b)   it appears to the enforcement authority that the risk mentioned in section 362J(2) applies in relation to the property, and

(c)   the enforcement authority believes that the property is in a country outside the United Kingdom (the receiving country).

(2)   The enforcement authority may send a request for assistance in relation to the property to the Secretary of State with a view to it being forwarded under this section.

(3)   The Secretary of State may forward the request for assistance to the government of the receiving country.

(4)   A request for assistance under this section is a request to the government of the receiving country –

(a)   to secure that any person is prohibited from dealing with the property;

(b)   for assistance in connection with the management of the property, including with securing its detention, custody or preservation.

362T   Enforcement abroad: receiver

(1)   This section applies if –

(a)   an interim freezing order has effect in relation to property, and

(b)   the receiver appointed under section 362N in respect of the property believes that it is in a country outside the United Kingdom (the receiving country).

(2)   The receiver may send a request for assistance in relation to the property to the Secretary of State with a view to it being forwarded under this section.

(3)   The Secretary of State must forward the request for assistance to the government of the receiving country.

(4)   A request for assistance under this section is a request to the government of the receiving country –

(a)   to secure that any person is prohibited from dealing with the property;

(b)   for assistance in connection with the management of the property, including with securing its detention, custody or preservation.'

Unexplained wealth orders: Scotland

4   Unexplained wealth orders: Scotland

In Chapter 3 of Part 8 of the Proceeds of Crime Act 2002 (investigations: Scotland), after section 396 insert –

'Unexplained wealth orders

396A   Unexplained wealth orders

(1)   The Court of Session may, on an application made by the Scottish Ministers, make an unexplained wealth order in respect of any property if the court is satisfied that each of the requirements for the making of the order is fulfilled.

(2)   An application for an order must –

(a)   specify or describe the property in respect of which the order is sought, and

(b)   specify the person whom the Scottish Ministers think holds the property ("the respondent") (and the person specified may include a person outside the United Kingdom).

(3)   An unexplained wealth order is an order requiring the respondent to provide a statement –

(a)   setting out the nature and extent of the respondent's interest in the property in respect of which the order is made,

(b)   explaining how the respondent obtained the property (including, in particular, how any costs incurred in obtaining it were met),

(c)   where the property is held by the trustees of a settlement, setting out such details of the settlement as may be specified in the order, and

(d)   setting out such other information in connection with the property as may be so specified.

(4)   The order must specify –

(a)   the form and manner in which the statement is to be given,

(b)   the person to whom it is to be given, and

(c)   the place at which it is to be given or, if it is to be given in writing, the address to which it is to be sent.

(5)   The order may, in connection with requiring the respondent to provide the statement mentioned in subsection (3), also require the respondent to produce documents of a kind specified or described in the order.

(6)   The respondent must comply with the requirements imposed by an unexplained wealth order within whatever period the court may specify (and different periods may be specified in relation to different requirements).

396B   Requirements for making of unexplained wealth order

(1)   These are the requirements for the making of an unexplained wealth order in respect of any property.

(2)   The Court of Session must be satisfied that there is reasonable cause to believe that –

(a)   the respondent holds the property, and

(b)   the value of the property is greater than £50,000.

(3)   The Court of Session must be satisfied that there are reasonable grounds for suspecting that the known sources of the respondent's lawfully obtained income would have been insufficient for the purposes of enabling the respondent to obtain the property.

(4)   The Court of Session must be satisfied that –

(a)   the respondent is a politically exposed person, or

(b)   there are reasonable grounds for suspecting that –

(i)   the respondent is, or has been, involved in serious crime (whether in a part of the United Kingdom or elsewhere), or

(ii)   a person connected with the respondent is, or has been, so involved.

(5)   It does not matter for the purposes of subsection (2)(a) –

(a)   whether or not there are other persons who also hold the property;

(b)   whether the property was obtained by the respondent before or after the coming into force of this section.

(6)   For the purposes of subsection (3) –

(a)   regard is to be had to any heritable security, charge or other kind of security that it is reasonable to assume was or may have been available to the respondent for the purposes of obtaining the property;

(b)   it is to be assumed that the respondent obtained the property for a price equivalent to its market value;

(c)   income is "lawfully obtained" if it is obtained lawfully under the laws of the country from where the income arises;

(d)   "known" sources of the respondent's income are the sources of income (whether arising from employment, assets or otherwise) that are reasonably ascertainable from available information at the time of the making of the application for the order;

    (e)   where the property is an interest in other property comprised in a settlement, the reference to the respondent obtaining the property is to be taken as if it were a reference to the respondent obtaining direct ownership of such share in the settled property as relates to, or is fairly represented by, that interest.

(7)   In subsection (4)(a), "politically exposed person" means a person who is –

    (a)   an individual who is, or has been, entrusted with prominent public functions by an international organisation or by a State other than the United Kingdom or another EEA State,

    (b)   a family member of a person within paragraph (a),

    (c)   known to be a close associate of a person within that paragraph, or

    (d)   otherwise connected with a person within that paragraph.

(8)   Article 3 of Directive 2015/849/EU of the European Parliament and of the Council of 20 May 2015 applies for the purposes of determining –

    (a)   whether a person has been entrusted with prominent public functions (see point (9) of that Article),

    (b)   whether a person is a family member (see point (10) of that Article), and

    (c)   whether a person is known to be a close associate of another (see point (11) of that Article).

(9)   For the purposes of this section –

    (a)   a person is involved in serious crime in a part of the United Kingdom or elsewhere if the person would be so involved for the purposes of Part 1 of the Serious Crime Act 2007 (see in particular sections 2, 2A and 3 of that Act);

    (b)   section 1122 of the Corporation Tax Act 2010 ("connected" persons) applies in determining whether a person is connected with another.

(10)   Where the property in respect of which the order is sought comprises more than one item of property, the reference in subsection (2)(b) to the value of the property is to the total value of those items.

396C   Effect of order: cases of non-compliance

(1)   This section applies in a case where the respondent fails, without reasonable excuse, to comply with the requirements imposed by an unexplained wealth order in respect of any property before the end of the response period.

(2)   The property is to be presumed to be recoverable property for the purposes of any proceedings taken in respect of the property under Part 5, unless the contrary is shown.

(3)   The presumption in subsection (2) applies in relation to property –

    (a)   only so far as relating to the respondent's interest in the property, and

    (b)   only if the value of that interest is greater than the sum specified in section 396B(2)(b).

It is for the court hearing the proceedings under Part 5 in relation to which reliance is placed on the presumption to determine the matters in this subsection.

(4)   The "response period" is whatever period the court specifies under section 396A(6) as the period within which the requirements imposed by the order

are to be complied with (or the period ending the latest, if more than one is specified in respect of different requirements).

(5)   For the purposes of subsection (1) –

(a)   a respondent who purports to comply with the requirements imposed by an unexplained wealth order is not to be taken to have failed to comply with the order (see instead section 396D);

(b)   where an unexplained wealth order imposes more than one requirement on the respondent, the respondent is to be taken to have failed to comply with the requirements imposed by the order unless each of the requirements is complied with or is purported to be complied with.

(6)   Subsections (7) and (8) apply in determining the respondent's interest for the purposes of subsection (3) in a case where the respondent to the unexplained wealth order –

(a)   is connected with another person who is, or has been, involved in serious crime (see subsection (4)(b)(ii) of section 396B), or

(b)   is a politically exposed person of a kind mentioned in paragraph (b), (c) or (d) of subsection (7) of that section (family member, known close associates etc of individual entrusted with prominent public functions).

(7)   In a case within subsection (6)(a), the respondent's interest is to be taken to include any interest in the property of the person involved in serious crime with whom the respondent is connected.

(8)   In a case within subsection (6)(b), the respondent's interest is to be taken to include any interest in the property of the person mentioned in subsection (7)(a) of section 396B.

(9)   Where an unexplained wealth order is made in respect of property comprising more than one item of property, the reference in subsection (3)(b) to the value of the respondent's interest in the property is to the total value of the respondent's interest in those items.

396D   Effect of order: cases of compliance or purported compliance

(1)   This section applies in a case where the respondent complies, or purports to comply, with the requirements imposed by an unexplained wealth order in respect of any property in relation to which the order is made before the end of the response period (as defined by section 396C(4)).

(2)   If an interim freezing order has effect in relation to the property (see section 396J), the Scottish Ministers must –

(a)   consider whether the Lord Advocate should be given an opportunity to determine what enforcement or investigatory proceedings, if any, the Lord Advocate considers ought to be taken by the Lord Advocate in relation to the property, and

(b)   determine whether they consider that any proceedings under Part 5 (civil recovery of the proceeds of unlawful conduct) or this Chapter ought to be taken by them in relation to the property.

(3)   If the Scottish Ministers consider that the Lord Advocate should be given an opportunity to make a determination as mentioned in subsection (2)(a), the Lord Advocate must determine what enforcement or investigatory proceedings, if any, the Lord Advocate considers ought to be taken by the Lord Advocate in relation to the property.

(4)   A determination under subsection (2)(b) or (3) must be made within the period of 60 days starting with the day of compliance.

(5)   If the determinations under subsections (2)(b) and (3) are that no further proceedings under Part 5 or this Chapter and no further enforcement or investigatory proceedings ought to be taken in relation to the property, the Scottish Ministers must notify the Court of Session of the nature of the determinations as soon as reasonably practicable (and in any event before the end of the 60 day period mentioned in subsection (4)).

(6)   If there is no interim freezing order in effect in relation to the property –

(a)   the Scottish Ministers may (at any time) determine whether they consider that any proceedings under Part 5 or this Chapter ought to be taken by them in relation to the property, and

(b)   the Lord Advocate may (at any time) determine what, if any, enforcement or investigatory proceedings the Lord Advocate considers ought to be taken by the Lord Advocate in relation to the property.

(7)   A determination under this section to take no further proceedings under Part 5 or this Chapter or no further enforcement or investigatory proceedings in relation to any property does not prevent any such proceedings being taken subsequently (whether as a result of new information or otherwise) in relation to the property.

(8)   For the purposes of this section –

(a)   the respondent complies with the requirements imposed by an unexplained wealth order only if all of the requirements are complied with,

(b)   references to the day of compliance are to the day on which the requirements imposed by the order are complied with (or, if the requirements are complied with over more than one day, the last of those days), and

(c)   where an order requires the sending of information in writing to, or the production of documents at, an address specified in the order, compliance with the order (so far as relating to that requirement) occurs when the written information is received, or the documents are produced, at that address,

and in paragraphs (a) to (c) references to compliance include purported compliance.

(9)   In this section "enforcement or investigatory proceedings" means any proceedings in relation to property taken under –

(a)   Part 3 (confiscation proceedings in Scotland), or

(b)   this Chapter.

396E   Offence

(1)   A person commits an offence if, in purported compliance with a requirement imposed by an unexplained wealth order, the person –

(a)   makes a statement that the person knows to be false or misleading in a material particular, or

(b)   recklessly makes a statement that is false or misleading in a material particular.

(2)   A person guilty of an offence under this section is liable –

(a)   on summary conviction, to imprisonment for a term not exceeding 12 months, or to a fine not exceeding the statutory maximum, or to both, or

(b)   on conviction on indictment, to imprisonment for a term not exceeding 2 years, or to a fine, or to both.

396F   Statements

(1)   A statement made by a person in response to a requirement imposed by an unexplained wealth order may not be used in evidence against that person in criminal proceedings.

(2)   Subsection (1) does not apply –

(a)   in the case of proceedings under Part 3,
(b)   on a prosecution for an offence under section 396E,
(c)   on a prosecution for perjury, or
(d)   on a prosecution for some other offence where, in giving evidence, the person makes a statement inconsistent with the statement mentioned in subsection (1).

(3)   A statement may not be used by virtue of subsection (2)(d) against a person unless –

(a)   evidence relating to it is adduced, or
(b)   a question relating to it is asked,

by the person or on the person's behalf in proceedings arising out of the prosecution.

396G   Disclosure of information, copying of documents, etc

(1)   An unexplained wealth order does not confer the right to require a person to answer any question, provide any information or produce any document which the person would be entitled to refuse to answer, provide or produce on grounds of legal privilege.

(2)   An unexplained wealth order has effect in spite of any restriction on the disclosure of information (however imposed).

(3)   The Scottish Ministers may take copies of any documents produced by the respondent in connection with complying with the requirements imposed by an unexplained wealth order.

(4)   Documents so produced may also be retained for so long as it is necessary to retain them (as opposed to a copy of them) in connection with an investigation of a kind mentioned in section 341 in relation to the property in respect of which the unexplained wealth order is made.

(5)   But if the Scottish Ministers have reasonable grounds to believe that the documents –

(a)   may need to be produced for the purposes of any legal proceedings, and
(b)   might otherwise be unavailable for those purposes, they may be retained until the proceedings are concluded.

396H   Holding of property: trusts and company arrangements etc

(1)   This section applies for the purposes of sections 396A and 396B.
(2)   The cases in which a person (P) is to be taken to "hold" property include those where –

(a)   P has effective control over the property;
(b)   P is the trustee of a settlement in which the property is comprised;
(c)   P is a beneficiary (whether actual or potential) in relation to such a settlement.

(3)   A person is to be taken to have "effective control" over property if, from all the circumstances, it is reasonable to conclude that the person –

(a)   exercises,

(b)   is able to exercise, or

(c)   is entitled to acquire, direct or indirect control over the property.

(4)   Where a person holds property by virtue of subsection (2) references to the person obtaining the property are to be read accordingly.

(5)   References to a person who holds or obtains property include any body corporate, whether incorporated or formed under the law of a part of the United Kingdom or in a country or territory outside the United Kingdom.

(6)   For further provision about how to construe references to the holding of property, see section 414.

396I   Supplementary

(1)   An application for an unexplained wealth order may be made without notice.

(2)   Provision may be made by rules of court as to the discharge and variation of unexplained wealth orders.

(3)   An application to discharge or vary an unexplained wealth order may be made to the Court of Session by –

(a)   the Scottish Ministers, or

(b)   any person affected by the order.

(4)   The Court of Session may –

(a)   discharge the order;

(b)   vary the order.'

5   Interim freezing orders

After section 396I of the Proceeds of Crime Act 2002 (inserted by section 4 above) insert –

'*Unexplained wealth orders: interim freezing of property*

396J   Application for interim freezing order

(1)   This section applies where the Court of Session makes an unexplained wealth order in respect of any property.

(2)   The court may make an interim freezing order in respect of the property if the court considers it necessary to do so for the purposes of avoiding the risk of any recovery order that might subsequently be obtained being frustrated.

(3)   An interim freezing order is an order that prohibits the respondent to the unexplained wealth order, and any other person with an interest in the property, from in any way dealing with the property (subject to any exclusions under section 396L).

(4)   An interim freezing order –

(a)   may be made only on the application of the Scottish Ministers,

(b)   must be made in the same proceedings as those in which the unexplained wealth order is made, and

(c)   may be combined in one document with the unexplained wealth order.

(5)   If an application for an unexplained wealth order in respect of any property is made without notice, an application for an interim freezing order in respect of the property must also be made without notice.

396K   Variation and recall of interim freezing order

(1)   The Court of Session may at any time vary or recall an interim freezing order.

(2)   The Court of Session must recall an interim freezing order, so far as it has effect in relation to any property, in each of the following three cases.

(3)   The first case is where –

(a)   the applicable 48 hour period has ended, and
(b)   a relevant application has not been made before the end of that period in relation to the property concerned.

(4)   The second case is where –

(a)   a relevant application has been made before the end of the applicable 48 hour period in relation to the property concerned, and
(b)   proceedings on the application (including any on appeal) have been determined or otherwise disposed of.

(5)   The third case is where the court has received a notification in relation to the property concerned under section 396D(5) (notification of no further proceedings).

(6)   References in this section to the "applicable 48 hour period" are to be read as follows –

(a)   in a case where the respondent complies, or purports to comply, with the requirements imposed by the unexplained wealth order before the end of the response period, it is the period of 48 hours beginning with the day after the day with which the 60 day period mentioned in section 396D(4) ends;
(b)   in any other case, it is the period of 48 hours beginning with the day after the day on which the response period ends.

(7)   In calculating a period of 48 hours for the purposes of subsection (6), no account is to be taken of –

(a)   any Saturday or Sunday,
(b)   Christmas Day,
(c)   Good Friday, or
(d)   any other day that is a bank holiday under the Banking and Financial Dealings Act 1971 in Scotland.

(8)   Section 396D(8) applies for the purposes of subsection (6) in determining whether a person complies, or purports to comply, with the requirements imposed by an unexplained wealth order and when such compliance, or purported compliance, takes place.

(9)   Before exercising power under this section to vary or recall an interim freezing order, the court must (as well as giving the parties to the proceedings an opportunity to be heard) give such an opportunity to any person who may be affected by its decision.

(10)   Subsection (9) does not apply where the court is acting as required by subsection (2).

(11)   In this section –

"relevant application" means an application for –

(a)   a restraint order under section 120,
(b)   a prohibitory property order under section 255A, or
(c)   an interim administration order under section 256;

"response period" has the meaning given by section 396C(4).

396L   Exclusions

(1)   The power to vary an interim freezing order includes (amongst other things) power to make exclusions as follows –

(a)   power to exclude property from the order, and

(b)   power, otherwise than by excluding property from the order, to make exclusions from the prohibition on dealing with the property to which the order applies.

(2)   Exclusions from the prohibition on dealing with the property to which the order applies (other than exclusions of property from the order) may also be made when the order is made.

(3)   An exclusion may (amongst other things) make provision for the purpose of enabling any person –

(a)   to meet the person's reasonable living expenses, or

(b)   to carry on any trade, business, profession or occupation.

(4)   An exclusion may be made subject to conditions.

(5)   An exclusion may not be made for the purpose of enabling any person to meet any legal expenses in respect of proceedings under this Chapter.

(6)   If excluded property is not specified in the order it must be described in the order in general terms.

396M   Restrictions on proceedings and remedies

(1)   While an interim freezing order has effect the Court of Session may sist any action, execution or other legal process in respect of the property to which the order applies.

(2)   If a court (whether the Court of Session or any other court) in which proceedings are pending in respect of any property is satisfied that an interim freezing order has been applied for or made in respect of the property, it may –

(a)   sist the proceedings, or

(b)   allow them to continue on any terms it thinks fit.

(3)   Before exercising a power conferred by this section, the court must (as well as giving the parties to any proceedings concerned an opportunity to be heard) give such an opportunity to any person who may be affected by the court's decision.

396N   Arrestment of property affected by interim freezing order

(1)   On the application of the Scottish Ministers the Court of Session may, in relation to moveable property to which an interim freezing order applies (whether generally or to such of it as is specified in the application), grant warrant for arrestment.

(2)   An application under subsection (1) may be made at the same time as the application for the interim freezing order or at any time afterwards.

(3)   A warrant for arrestment may be granted only if the property would be arrestable if the person entitled to it were a debtor.

(4)   A warrant under subsection (1) has effect as if granted on the dependence of an action for debt at the instance of the Scottish Ministers against the person and may be executed, recalled, loosed or restricted accordingly.

(5)   An arrestment executed under this section ceases to have effect when, or in so far as, the interim freezing order ceases to apply in respect of the property in relation to which the warrant for arrestment was granted.

(6)   If an arrestment ceases to have effect to any extent by virtue of subsection (5), the Scottish Ministers must apply to the Court of Session for an order recalling or, as the case may be, restricting the arrestment.

396O   Inhibition of property affected by interim freezing order

(1)   On the application of the Scottish Ministers, the Court of Session may, in relation to the property mentioned in subsection (2), grant warrant for inhibition against any person specified in an interim freezing order.

(2)   The property is heritable property situated in Scotland to which the interim freezing order applies (whether generally or to such of it as is specified in the application).

(3)   The warrant for inhibition –

  (a)   has effect as if granted on the dependence of an action for debt by the Scottish Ministers against the person and may be executed, recalled, loosed or restricted accordingly, and

  (b)   has the effect of letters of inhibition and must forthwith be registered by the Scottish Ministers in the register of inhibitions and adjudications.

(4)   Section 155 of the Titles to Land Consolidation (Scotland) Act 1868 (effective date of inhibition) applies in relation to an inhibition for which warrant is granted under subsection (1) as it applies to an inhibition by separate letters or contained in a summons.

(5)   An inhibition executed under this section ceases to have effect when, or in so far as, the interim freezing order ceases to apply in respect of the property in relation to which the warrant for inhibition was granted.

(6)   If an inhibition ceases to have effect to any extent by virtue of subsection (5), the Scottish Ministers must –

  (a)   apply for the recall or, as the case may be, the restriction of the inhibition, and

  (b)   ensure that the recall or restriction is reflected in the register of inhibitions and adjudications.

396P   Receivers in connection with interim freezing orders

(1)   This section applies where the Court of Session makes an interim freezing order on an application by the Scottish Ministers.

(2)   The Court of Session may, on an application by the Scottish Ministers, by order appoint a receiver in respect of any property to which the interim freezing order applies.

(3)   An application under subsection (2) may be made at the same time as the application for the interim freezing order or at any time afterwards.

(4)   The application may be made without notice if the circumstances of the case are such that notice of the application would prejudice the right of the Scottish Ministers to obtain a recovery order in respect of the property.

(5)   In their application the Scottish Ministers must nominate a suitably qualified person for appointment as a receiver.

(6)   The person nominated may be a member of staff of the Scottish Ministers.

(7)   The Scottish Ministers may apply a sum received by them under section 280(2) in making payment of the remuneration and expenses of a receiver appointed under this section.

(8)   Subsection (7) does not apply in relation to the remuneration of the receiver if that person is a member of staff of the Scottish Ministers (but it does apply in relation to such remuneration if the receiver is a person providing services under arrangements made by the Scottish Ministers).

396Q   Powers of receivers appointed under section 396P

(1)   If the Court of Session appoints a receiver under section 396P, the court may act under this section on the application of the Scottish Ministers.

(2)   The court may by order authorise or require the receiver –

(a)   to exercise any of the powers mentioned in paragraph 5 of Schedule 6 (management powers) in relation to any property in respect of which the receiver is appointed;

(b)   to take any other steps the court thinks appropriate in connection with the management of any such property (including securing the detention, custody or preservation of the property in order to manage it).

(3)   The court may by order require any person in respect of whose property the receiver is appointed –

(a)   to bring the property to a place in Scotland specified by the receiver or to place it in the custody of the receiver (if in either case the person is able to do so);

(b)   to do anything the person is reasonably required to do by the receiver for the preservation of the property.

(4)   The court may by order require any person in respect of whose property the receiver is appointed to bring any documents relating to the property which are in that person's possession or control to a place in Scotland specified by the receiver or to place them in the custody of the receiver.

(5)   In subsection (4) "document" means anything in which information of any description is recorded.

(6)   Any prohibition on dealing with property imposed by an interim freezing order does not prevent a person from complying with any requirements imposed by virtue of this section.

(7)   Subsection (8) applies in a case where –

(a)   the receiver deals with property that is not property in respect of which the receiver was appointed under section 396P, but

(b)   at the time of dealing with the property the receiver believed on reasonable grounds that he or she was entitled to do so by virtue of his or her appointment.

(8)   The receiver is not liable to any person in respect of any loss or damage resulting from the receiver's dealing with the property.

(9)   But subsection (8) does not apply to the extent that the loss or damage is caused by the receiver's negligence.

396R   Supervision of section 396P receiver and variations

(1)   Any of the following persons may at any time apply to the Court of Session for directions as to the exercise of the functions of a receiver appointed under section 396P –

(a)   the receiver;

(b)   a party to the proceedings for the appointment of the receiver or the interim freezing order concerned;

(c)   a person affected by an action taken by the receiver;

(d)   a person who may be affected by an action proposed to be taken by the receiver.

(2)   Before it gives directions under subsection (1), the court must give an opportunity to be heard to –

(a)   the receiver;

(b)   the parties to the proceedings for the appointment of the receiver and for the interim freezing order concerned;

        (c)   any person who may be interested in the application under subsection (1).

(3)   The court may at any time vary or recall –

        (a)   the appointment of a receiver under section 396P,
        (b)   an order under section 396Q, or
        (c)   directions under this section.

(4)   Before exercising a power under subsection (3) the court must give an opportunity to be heard to –

        (a)   the receiver;
        (b)   the parties to the proceedings for the appointment of the receiver, for the order under section 396Q or (as the case may be) for the directions under this section;
        (c)   the parties to the proceedings for the interim freezing order concerned;
        (d)   any person who may be affected by the court's decision.

396S   Compensation

(1)   Where an interim freezing order in respect of any property is recalled, the person to whom the property belongs may make an application to the Court of Session for the payment of compensation.

(2)   The application must be made within the period of three months beginning with the recall of the interim freezing order.

(3)   The court may order compensation to be paid to the applicant only if satisfied that –

        (a)   the applicant has suffered loss as a result of the making of the interim freezing order,
        (b)   there has been a serious default on the part of the Scottish Ministers in applying for the order, and
        (c)   the order would not have been made had the default not occurred.

(4)   Where the court orders the payment of compensation –

        (a)   the compensation is payable by the Scottish Ministers, and
        (b)   the amount of compensation to be paid is the amount that the court thinks reasonable, having regard to the loss suffered and any other relevant circumstances.'

6   External assistance

After section 396S of the Proceeds of Crime Act 2002 (inserted by section 5 above) insert –

'Unexplained wealth orders: enforcement abroad

396T   Enforcement abroad: Scottish Ministers

(1)   This section applies if –

        (a)   the Court of Session makes an unexplained wealth order in respect of any property,
        (b)   it appears to the Scottish Ministers that the risk mentioned in section 396J(2) applies in relation to the property, and
        (c)   the Scottish Ministers believe that the property is in a country outside the United Kingdom (the receiving country).

(2)   The Scottish Ministers may send a request for assistance in relation to the property to the Secretary of State with a view to it being forwarded under this section.

(3)   The Secretary of State may forward the request for assistance to the government of the receiving country.

(4)   A request for assistance under this section is a request to the government of the receiving country –

   (a)   to secure that any person is prohibited from dealing with the property;

   (b)   for assistance in connection with the management of the property, including with securing its detention, custody or preservation.

396U   Enforcement abroad: receiver

(1)   This section applies if –

   (a)   an interim freezing order has effect in relation to property, and

   (b)   the receiver appointed under section 396P in respect of the property believes that it is in a country outside the United Kingdom (the receiving country).

(2)   The receiver may send a request for assistance in relation to the property to the Secretary of State with a view to it being forwarded under this section.

(3)   The Secretary of State must forward the request for assistance to the government of the receiving country.

(4)   A request for assistance under this section is a request to the government of the receiving country –

   (a)   to secure that any person is prohibited from dealing with the property;

   (b)   for assistance in connection with the management of the property, including with securing its detention, custody or preservation.'

Disclosure orders

7   Disclosure orders: England and Wales and Northern Ireland

(1)   Chapter 2 of Part 8 of the Proceeds of Crime Act 2002 (investigations: England and Wales and Northern Ireland) is amended as follows.

(2)   In section 357 (disclosure orders) –

   (a)   in subsection (2) omit 'or a money laundering investigation';

   (b)   omit subsection (2A);

   (c)   in subsection (3), after paragraph (b) insert –

   '(ba) a person specified in the application is subject to a money laundering investigation which is being carried out by an appropriate officer and the order is sought for the purposes of the investigation, or;'

   (d)   in subsection (7) –

      (i)   in paragraph (a) for 'a prosecutor' substitute 'an appropriate officer';

      (ii)   after paragraph (b) insert –

      '(ba) in relation to a money laundering investigation, an appropriate officer, and;'

   (e)   omit subsections (8) and (9).

(3)   In section 358 (requirements for making a disclosure order), in subsection (2) after paragraph (b) insert –

'(ba)   in the case of a money laundering investigation, the person specified in the
      application for the order has committed a money laundering offence;'

(4)   In section 362 (supplementary) –

    (a)   for subsection (4A) substitute –

        '(4A)   An application to discharge or vary a disclosure order need not be
            made by the same appropriate officer or (as the case may be) the same
            National Crime Agency officer that applied for the order (but must be
            made by an appropriate officer of the same description or (as the case
            may be) by another National Crime Agency officer).

        (4AA)If the application for the order was, by virtue of an order under section
            453, made by an accredited financial investigator of a particular
            description, the reference in subsection (4A) to an appropriate officer
            of the same description is to another accredited financial investigator
            of that description.'

    (b)   after subsection (5) insert –

        '(6)   An appropriate officer may not make an application for a disclosure
            order, or an application for the discharge or variation of such an order,
            unless the officer is a senior appropriate officer or is authorised to do
            so by a senior appropriate officer.'

8   Disclosure orders: Scotland

(1)   Chapter 3 of Part 8 of the Proceeds of Crime Act 2002 (investigations: Scotland) is
    amended as follows.

(2)   In section 391(disclosure orders) –

    (a)   in subsection (1) after 'confiscation investigations' insert 'or money laundering
      investigations';

    (b)   in subsection (2) omit 'or a money laundering investigation';

    (c)   in subsection (3) after paragraph (a) insert –

        '(aa)   a person specified in the application is subject to a money laundering
            investigation and the order is sought for the purposes of the investiga-
            tion, or'

(3)   In section 392 (requirements for making a disclosure order), in subsection (2) after
    paragraph (a) insert –

    '(aa)   in the case of a money laundering investigation, the person specified in the
      application for the order has committed a money laundering offence;'

(4)   In section 396 (supplementary) –

    (a)   in subsection (1) in paragraph (a) after 'confiscation investigation' insert 'or a
      money laundering investigation';

    (b)   in subsection (3) in paragraph (a) after 'confiscation investigation' insert 'or a
      money laundering investigation'.

Beneficial ownership

9   Co-operation: beneficial ownership information

In Part 11 of the Proceeds of Crime Act 2002 (co-operation), after section 445 insert –

'445A   Sharing of beneficial ownership information

    (1)   The relevant Minister must prepare a report about the arrangements in place
        between –

(a)   the government of the United Kingdom, and

(b)   the government of each relevant territory, for the sharing of beneficial ownership information.

(2)   The report must include an assessment of the effectiveness of those arrangements, having regard to such international standards as appear to the relevant Minister to be relevant.

(3)   The report –

(a)   must be prepared before 1 July 2019, and

(b)   must relate to the arrangements in place during the period of 18 months from 1 July 2017 to 31 December 2018.

(4)   The relevant Minister must –

(a)   publish the report, and

(b)   lay a copy of it before Parliament.

(5)   The reference in subsection (1) to arrangements in place for the sharing of beneficial ownership information between the government of the United Kingdom and the government of a relevant territory is to such arrangements as are set out in an exchange of notes –

(a)   for the provision of beneficial ownership information about a person incorporated in a part of the United Kingdom to a law enforcement authority of the relevant territory at the request of the authority, and

(b)   for the provision of beneficial ownership information about a person incorporated in a relevant territory to a law enforcement authority of the United Kingdom at the request of the authority.

(6)   In this section –

"beneficial ownership information" means information in relation to the beneficial ownership of persons incorporated in a part of the United Kingdom or (as the case may be) in a relevant territory;

"exchange of notes" means written documentation signed on behalf of the government of the United Kingdom and the government of a relevant territory setting out details of the agreement reached in respect of the arrangements for the matters mentioned in subsection (5)(a) and (b);

"relevant Minister" means the Secretary of State or the Minister for the Cabinet Office;

"relevant territory" means any of the Channel Islands, the Isle of Man or any British overseas territory.'

CHAPTER 2   MONEY LAUNDERING

10   Power to extend moratorium period

(1) Part 7 of the Proceeds of Crime Act 2002 (money laundering) is amended as follows.

(2) In section 335 (appropriate consent), after subsection (6) insert –

'(6A) Subsection (6) is subject to –

(a)   section 336A, which enables the moratorium period to be extended by court order in accordance with that section, and

(b)   section 336C, which provides for an automatic extension of the moratorium period in certain cases (period extended if it would otherwise end before determination of application or appeal proceedings etc).'

(3) In section 336 (nominated officer: consent), after subsection (8) insert –

'(8A) Subsection (8) is subject to –

> (a)   section 336A, which enables the moratorium period to be extended by court order in accordance with that section, and
>
> (b)   section 336C, which provides for an automatic extension of the moratorium period in certain cases (period extended if it would otherwise end before determination of application or appeal proceedings etc).'

(4) After section 336 insert –

'336A Power of court to extend the moratorium period

(1)   The court may, on an application under this section, grant an extension of a moratorium period if satisfied that –

> (a)   an investigation is being carried out in relation to a relevant disclosure (but has not been completed),
>
> (b)   the investigation is being conducted diligently and expeditiously,
>
> (c)   further time is needed for conducting the investigation, and
>
> (d)   it is reasonable in all the circumstances for the moratorium period to be extended.

(2)   An application under this section may be made only by a senior officer.

(3)   The application must be made before the moratorium period would otherwise end.

(4)   An extension of a moratorium period must end no later than 31 days beginning with the day after the day on which the period would otherwise end.

(5)   Where a moratorium period is extended by the court under this section, it may be further extended by the court (on one or more occasions) on the making of another application.

(6)   A moratorium period extended in accordance with subsection (2) or (4) of section 336C may also be further extended by the court on the making of an application under this section.

(7)   But the court may not grant a further extension of a moratorium period if the effect would be to extend the period by more than 186 days (in total) beginning with the day after the end of the 31 day period mentioned in section 335(6) or (as the case may be) section 336(8).

(8)   Subsections (1) to (4) apply to any further extension of a moratorium period as they apply to the first extension of the period under this section.

(9)   An application under this section may be made by an immigration officer only if the officer has reasonable grounds for suspecting that conduct constituting the prohibited act in relation to which the moratorium period in question applies –

> (a)   relates to the entitlement of one or more persons who are not nationals of the United Kingdom to enter, transit across, or be in, the United Kingdom (including conduct which relates to conditions or other controls on any such entitlement), or
>
> (b)   is undertaken for the purposes of, or otherwise in relation to, a relevant nationality enactment.

(10) In subsection (9) –

> "prohibited act" has the meaning given by section 335(8) or (as the case may be) section 336(10);

"relevant nationality enactment" means any enactment in –

    (a)   the British Nationality Act 1981,

    (b)   the Hong Kong Act 1985,

    (c)   the Hong Kong (War Wives and Widows) Act 1996,

    (d)   the British Nationality (Hong Kong) Act 1997,

    (e)   the British Overseas Territories Act 2002, or

    (f)   an instrument made under any of those Acts.

336B   Proceedings under section 336A: supplementary

(1)   This section applies to proceedings on an application under section 336A.

(2)   The court must determine the proceedings as soon as reasonably practicable.

(3)   The court may exclude from any part of the hearing –

    (a)   an interested person;

    (b)   anyone representing that person.

(4)   The person who made the application may apply to the court for an order that specified information upon which he or she intends to rely be withheld from –

    (a)   an interested person;

    (b)   anyone representing that person.

(5)   The court may make such an order only if satisfied that there are reasonable grounds to believe that if the specified information were disclosed –

    (a)   evidence of an offence would be interfered with or harmed,

    (b)   the gathering of information about the possible commission of an offence would be interfered with,

    (c)   a person would be interfered with or physically injured,

    (d)   the recovery of property under this Act would be hindered, or

    (e)   national security would be put at risk.

(6)   The court must direct that the following be excluded from the hearing of an application under subsection (4) –

    (a)   the interested person to whom that application relates;

    (b)   anyone representing that person.

(7)   Subject to this section, rules of court may make provision as to the practice and procedure to be followed in connection with proceedings in relation to applications under section 336A.

(8)   An appeal lies to the appropriate appeal court on a point of law arising from a decision made by the Crown Court in Northern Ireland or by the sheriff.

(9)   The appropriate appeal court may on such an appeal make any order that it considers appropriate (subject to the restriction mentioned in section 336A(7)).

(10)   The appropriate appeal court is –

    (a)   in the case of a decision of the Crown Court in Northern Ireland, the Court of Appeal in Northern Ireland;

    (b)   in the case of a decision of the sheriff, the Sheriff Appeal Court.

(11)   For rights of appeal in the case of decisions made by the Crown Court in England and Wales, see section 28 of the Senior Courts Act 1981 (appeals from Crown Court and inferior courts).

336C   Extension of moratorium period pending determination of proceedings etc

(1)   A moratorium period is extended in accordance with subsection (2) where –

(a)   an application is made to the court under section 336A for the extension (or further extension) of the moratorium period, and

(b)   the period would (apart from that subsection) end before the court determines the application or it is otherwise disposed of.

(2)   The moratorium period is extended from the time when it would otherwise end until the court determines the application or it is otherwise disposed of.

(3)   A moratorium period is extended in accordance with subsection (4) where –

(a)   proceedings on an appeal in respect of a decision on an application under section 336A have been brought, and

(b)   the period would (apart from that subsection) end before the proceedings are finally determined or otherwise disposed of.

(4)   The moratorium period is extended from the time when it would otherwise end until the proceedings are finally determined or otherwise disposed of.

(5)   But the maximum period by which the moratorium period is extended by virtue of subsection (2) or (4) is 31 days beginning with the day after the day on which the period would otherwise have ended.

(6)   A moratorium period is extended in accordance with subsection (7) where –

(a)   an application is made to the court under section 336A for an extension of the period,

(b)   the court refuses to grant the application, and

(c)   the period would (apart from that subsection) end before the end of the 5 day period.

(7)   The moratorium period is extended from the time when it would otherwise end until –

(a)   the end of the 5 day period, or

(b)   if proceedings on an appeal against the decision are brought before the end of the 5 day period, the time when those proceedings are brought.

(8)   The "5 day period" is the period of 5 working days beginning with the day on which the court refuses to grant the application.

(9)   This restriction on the overall extension of a moratorium period mentioned in section 336A(7) applies to an extension of a moratorium period in accordance with any provision of this section as it applies to an extension under an order of the court.

336D   Sections 336A to 336C: interpretation

(1)   This section provides for the meaning of terms used in sections 336A to 336C (and in this section).

(2)   "The court" means –

(a)   in relation to England and Wales or Northern Ireland, the Crown Court;

(b)   in relation to Scotland, the sheriff.

(3)   "Interested person" means –

(a)   the person who made the relevant disclosure, and

(b)   any other person who appears to the person making the application under section 336A to have an interest in the relevant property.

(4)   "Moratorium period" means the period of 31 days mentioned in section 335(6) or (as the case may be) section 336(8), or any such period as extended or further extended by virtue of an order under section 336A or in accordance with any provision of section 336C.

(5)   "Relevant disclosure" means –

(a)   where the application under section 336A relates to the moratorium period mentioned in section 335(6), the authorised disclosure mentioned in section 335(2)(a);

(b)   where the application under section 336A relates to the moratorium period mentioned in section 336(8), the disclosure mentioned in section 336(4)(a).

(6)   "Relevant property" means any property that would be the subject of the prohibited act (within the meaning of section 335(8) or (as the case may be) section 336(10)) in relation to which the moratorium period in question applies.

(7)   In the case of an application to the Crown Court, "senior officer" means –

(a)   the Director General of the National Crime Agency,

(b)   any other National Crime Agency officer authorised by the Director General (whether generally or specifically) for this purpose,

(c)   a police officer of at least the rank of inspector,

(d)   an officer of Revenue and Customs who is not below such grade as is designated by the Commissioners for Her Majesty's Revenue and Customs as equivalent to that rank,

(e)   an immigration officer who is not below such grade as is designated by the Secretary of State as equivalent to that rank,

(f)   a member of staff of the Financial Conduct Authority who is not below such grade as is designated by the Treasury for the purposes of this Part,

(g)   the Director of the Serious Fraud Office (or a member of staff of that Office authorised for the purposes of section 336A by virtue of section 2C(2)), or

(h)   an accredited financial investigator who falls within a description specified in an order made for the purposes of section 336A by the Secretary of State under section 453.

(8)   In the case of an application to the sheriff, "senior officer" means a procurator fiscal.

(9)   "Working day" means a day other than –

(a)   a Saturday,

(b)   a Sunday,

(c)   Christmas Day,

(d)   Good Friday, or

(e)   a day which is a bank holiday under the Banking and Financial Dealings Act 1971 in the part of the United Kingdom in which the application in question under section 336A is made.'

11 Sharing of information within the regulated sector

After section 339ZA of the Proceeds of Crime Act 2002 insert –

'339ZB Voluntary disclosures within the regulated sector

(1)   A person (A) may disclose information to one or more other persons if conditions 1 to 4 are met.

(2)   Condition 1 is that –

(a)   A is carrying on a business in the regulated sector as a relevant undertaking,

(b)   the information on which the disclosure is based came to A in the course of carrying on that business, and

(c)   the person to whom the information is to be disclosed (or each of them, where the disclosure is to more than one person) is also carrying on a business in the regulated sector as a relevant undertaking (whether or not of the same kind as A).

(3)   Condition 2 is that –

(a)   an NCA authorised officer has requested A to make the disclosure, or

(b)   the person to whom the information is to be disclosed (or at least one of them, where the disclosure is to more than one person) has requested A to do so.

(4)   Condition 3 is that, before A makes the disclosure, the required notification has been made to an NCA authorised officer (see section 339ZC(3) to (5)).

(5)   Condition 4 is that A is satisfied that the disclosure of the information will or may assist in determining any matter in connection with a suspicion that a person is engaged in money laundering.

(6)   A person may disclose information to A for the purposes of making a disclosure request if, and to the extent that, the person has reason to believe that A has in A's possession information that will or may assist in determining any matter in connection with a suspicion that a person is engaged in money laundering.

339ZC   Section 339ZB: disclosure requests and required notifications

(1)   A disclosure request must –

(a)   state that it is made in connection with a suspicion that a person is engaged in money laundering,

(b)   identify the person (if known),

(c)   describe the information that is sought from A, and

(d)   specify the person or persons to whom it is requested that the information is disclosed.

(2)   Where the disclosure request is made by a person mentioned in section 339ZB(3)(b), the request must also –

(a)   set out the grounds for the suspicion that a person is engaged in money laundering, or

(b)   provide such other information as the person making the request thinks appropriate for the purposes of enabling A to determine whether the information requested ought to be disclosed under section 339ZB(1).

(3)   A required notification must be made –

(a)   in the case of a disclosure request made by an NCA authorised officer, by the person who is to disclose information under section 339ZB(1) as a result of the request;

(b)   in the case of a disclosure request made by a person mentioned in section 339ZB(3)(b), by the person who made the request.

(4)   In a case within subsection (3)(a), the required notification must state that information is to be disclosed under section 339ZB(1).

(5)   In a case within subsection (3)(b), the required notification must –

(a)   state that a disclosure request has been made,

(b)   specify the person to whom the request was made,

(c)   identify any person (if known) suspected of being engaged in money laundering in connection with whom the request was made, and

(d)   provide all such other information that the person giving the notification would be required to give if making the required disclosure for the purposes of section 330 (see in particular subsection (5)(b) and (c) of that section).

339ZD   Section 339ZB: effect on required disclosures under section 330 or 331

(1)   This section applies if in any proceedings a question arises as to whether the required disclosure has been made for the purposes of section 330(4) or 331(4) –

(a)   by a person (A) who discloses information under section 339ZB(1) as a result of a disclosure request,

(b)   by a person (B) who makes a required notification in accordance with section 339ZC(3)(b) in connection with that request, or

(c)   by any other person (C) to whom A discloses information under section 339ZB(1) as a result of that request.

(2)   The making of a required notification in good faith is to be treated as satisfying any requirement to make the required disclosure on the part of A, B and C.

This is subject to section 339ZE(1) to (8).

(3)   The making of a joint disclosure report in good faith is to be treated as satisfying any requirement to make the required disclosure on the part of the persons who jointly make the report.

This is subject to section 339ZE(10).

(4)   A joint disclosure report is a report to an NCA authorised officer that –

(a)   is made jointly by A and B (whether or not also jointly with other persons to whom A discloses information under section 339ZB(1)),

(b)   satisfies the requirements as to content mentioned in subsection (5),

(c)   is prepared after the making of a disclosure by A to B under section 339ZB(1) in connection with a suspicion of a person's engagement in money laundering, and

(d)   is sent to the NCA authorised officer before the end of the applicable period.

(5)   The requirements as to content are that the report must –

(a)   explain the extent to which there are continuing grounds to suspect that the person mentioned in subsection (4)(c) is engaged in money laundering,

(b)   identify the person (if known),

(c)   set out the grounds for the suspicion, and

(d)   provide any other information relevant to the matter.

(6)   The applicable period is –

(a)   in a case where the disclosure under section 339ZB was made as a result of a disclosure request from an NCA authorised officer by virtue of subsection (3)(a) of that section, whatever period may be specified by the officer when making the request;

(b)   in a case where the disclosure was made as a result of a disclosure request from another person by virtue of subsection (3)(b) of that section, the period of 84 days beginning with the day on which a required notification is made in connection with the request.

(7)   A joint disclosure report must be –

(a)   approved by the nominated officer of each person that jointly makes the report, and

(b)   signed by the nominated officer on behalf of each such person.

If there is no nominated officer the report must be approved and signed by another senior officer.

(8)   References in this section to A, B or C include –

(a)   a nominated officer acting on behalf of A, B or C, and

(b)   any other person who is an employee, officer or partner of A, B or C.

339ZE   Limitations on application of section 339ZD(2) and (3)

(1)   Subsections (2) and (3) apply in a case where the required notification is made by A (notification made as a result of disclosure request received from NCA authorised officer).

(2)   Section 339ZD(2) has effect in the case of A, B or C only so far as relating to –

(a)   the suspicion in connection with which the required notification is made, and

(b)   matters known, suspected or believed as a result of the making of the disclosure request concerned.

(3)   Accordingly, section 339ZD(2) does not remove any requirement to make the required disclosure in relation to anything known, suspected or believed that does not result only from the making of the disclosure request.

(4)   Subsections (5) to (7) apply in a case where the required notification is made by B (notification made as a result of disclosure request received from another undertaking in the regulated sector).

(5)   Section 339ZD(2) has effect in the case of A or C only so far as relating to –

(a)   the suspicion in connection with which the notification by B is made, and

(b)   matters known, suspected or believed by A or C as a result of the making of that notification.

(6)   Accordingly, section 339ZD(2) does not remove any requirement to make the required disclosure in relation to anything known, suspected or believed that does not result only from the making of the notification.

(7)   Section 339ZD(2) has effect in the case of B only so far as relating to –

(a)   the suspicion in connection with which the notification is made, and

(b)   matters known, suspected or believed by B at the time of the making of the notification.

(8)   If a joint disclosure report is not made before the end of the applicable period (whether the required notification was made by A or B), section 339ZD(2) –

(a)   has effect only so far as relating to any requirement to make the required disclosure that would have otherwise arisen within that period, and

(b)   does not remove a requirement to make the required disclosure so far as arising after the end of that period on the part of any person in respect of matters that may become known, suspected or believed by the person after the time when the required notification was made.

(9)   If a joint disclosure report is not made before the end of the applicable

period, the person who made the required notification must notify an NCA authorised officer that a report is not being made as soon as reasonably practicable after the period ends.

(10)   Section 339ZD(3) has effect only so far as relating to –

(a)   the suspicion in connection with which the report is made, and

(b)   matters known, suspected or believed at the time of the making of the report.

(11)   Terms used in this section have the same meanings as in section 339ZD.

339ZF   Section 339ZB: supplementary

(1)   A relevant disclosure made in good faith does not breach –

(a)   an obligation of confidence owed by the person making the disclosure, or

(b)   any other restriction on the disclosure of information, however imposed.

(2)   But a relevant disclosure may not include information obtained from a UK law enforcement agency unless that agency consents to the disclosure.

(3)   In a case where a person is acting on behalf of another ("the undertaking") as a nominated officer –

(a)   a relevant disclosure by the undertaking must be made by the nominated officer on behalf of the undertaking, and

(b)   a relevant disclosure to the undertaking must be made to that officer.

(4)   Subsection (1) applies whether or not the conditions in section 339ZB were met in respect of the disclosure if the person making the disclosure did so in the reasonable belief that the conditions were met.

(5)   In this section –

"relevant disclosure" means any disclosure made in compliance, or intended compliance, with section 339ZB;

"UK law enforcement agency" means –

(a)   the National Crime Agency;

(b)   a police force in England, Scotland, Northern Ireland or Wales;

(c)   any other person operating in England, Scotland, Northern Ireland or Wales charged with the duty of preventing, detecting, investigating or prosecuting offences.

339ZG   Sections 339ZB to 339ZF: interpretation

(1)   This section applies for the purposes of sections 339ZB to 339ZF.

(2)   "Disclosure request" means a request made for the purposes of condition 2 in section 339ZB(3).

(3)   "NCA authorised officer" means a person authorised for the purposes of this Part by the Director General of the National Crime Agency.

(4)   "Nominated officer" means a person nominated to receive disclosures under section 330.

(5)   "Relevant undertaking" means any of the following –

(a)   a credit institution;

(b)   a financial institution;

(c)   a professional legal adviser;

(d)   a relevant professional adviser;

(e)   other persons (not within paragraphs (a) to (d)) whose business consists of activities listed in paragraph 1(1) of Schedule 9.

(6)   "Required disclosure" has the same meaning as in section 330(5) or (as the case may be) section 331(5).

(7)   "Required notification" means a notification made for the purposes of condition 3 in section 339ZB(4).

(8)   For the purposes of subsection (5) –

(a)   "credit institution" has the same meaning as in Schedule 9;

(b)   "financial institution" means an undertaking that carries on a business in the regulated sector by virtue of any of paragraphs (b) to (i) of paragraph 1(1) of that Schedule;

(c)   "relevant professional adviser" has the meaning given by section 333E(5).

(9)   Schedule 9 has effect for determining what is a business in the regulated sector.'

12   Further information orders

After section 339ZG of the Proceeds of Crime Act 2002 (inserted by section 11 above) insert –

'Further information orders

339ZH   Further information orders

(1)   A magistrates' court or (in Scotland) the sheriff may, on an application made by a relevant person, make a further information order if satisfied that either condition 1 or condition 2 is met.

(2)   The application must –

(a)   specify or describe the information sought under the order, and

(b)   specify the person from whom the information is sought ("the respondent").

(3)   A further information order is an order requiring the respondent to provide –

(a)   the information specified or described in the application for the order, or

(b)   such other information as the court or sheriff making the order thinks appropriate,

so far as the information is in the possession, or under the control, of the respondent.

(4)   Condition 1 for the making of a further information order is met if –

(a)   the information required to be given under the order would relate to a matter arising from a disclosure made under this Part,

(b)   the respondent is the person who made the disclosure or is otherwise carrying on a business in the regulated sector,

(c)   the information would assist in investigating whether a person is engaged in money laundering or in determining whether an investigation of that kind should be started, and

(d)   it is reasonable in all the circumstances for the information to be provided.

(5)   Condition 2 for the making of a further information order is met if –

(a)   the information required to be given under the order would relate to a matter arising from a disclosure made under a corresponding disclosure requirement,

(b)   an external request has been made to the National Crime Agency for the provision of information in connection with that disclosure,

(c)   the respondent is carrying on a business in the regulated sector,

(d)   the information is likely to be of substantial value to the authority that made the external request in determining any matter in connection with the disclosure, and

(e)   it is reasonable in all the circumstances for the information to be provided.

(6)   For the purposes of subsection (5), "external request" means a request made by an authority of a foreign country which has responsibility in that country for carrying out investigations into whether a corresponding money laundering offence has been committed.

(7)   A further information order must specify –

(a)   how the information required under the order is to be provided, and

(b)   the date by which it is to be provided.

(8)   If a person fails to comply with a further information order made by a magistrates' court, the magistrates' court may order the person to pay an amount not exceeding £5,000.

(9)   The sum mentioned in subsection (8) is to be treated as adjudged to be paid by a conviction of the court for the purposes of the Magistrates' Courts Act 1980 or (as the case may be) the Magistrates' Courts (Northern Ireland) Order 1981 (S.I. 1981/1675 (N.I. 26)).

(10)   In order to take account of changes in the value of money the Secretary of State may by regulations substitute another sum for the sum for the time being specified in subsection (8).

(11)   Schedule 9 has effect for the purposes of this section in determining what is a business in the regulated sector.

(12)   In this section –

"corresponding disclosure requirement" means a requirement to make a disclosure under the law of the foreign country concerned that corresponds to a requirement imposed by virtue of this Part;

"corresponding money laundering offence" means an offence under the law of the foreign country concerned that would, if done in the United Kingdom, constitute an offence specified in paragraph (a), (b) or (c) of section 340(11);

"foreign country" means a country or territory outside the United Kingdom;

"relevant person" means –

(a)   in the case of an application to a magistrates' court, the Director General of the National Crime Agency or any other National Crime Agency officer authorised by the Director General (whether generally or specifically) for this purpose, or

(b)   in the case of an application to the sheriff, a procurator fiscal.

339ZI   Statements

(1)   A statement made by a person in response to a further information order may not be used in evidence against the person in criminal proceedings.

(2)   Subsection (1) does not apply –

(a)   in the case of proceedings under this Part,

(b)   on a prosecution for perjury, or

(c)   on a prosecution for some other offence where, in giving evidence, the person makes a statement inconsistent with the statement mentioned in subsection (1).

(3)   A statement may not be used by virtue of subsection (2)(c) unless –

(a)   evidence relating to it is adduced, or
(b)   a question relating to it is asked,

by or on behalf of the person in the proceedings arising out of the prosecution.

(4)   In subsection (2)(b) the reference to a prosecution for perjury is –

(a)   in the case of England and Wales, a reference to a prosecution for an offence under section 5 of the Perjury Act 1911;
(b)   in the case of Northern Ireland, a reference to a prosecution for an offence under Article 10 of the Perjury (Northern Ireland) Order 1979 (S.I. 1979/1714 (N.I. 19)).

339ZJ   Appeals

(1)   An appeal from a decision on an application for a further information order lies to the relevant appeal court.
(2)   An appeal under this section lies at the instance of any person who was a party to the proceedings on the application.
(3)   The "relevant appeal court" is –

(a)   the Crown Court, in the case of a decision made by a magistrates' court in England and Wales;
(b)   a county court, in the case of a decision made by a magistrates' court in Northern Ireland;
(c)   the Sheriff Appeal Court, in the case of a decision made by the sheriff.

(4)   On an appeal under this section the relevant appeal court may –

(a)   make or (as the case may be) discharge a further information order, or
(b)   vary the order.

339ZK   Supplementary

(1)   A further information order does not confer the right to require a person to provide privileged information.
(2)   "Privileged information" is information which a person would be entitled to refuse to provide on grounds of legal professional privilege in proceedings in the High Court or, in Scotland, legal privilege as defined by section 412.
(3)   Information provided in pursuance of a further information order is not to be taken to breach any restriction on the disclosure of information (however imposed).
(4)   An application for a further information order may be heard and determined in private.
(5)   Rules of court may make provision as to the practice and procedure to be followed in connection with proceedings relating to further information orders.'

CHAPTER 3   CIVIL RECOVERY

Meaning of 'unlawful conduct': gross human rights abuses or violations

13   Unlawful conduct: gross human rights abuses or violations

(1)   Part 5 of the Proceeds of Crime Act 2002 (civil recovery of the proceeds etc of unlawful conduct) is amended as follows.

(2) In section 241 (meaning of 'unlawful conduct'), after subsection (2) insert –

'(2A) Conduct which –

    (a) occurs in a country or territory outside the United Kingdom,

    (b) constitutes, or is connected with, the commission of a gross human rights abuse or violation (see section 241A), and

    (c) if it occurred in a part of the United Kingdom, would be an offence triable under the criminal law of that part on indictment only or either on indictment or summarily,

is also unlawful conduct.'

(3) After that section insert –

'**241A "Gross human rights abuse or violation"**

(1) Conduct constitutes the commission of a gross human rights abuse or violation if each of the following three conditions is met.

(2) The first condition is that –

    (a) the conduct constitutes the torture of a person who has sought –

        (i) to expose illegal activity carried out by a public official or a person acting in an official capacity, or

        (ii) to obtain, exercise, defend or promote human rights and fundamental freedoms, or

    (b) the conduct otherwise involves the cruel, inhuman or degrading treatment or punishment of such a person.

(3) The second condition is that the conduct is carried out in consequence of that person having sought to do anything falling within subsection (2)(a)(i) or (ii).

(4) The third condition is that the conduct is carried out –

    (a) by a public official, or a person acting in an official capacity, in the performance or purported performance of his or her official duties, or

    (b) by a person not falling within paragraph (a) at the instigation or with the consent or acquiescence –

        (i) of a public official, or

        (ii) of a person acting in an official capacity,

who in instigating the conduct, or in consenting to or acquiescing in it, is acting in the performance or purported performance of his or her official duties.

(5) Conduct is connected with the commission of a gross human rights abuse or violation if it is conduct by a person that involves –

    (a) acting as an agent for another in connection with activities relating to conduct constituting the commission of a gross human rights abuse or violation,

    (b) directing, or sponsoring, such activities,

    (c) profiting from such activities, or

    (d) materially assisting such activities.

(6) Conduct that involves the intentional infliction of severe pain or suffering on another person is conduct that constitutes torture for the purposes of subsection (2)(a).

(7) It is immaterial whether the pain or suffering is physical or mental and whether it is caused by an act or omission.

(8)   The cases in which a person materially assists activities for the purposes of subsection (5)(d) include those where the person –

    (a)   provides goods or services in support of the carrying out of the activities, or

    (b)   otherwise provides any financial or technological support in connection with their carrying out.'

(4)   The amendments made by this section –

    (a)   apply in relation to conduct, so far as that conduct constitutes or is connected with the torture of a person (see section 241A(2)(a) of the Proceeds of Crime Act 2002 as inserted by subsection (3) above), whether the conduct occurs before or after the coming into force of this section;

    (b)   apply in relation to property obtained through such conduct whether the property is obtained before or after the coming into force of this section;

    (c)   apply in relation to conduct, so far as that conduct involves or is connected with the cruel, inhuman or degrading treatment or punishment of a person (see section 241A(2)(b) of that Act as inserted by subsection (3) above), only if the conduct occurs after the coming into force of this section.

This is subject to subsection (5).

(5)   Proceedings under Chapter 2 of Part 5 of the Proceeds of Crime Act 2002 may not be brought in respect of property obtained through unlawful conduct of the kind mentioned in section 241(2A) of the Proceeds of Crime Act 2002 (as inserted by subsection (2) above) after the end of the period of 20 years from the date on which the conduct constituting the commission of the gross human rights abuse or violation concerned occurs.

(6)   Proceedings under that Chapter are brought in England and Wales or Northern Ireland when –

    (a)   a claim form is issued,

    (b)   an application is made for a property freezing order under section 245A of that Act, or

    (c)   an application is made for an interim receiving order under section 246 of that Act,

whichever is the earliest.

(7)   Proceedings under that Chapter are brought in Scotland when –

    (a)   the proceedings are served,

    (b)   an application is made for a prohibitory property order under section 255A of that Act, or

    (c)   an application is made for an interim administration order under section 256 of that Act,

whichever is the earliest.

Forfeiture

14   Forfeiture of cash

(1)   In section 289(6) of the Proceeds of Crime Act 2002 (meaning of cash for purposes of Chapter 3 of Part 5 of that Act), after paragraph (e) insert –

    '(f)   gaming vouchers,

    (g)   fixed-value casino tokens,

    (h)   betting receipts,'

(2)   After section 289(7) of that Act insert –

    '(7A)   For the purposes of subsection (6) –

(a)   "gaming voucher" means a voucher in physical form issued by a gaming machine that represents a right to be paid the amount stated on it;

(b)   "fixed-value casino token" means a casino token that represents a right to be paid the amount stated on it;

(c)   "betting receipt" means a receipt in physical form that represents a right to be paid an amount in respect of a bet placed with a person holding a betting licence.

(7B)   In subsection (7A) –

"bet" –

(a)   in relation to England and Wales and Scotland, has the same meaning as in section 9(1) of the Gambling Act 2005;

(b)   in relation to Northern Ireland, has the same meaning as in the Betting, Gaming, Lotteries and Amusements (Northern Ireland) Order 1985 (S.I. 1985/1204 (N.I. 11)) (see Article 2 of that Order);

"betting licence" –

(a)   in relation to England and Wales and Scotland, means a general betting operating licence issued under Part 5 of the Gambling Act 2005;

(b)   in relation to Northern Ireland, means a bookmaker's licence as defined in Article 2 of the Betting, Gaming, Lotteries and Amusements (Northern Ireland) Order 1985;

"gaming machine" –

(a)   in relation to England and Wales and Scotland, has the same meaning as in the Gambling Act 2005 (see section 235 of that Act);

(b)   in relation to Northern Ireland, has the same meaning as in the Betting, Gaming, Lotteries and Amusements (Northern Ireland) Order 1985 (see Article 2 of that Order).

(7C)   In the application of subsection (7A) to Northern Ireland references to a right to be paid an amount are to be read as references to the right that would exist but for Article 170 of the Betting, Gaming, Lotteries and Amusements (Northern Ireland) Order 1985 (gaming and wagering contracts void).'

15   Forfeiture of certain personal (or moveable) property

In Part 5 of the Proceeds of Crime Act 2002 (civil recovery of the proceeds etc of unlawful conduct), after section 303A insert –

'Chapter 3A   RECOVERY OF LISTED ASSETS IN SUMMARY PROCEEDINGS

Definition of listed asset

303B   "Listed asset"

(1)   In this Chapter, a "listed asset" means an item of property that falls within one of the following descriptions of property –

(a)   precious metals;
(b)   precious stones;
(c)   watches;
(d)   artistic works;
(e)   face-value vouchers;
(f)   postage stamps.

(2)   The Secretary of State may by regulations amend subsection (1) –

(a)   by removing a description of property;
(b)   by adding a description of tangible personal (or corporeal moveable) property.

(3)   The Secretary of State must consult the Scottish Ministers and the Department of Justice before making regulations under subsection (2).

(4)   In this section –

(a)   "precious metal" means gold, silver or platinum (whether in an unmanufactured or a manufactured state);
(b)   "artistic work" means a piece of work falling within section 4(1)(a) of the Copyright, Designs and Patents Act 1988;
(c)   "face-value voucher" means a voucher in physical form that represents a right to receive goods or services to the value of an amount stated on it.

Searches

303C   Searches

(1)   If a relevant officer is lawfully on any premises and has reasonable grounds for suspecting that there is on the premises a seizable listed asset, the relevant officer may search for the listed asset there.

(2)   The powers conferred by subsection (5) are exercisable by a relevant officer if –

(a)   the relevant officer has reasonable grounds for suspecting that there is a seizable listed asset in a vehicle,
(b)   it appears to the officer that the vehicle is under the control of a person (the suspect) who is in or in the vicinity of the vehicle, and
(c)   the vehicle is in a place falling within subsection (3).

(3)   The places referred to in subsection (2)(c) are –

(a)   a place to which, at the time of the proposed exercise of the powers, the public or any section of the public has access, on payment or otherwise, as of right or by virtue of express or implied permission, and
(b)   any other place to which at that time people have ready access but which is not a dwelling.

(4)   But if the vehicle is in a garden or yard or other land occupied with and used for the purposes of a dwelling, the relevant officer may exercise the powers conferred by subsection (5) only if the relevant officer has reasonable grounds for believing –

(a)   that the suspect does not reside in the dwelling, and
(b)   that the vehicle is not in the place in question with the express or implied permission of a person who resides in the dwelling.

(5)   The powers conferred by this subsection are –

(a)   power to require the suspect to permit entry to the vehicle;
(b)   power to require the suspect to permit a search of the vehicle.

(6)   If a relevant officer has reasonable grounds for suspecting that a person (the suspect) is carrying a seizable listed asset, the relevant officer may require the suspect –

(a)   to permit a search of any article the suspect has with him or her;

(b)   to permit a search of the suspect's person.

(7)   The powers conferred by subsections (5) and (6) are exercisable only so far as the relevant officer thinks it necessary or expedient.

(8)   A relevant officer may –

(a)   in exercising powers conferred by subsection (5), detain the vehicle for so long as is necessary for their exercise;

(b)   in exercising powers conferred by subsection (6)(b), detain the suspect for so long as is necessary for their exercise.

(9)   In this Chapter, a "relevant officer" means –

(a)   an officer of Revenue and Customs,

(b)   a constable,

(c)   an SFO officer, or

(d)   an accredited financial investigator who falls within a description specified in an order made for the purposes of this Chapter by the Secretary of State under section 453.

(10)   For the purposes of this section a listed asset is a seizable listed asset if –

(a)   all or part of it is recoverable property or is intended by any person for use in unlawful conduct, and

(b)   the value of the asset, or the part of it that falls within paragraph (a), is not less than the minimum value.

(11)   Where a power conferred by this section is being exercised in respect of more than one seizable listed asset, this section is to apply as if the value of each asset or (as the case may be) part of an asset was equal to the aggregate value of all of those assets or parts.

303D   Searches: supplemental provision

(1)   The powers conferred by section 303C –

(a)   are exercisable only so far as reasonably required for the purpose of finding a listed asset;

(b)   include the power to carry out (or arrange for the carrying out of) tests on anything found during the course of the search for the purpose of establishing whether it is a listed asset;

(c)   are exercisable by an officer of Revenue and Customs only if the officer has reasonable grounds for suspecting that the unlawful conduct in question relates to an assigned matter (within the meaning of the Customs and Excise Management Act 1979);

(d)   are exercisable by an SFO officer or an accredited financial investiga-tor only in relation to the following –

(i)   premises in England, Wales or Northern Ireland (in the case of section 303C(1));

(ii)   vehicles and suspects in England, Wales or Northern Ireland (in the case of section 303C(5) and (8)(a));

(iii)   suspects in England, Wales or Northern Ireland (in the case of section 303C(6) and (8)(b)).

(2)   Section 303C does not require a person to submit to an intimate search or strip search (within the meaning of section 164 of the Customs and Excise Management Act 1979).

303E   Prior approval

(1)   The powers conferred by section 303C may be exercised only with the

appropriate approval unless, in the circumstances, it is not practicable to obtain that approval before exercising the power.

(2)   The appropriate approval means the approval of a judicial officer or (if that is not practicable in any case) the approval of a senior officer.

(3)   A judicial officer means –

(a)   in relation to England and Wales and Northern Ireland, a justice of the peace;

(b)   in relation to Scotland, the sheriff.

(4)   A senior officer means –

(a)   in relation to the exercise of a power by an officer of Revenue and Customs, such an officer of a rank designated by the Commissioners for Her Majesty's Revenue and Customs as equivalent to that of a senior police officer;

(b)   in relation to the exercise of a power by a constable, a senior police officer;

(c)   in relation to the exercise of a power by an SFO officer, the Director of the Serious Fraud Office;

(d)   in relation to the exercise of a power by a National Crime Agency officer, the Director General of the National Crime Agency or any other National Crime Agency officer authorised by the Director General (whether generally or specifically) for this purpose;

(e)   in relation to the exercise of a power by an accredited financial investigator who is –

(i)   a member of the civilian staff of a police force in England and Wales (including the metropolitan police force), within the meaning of Part 1 of the Police Reform and Social Responsibility Act 2011,

(ii)   a member of staff of the City of London police force, or

(iii)   a member of staff of the Police Service of Northern Ireland, a senior police officer;

(f)   in relation to the exercise of a power by an accredited financial investigator who does not fall within any of the preceding paragraphs, an accredited financial investigator who falls within a description specified in an order made for this purpose by the Secretary of State under section 453.

(5)   A senior police officer means a police officer of at least the rank of inspector.

(6)   If the powers are exercised without the approval of a judicial officer in a case where –

(a)   no property is seized by virtue of section 303J, or

(b)   any property so seized is not detained for more than 48 hours (calculated in accordance with section 303K(5)),

the relevant officer who exercised the power must give a written report to the appointed person.

(7)   But the duty in subsection (6) does not apply if, during the course of exercising the powers conferred by section 303C, the relevant officer seizes cash by virtue of section 294 and the cash so seized is detained for more than 48 hours (calculated in accordance with section 295(1B)).

(8)   A report under subsection (6) must give particulars of the circumstances which led the relevant officer to believe that –

(a)   the powers were exercisable, and

(b)   it was not practicable to obtain the approval of a judicial officer.

(9)   In this section and section 303F, the appointed person means –

(a)   in relation to England and Wales, a person appointed by the Secretary of State;

(b)   in relation to Scotland, a person appointed by the Scottish Ministers;

(c)   in relation to Northern Ireland, a person appointed by the Department of Justice.

(10)   The appointed person must not be a person employed under or for the purposes of a government department or of the Scottish Administration; and the terms and conditions of the person's appointment, including any remuneration or expenses to be paid to the person, are to be determined by the person making the appointment.

303F   Report on exercise of powers

(1)   As soon as possible after the end of each financial year, the appointed person must prepare a report for that year.

(2)   "Financial year" means –

(a)   the period beginning with the day on which section 15 of the Criminal Finances Act 2017 (which inserted this section) came into force and ending with the next 31 March (which is the first financial year), and

(b)   each subsequent period of 12 months beginning with 1 April.

(3)   The report must give the appointed person's opinion as to the circumstances and manner in which the powers conferred by section 303C are being exercised in cases where the relevant officer who exercised them is required to give a report under section 303E(6).

(4)   In the report, the appointed person may make any recommendations he or she considers appropriate.

(5)   The appointed person must send a copy of the report to whichever of the Secretary of State, the Scottish Administration or the Department of Justice appointed the person.

(6)   The Secretary of State must lay a copy of any report the Secretary of State receives under this section before Parliament and arrange for it to be published.

(7)   The Scottish Ministers must lay a copy of any report they receive under this section before the Scottish Parliament and arrange for it to be published.

(8)   The Department of Justice must lay a copy of any report it receives under this section before the Northern Ireland Assembly and arrange for it to be published.

(9)   Section 41(3) of the Interpretation Act (Northern Ireland) 1954 applies for the purposes of subsection (8) in relation to the laying of a copy of a report as it applies in relation to the laying of a statutory document under an enactment.

303G   Code of practice: Secretary of State

(1)   The Secretary of State must make a code of practice in connection with the exercise by officers of Revenue and Customs, SFO officers and (in relation to England and Wales) constables and accredited financial investigators of the powers conferred by section 303C.

(2)   Where the Secretary of State proposes to issue a code of practice, the Secretary of State must –

(a)   publish a draft,

      (b)   consider any representations made about the draft by the Scottish Ministers, the Department of Justice or any other person, and

      (c)   if the Secretary of State thinks it appropriate, modify the draft in the light of any such representations.

(3)   The Secretary of State must also consult the Attorney General about the draft in its application to the exercise of powers by SFO officers and the Director of the Serious Fraud Office.

(4)   The Secretary of State must lay a draft of the code before Parliament.

(5)   When the Secretary of State has laid a draft of the code before Parliament, the Secretary of State may bring it into operation by regulations.

(6)   The Secretary of State may revise the whole or any part of the code and issue the code as revised; and subsections (2) to (5) apply to such a revised code as they apply to the original code.

(7)   A failure by an officer of Revenue and Customs, an SFO officer, a constable or an accredited financial investigator to comply with a provision of the code does not of itself make him or her liable to criminal or civil proceedings.

(8)   The code is admissible in evidence in criminal or civil proceedings and is to be taken into account by a court or tribunal in any case in which it appears to the court or tribunal to be relevant.

303H   Code of practice: Scotland

(1)   The Scottish Ministers must make a code of practice in connection with the exercise by constables in relation to Scotland of the powers conferred by section 303C.

(2)   Where the Scottish Ministers propose to issue a code of practice, they must –

      (a)   publish a draft,

      (b)   consider any representations made about the draft, and

      (c)   if they think it appropriate, modify the draft in the light of any such representations.

(3)   The Scottish Ministers must lay a draft of the code before the Scottish Parliament.

(4)   When the Scottish Ministers have laid a draft of the code before the Scottish Parliament, they may bring it into operation by order.

(5)   The Scottish Ministers may revise the whole or any part of the code and issue the code as revised; and subsections (2) to (4) apply to such a revised code as they apply to the original code.

(6)   A failure by a constable to comply with a provision of the code does not of itself make the constable liable to criminal or civil proceedings.

(7)   The code is admissible in evidence in criminal or civil proceedings and is to be taken into account by a court or tribunal in any case in which it appears to the court or tribunal to be relevant.

303I   Code of practice: Northern Ireland

(1)   The Department of Justice must make a code of practice in connection with the exercise by constables and accredited financial investigators, in relation to Northern Ireland, of the powers conferred by section 303C.

(2)   Where the Department of Justice proposes to issue a code of practice, it must –

      (a)   publish a draft,

      (b)   consider any representations made about the draft, and

      (c)   if the Department of Justice thinks it appropriate, modify the draft in the light of any such representations.

(3)   The Department of Justice must lay a draft of the code before the Northern Ireland Assembly.

(4)   When the Department of Justice has laid a draft of the code before the Northern Ireland Assembly, the Department of Justice may bring it into operation by order.

(5)   Section 41(3) of the Interpretation Act (Northern Ireland) 1954 applies for the purposes of subsections (3) and (4) in relation to the laying of a draft as it applies in relation to the laying of a statutory document under an enactment.

(6)   The Department of Justice may revise the whole or any part of the code and issue the code as revised; and subsections (2) to (5) apply to such a revised code as they apply to the original code.

(7)   A failure by a constable or accredited financial investigator to comply with a provision of the code does not of itself make him or her liable to criminal or civil proceedings.

(8)   The code is admissible in evidence in criminal or civil proceedings and is to be taken into account by a court or tribunal in any case in which it appears to the court or tribunal to be relevant.

Seizure and detention

303J   Seizure of listed assets

(1)   A relevant officer may seize any item of property if the relevant officer has reasonable grounds for suspecting that –

   (a)   it is a listed asset,

   (b)   it is recoverable property or intended by any person for use in unlawful conduct, and

   (c)   the value of it is not less than the minimum value.

(2)   A relevant officer may also seize any item of property if –

   (a)   the relevant officer has reasonable grounds for suspecting the item to be a listed asset,

   (b)   the relevant officer has reasonable grounds for suspecting that part of the item is recoverable property or intended by any person for use in unlawful conduct,

   (c)   the relevant officer has reasonable grounds for suspecting that the value of the part to which the suspicion relates is not less than the minimum value, and

   (d)   it is not reasonably practicable to seize only that part.

(3)   Where the powers conferred by this section are being exercised by a relevant officer in respect of more than one item of property, this section is to apply as if the value of each item was equal to the aggregate value of all of those items.

(4)   The references in subsection (3) to the value of an item are to be read as including references to the value of part of an item where the power conferred by subsection (2) is being exercised (whether alone or in conjunction with the power conferred by subsection (1)).

(5)   This section does not authorise the seizure by an SFO officer or an accredited financial investigator of an item of property found in Scotland.

303K   Initial detention of seized property

(1)   Property seized under section 303J may be detained for an initial period of 6 hours.

(2)   Property seized under section 303J may be detained beyond the initial period of 6 hours only if its continued detention is authorised by a senior officer.

(3)   If the continued detention of property seized under section 303J is authorised under subsection (2), the property may be detained for a further period of 42 hours.

(4)   Subsections (1) to (3) authorise the detention of property only for so long as a relevant officer continues to have reasonable grounds for suspicion in relation to that property as described in section 303J(1) or (2) (as the case may be).

(5)   In calculating a period of hours for the purposes of this section, no account shall be taken of –

(a)   any Saturday or Sunday,
(b)   Christmas Day,
(c)   Good Friday,
(d)   any day that is a bank holiday under the Banking and Financial Dealings Act 1971 in the part of the United Kingdom within which the property is seized, or
(e)   any day prescribed under section 8(2) of the Criminal Procedure (Scotland) Act 1995 as a court holiday in a sheriff court in the sheriff court district within which the property is seized.

(6)   "Senior officer" has the same meaning in this section as it has in section 303E.

303L   Further detention of seized property

(1)   The period for which property seized under section 303J, or any part of that property, may be detained may be extended by an order made –

(a)   in England and Wales or Northern Ireland, by a magistrates' court;
(b)   in Scotland, by the sheriff.

(2)   An order under subsection (1) may not authorise the detention of any property –

(a)   beyond the end of the period of 6 months beginning with the date of the order, and
(b)   in the case of any further order under this section, beyond the end of the period of 2 years beginning with the date of the first order.

(3)   A justice of the peace may also exercise the power of a magistrates' court to make the first order under subsection (1) extending a particular period of detention.

(4)   An application for an order under subsection (1) may be made –

(a)   in relation to England and Wales and Northern Ireland, by a person specified in subsection (5);
(b)   in relation to Scotland, by the Scottish Ministers in connection with their functions under section 303O or by a procurator fiscal.

(5)   The persons referred to in subsection (4)(a) are –

(a)   the Commissioners for Her Majesty's Revenue and Customs,
(b)   a constable,
(c)   an SFO officer, or
(d)   an accredited financial investigator who falls within a description specified in an order made for the purposes of this Chapter by the Secretary of State under section 453.

(6)   The court, sheriff or justice may make the order if satisfied, in relation to the item of property to be further detained, that –

(a) it is a listed asset,
(b) the value of it is not less than the minimum value, and
(c) condition 1 or condition 2 is met.

(7) Subsection (6)(b) does not apply where the application is for a second or subsequent order under this section.

(8) Condition 1 is that there are reasonable grounds for suspecting that the property is recoverable property and that either –

   (a) its continued detention is justified while its derivation is further investigated or consideration is given to bringing (in the United Kingdom or elsewhere) proceedings against any person for an offence with which the property is connected, or
   (b) proceedings against any person for an offence with which the property is connected have been started and have not been concluded.

(9) Condition 2 is that there are reasonable grounds for suspecting that the property is intended to be used in unlawful conduct and that either –

   (a) its continued detention is justified while its intended use is further investigated or consideration is given to bringing (in the United Kingdom or elsewhere) proceedings against any person for an offence with which the property is connected, or
   (b) proceedings against any person for an offence with which the property is connected have been started and have not been concluded.

(10) Where an application for an order under subsection (1) relates to an item of property seized under section 303J(2), the court, sheriff or justice may make the order if satisfied that –

   (a) the item of property is a listed asset,
   (b) condition 1 or 2 is met in respect of part of the item,
   (c) the value of that part is not less than the minimum value, and
   (d) it is not reasonably practicable to detain only that part.

(11) Subsection (10)(c) does not apply where the application is for a second or subsequent order under this section.

(12) Where an application for an order under subsection (1) is made in respect of two or more items of property that were seized at the same time and by the same person, this section is to apply as if the value of each item was equal to the aggregate value of all of those items.

(13) The references in subsection (12) to the value of an item are to be read as including references to the value of part of an item where subsection (10) applies in relation to one or more of the items in respect of which the application under subsection (1) is made.

(14) An order under subsection (1) must provide for notice to be given to persons affected by it.

303M Testing and safekeeping of property seized under section 303J

(1) A relevant officer may carry out (or arrange for the carrying out of) tests on any item of property seized under section 303J for the purpose of establishing whether it is a listed asset.

(2) A relevant officer must arrange for any item of property seized under section 303J to be safely stored throughout the period during which it is detained under this Chapter.

303N Release of detained property

(1) This section applies while any property is detained under section 303K or 303L.

(2)   A magistrates' court or (in Scotland) the sheriff may direct the release of the whole or any part of the property if the following condition is met.

(3)   The condition is that the court or sheriff is satisfied, on an application by the person from whom the property was seized, that the conditions in section 303K or 303L (as the case may be) for the detention of the property are no longer met in relation to the property to be released.

(4)   A relevant officer or (in Scotland) a procurator fiscal may, after notifying the magistrates' court, sheriff or justice under whose order property is being detained, release the whole or any part of it if satisfied that the detention of the property to be released is no longer justified.

Forfeiture

303O   Forfeiture

(1)   While property is detained under this Chapter, an application for the forfeiture of the whole or any part of it may be made –

(a)   to a magistrates' court by a person specified in subsection (2);
(b)   to the sheriff by the Scottish Ministers.

(2)   The persons referred to in subsection (1)(a) are –

(a)   the Commissioners for Her Majesty's Revenue and Customs,
(b)   a constable,
(c)   an SFO officer, or
(d)   an accredited financial investigator who falls within a description specified in an order made for the purposes of this Chapter by the Secretary of State under section 453.

(3)   The court or sheriff may order the forfeiture of the property or any part of it if satisfied that –

(a)   the property is a listed asset, and
(b)   what is to be forfeited is recoverable property or intended by any person for use in unlawful conduct.

(4)   An order under subsection (3) made by a magistrates' court may provide for payment under section 303U of reasonable legal expenses that a person has reasonably incurred, or may reasonably incur, in respect of –

(a)   the proceedings in which the order is made, or
(b)   any related proceedings under this Chapter.

(5)   A sum in respect of a relevant item of expenditure is not payable under section 303U in pursuance of provision under subsection (4) unless –

(a)   the person who applied for the order under subsection (3) agrees to its payment, or
(b)   the court has assessed the amount allowed in respect of that item and the sum is paid in respect of the assessed amount.

(6)   For the purposes of subsection (5) –

(a)   a "relevant item of expenditure" is an item of expenditure to which regulations under section 286B would apply if the order under subsection (3) had instead been a recovery order;
(b)   an amount is "allowed" in respect of a relevant item of expenditure if it would have been allowed by those regulations;
(c)   if the person who applied for the order under subsection (3) was a constable, an SFO officer or an accredited financial investigator, that

person may not agree to the payment of a sum unless the person is a senior officer or is authorised to do so by a senior officer.

(7)   "Senior officer" has the same meaning in subsection (6)(c) as it has in section 303E.

(8)   Subsection (3) ceases to apply on the transfer of an application made under this section in accordance with section 303R(1)(a) or (b).

(9)   Where an application for the forfeiture of any property is made under this section, the property is to be detained (and may not be released under any power conferred by this Chapter) until any proceedings in pursuance of the application (including any proceedings on appeal) are concluded.

(10)   Where the property to which the application relates is being detained under this Chapter as part of an item of property, having been seized under section 303J(2), subsection (9) is to be read as if it required the continued detention of the whole of the item of property.

303P   Associated and joint property

(1)   Sections 303Q and 303R apply if –

(a)   an application is made under section 303O in respect of property detained under this Chapter,

(b)   the court or sheriff is satisfied that the property is a listed asset,

(c)   the court or sheriff is satisfied that all or part of the property is recoverable property or intended by any person for use in unlawful conduct, and

(d)   there exists property that is associated with the property in relation to which the court or sheriff is satisfied as mentioned in paragraph (c).

(2)   Sections 303Q and 303R also apply in England and Wales and Northern Ireland if –

(a)   an application is made under section 303O in respect of property detained under this Chapter,

(b)   the court is satisfied that the property is a listed asset,

(c)   the court is satisfied that all or part of the property is recoverable property, and

(d)   the property in relation to which the court is satisfied as mentioned in paragraph (c) belongs to joint tenants and one of the tenants is an excepted joint owner.

(3)   In this section and sections 303Q and 303R "associated property" means property of any of the following descriptions that is not itself the forfeitable property –

(a)   any interest in the forfeitable property;

(b)   any other interest in the property in which the forfeitable property subsists;

(c)   if the forfeitable property is a tenancy in common, the tenancy of the other tenant;

(d)   if (in Scotland) the forfeitable property is owned in common, the interest of the other owner;

(e)   if the forfeitable property is part of a larger property, but not a separate part, the remainder of that property.

References to property being associated with forfeitable property are to be read accordingly.

(4)   In this section and sections 303Q and 303R the "forfeitable property" means

the property in relation to which the court or sheriff is satisfied as mentioned in subsection (1)(c) or (2)(c) (as the case may be).

303Q   Agreements about associated and joint property

(1)   Where –

    (a)   this section applies, and

    (b)   the person who applied for the order under section 303O (on the one hand) and the person who holds the associated property or who is the excepted joint owner (on the other hand) agree,

the magistrates' court or sheriff may, instead of making an order under section 303O(3), make an order requiring the person who holds the associated property or who is the excepted joint owner to make a payment to a person identified in the order.

(2)   The amount of the payment is (subject to subsection (3)) to be the amount which the persons referred to in subsection (1)(b) agree represents –

    (a)   in a case where this section applies by virtue of section 303P(1), the value of the forfeitable property;

    (b)   in a case where this section applies by virtue of section 303P(2), the value of the forfeitable property less the value of the excepted joint owner's share.

(3)   The amount of the payment may be reduced if the person who applied for the order under section 303O agrees that the other party to the agreement has suffered loss as a result of the seizure of the forfeitable property and any associated property under section 303J and its subsequent detention.

(4)   The reduction that is permissible by virtue of subsection (3) is such amount as the parties to the agreement agree is reasonable, having regard to the loss suffered and any other relevant circumstances.

(5)   An order under subsection (1) may, so far as required for giving effect to the agreement, include provision for vesting, creating or extinguishing any interest in property.

(6)   An order under subsection (1) made by a magistrates' court may provide for payment under subsection (12) of reasonable legal expenses that a person has reasonably incurred, or may reasonably incur, in respect of –

    (a)   the proceedings in which the order is made, or

    (b)   any related proceedings under this Chapter.

(7)   A sum in respect of a relevant item of expenditure is not payable under subsection (12) in pursuance of provision under subsection (6) unless –

    (a)   the person who applied for the order under section 303O agrees to its payment, or

    (b)   the court has assessed the amount allowed in respect of that item and the sum is paid in respect of the assessed amount.

(8)   For the purposes of subsection (7) –

    (a)   a "relevant item of expenditure" is an item of expenditure to which regulations under section 286B would apply if the order under subsection (1) had instead been a recovery order;

    (b)   an amount is "allowed" in respect of a relevant item of expenditure if it would have been allowed by those regulations.

(9)   For the purposes of section 308(2), on the making of an order under subsection (1), the forfeitable property is to be treated as if it had been forfeited.

(10) If there is more than one item of associated property or more than one excepted joint owner, the total amount to be paid under subsection (1), and the part of that amount which is to be provided by each person who holds any such associated property or who is an excepted joint owner, is to be agreed between both (or all) of them and the person who applied for the order under section 303O.

(11) If the person who applied for the order under section 303O was a constable, an SFO officer or an accredited financial investigator, that person may enter into an agreement for the purposes of any provision of this section only if the person is a senior officer or is authorised to do so by a senior officer.

"Senior officer" has the same meaning in this subsection as it has in section 303E.

(12) An amount received under an order under subsection (1) must be applied as follows –

(a) first, it must be applied in making any payment of legal expenses which, after giving effect to subsection (7), are payable under this subsection in pursuance of provision under subsection (6);

(b) second, it must be applied in payment or reimbursement of any reasonable costs incurred in storing or insuring the forfeitable property and any associated property whilst detained under this Part;

(c) third, it must be paid –

(i) if the order was made by a magistrates' court, into the Consolidated Fund;

(ii) if the order was made by the sheriff, into the Scottish Consolidated Fund.

303R   Associated and joint property: default of agreement

(1) Where this section applies and there is no agreement under section 303Q, the magistrates' court or sheriff –

(a) must transfer the application made under section 303O to the relevant court if satisfied that the value of the forfeitable property and any associated property is £10,000 or more;

(b) may transfer the application made under section 303O to the relevant court if satisfied that the value of the forfeitable property and any associated property is less than £10,000.

(2) The "relevant court" is –

(a) the High Court, where the application under section 303O was made to a magistrates' court;

(b) the Court of Session, where the application under section 303O was made to the sheriff.

(3) Where (under subsection (1)(a) or (b)) an application made under section 303O is transferred to the relevant court, the relevant court may order the forfeiture of the property to which the application relates, or any part of that property, if satisfied that –

(a) the property is a listed asset, and

(b) what is to be forfeited is recoverable property or intended by any person for use in unlawful conduct.

(4) An order under subsection (3) made by the High Court may include provision of the type that may be included in an order under section 303O(3) made by a magistrates' court by virtue of section 303O(4).

(5)   If provision is included in an order of the High Court by virtue of subsection (4) of this section, section 303O(5) and (6) apply with the necessary modifications.

(6)   The relevant court may, as well as making an order under subsection (3), make an order –

(a)   providing for the forfeiture of the associated property or (as the case may be) for the excepted joint owner's interest to be extinguished, or

(b)   providing for the excepted joint owner's interest to be severed.

(7)   Where (under subsection (1)(b)) the magistrates' court or sheriff decides not to transfer an application made under section 303O to the relevant court, the magistrates' court or sheriff may, as well as making an order under section 303O(3), make an order –

(a)   providing for the forfeiture of the associated property or (as the case may be) for the excepted joint owner's interest to be extinguished, or

(b)   providing for the excepted joint owner's interest to be severed.

(8)   An order under subsection (6) or (7) may be made only if the relevant court, the magistrates' court or the sheriff (as the case may be) thinks it just and equitable to do so.

(9)   An order under subsection (6) or (7) must provide for the payment of an amount to the person who holds the associated property or who is an excepted joint owner.

(10)   In making an order under subsection (6) or (7), and including provision in it by virtue of subsection (9), the relevant court, the magistrates' court or the sheriff (as the case may be) must have regard to –

(a)   the rights of any person who holds the associated property or who is an excepted joint owner and the value to that person of that property or (as the case may) of that person's share (including any value that cannot be assessed in terms of money), and

(b)   the interest of the person who applied for the order under section 303O in realising the value of the forfeitable property.

(11)   If the relevant court, the magistrates' court or the sheriff (as the case may be) is satisfied that –

(a)   the person who holds the associated property or who is an excepted joint owner has suffered loss as a result of the seizure of the forfeitable property and any associated property under section 303J and its subsequent detention, and

(b)   the circumstances are exceptional,

an order under subsection (6) or (7) may require the payment of compensation to that person.

(12)   The amount of compensation to be paid by virtue of subsection (11) is the amount the relevant court, the magistrates' court or the sheriff (as the case may be) thinks reasonable, having regard to the loss suffered and any other relevant circumstances.

(13)   Compensation to be paid by virtue of subsection (11) is to be paid in the same way that compensation is to be paid under section 303W.

303S   Sections 303O to 303R: appeals

(1)   Any party to proceedings for an order for the forfeiture of property under section 303O may appeal against –

(a)   the making of an order under section 303O;

(b)   the making of an order under section 303R(7);

(c)   a decision not to make an order under section 303O unless the reason that no order was made is that an order was instead made under section 303Q;

(d)   a decision not to make an order under section 303R(7).

Paragraphs (c) and (d) do not apply if the application for the order under section 303O was transferred in accordance with section 303R(1)(a) or (b).

(2)   Where an order under section 303Q is made by a magistrates' court, any party to the proceedings for the order (including any party to the proceedings under section 303O that preceded the making of the order) may appeal against a decision to include, or not to include, provision in the order under subsection (6) of section 303Q.

(3)   An appeal under this section lies –

(a)   in relation to England and Wales, to the Crown Court;

(b)   in relation to Scotland, to the Sheriff Appeal Court;

(c)   in relation to Northern Ireland, to a county court.

(4)   An appeal under this section must be made before the end of the period of 30 days starting with the day on which the court makes the order or decision.

(5)   The court hearing the appeal may make any order it thinks appropriate.

(6)   If the court upholds an appeal against an order forfeiting property, it may order the release of the whole or any part of the property.

303T   Realisation of forfeited property

(1)   If property is forfeited under section 303O or 303R, a relevant officer must realise the property or make arrangements for its realisation.

(2)   But the property is not to be realised –

(a)   before the end of the period within which an appeal may be made (whether under section 303S or otherwise), or

(b)   if an appeal is made within that period, before the appeal is determined or otherwise disposed of.

(3)   The realisation of property under subsection (1) must be carried out, so far as practicable, in the manner best calculated to maximise the amount obtained for the property.

303U   Proceeds of realisation

(1)   The proceeds of property realised under section 303T must be applied as follows –

(a)   first, they must be applied in making any payment required to be made by virtue of section 303R(9);

(b)   second, they must be applied in making any payment of legal expenses which, after giving effect to section 303O(5) (including as applied by section 303R(5)), are payable under this subsection in pursuance of provision under section 303O(4) or, as the case may be, 303R(4);

(c)   third, they must be applied in payment or reimbursement of any reasonable costs incurred in storing or insuring the property whilst detained under this Part and in realising the property;

(d)   fourth, they must be paid –

(i)   if the property was forfeited by a magistrates' court or the High Court, into the Consolidated Fund;

(ii)   if the property was forfeited by the sheriff or the Court of Session, into the Scottish Consolidated Fund.

(2)   If what is realised under section 303T represents part only of an item of property seized under section 303J and detained under this Chapter, the reference in subsection (1)(c) to costs incurred in storing or insuring the property is to be read as a reference to costs incurred in storing or insuring the whole of the item of property.

Supplementary

303V   Victims and other owners

(1)   A person who claims that any property detained under this Chapter, or any part of it, belongs to him or her may apply for the property or part to be released.

(2)   An application under subsection (1) is to be made –

(a)   in England and Wales or Northern Ireland, to a magistrates' court;
(b)   in Scotland, to the sheriff.

(3)   The application may be made in the course of proceedings under section 303L or 303O or at any other time.

(4)   The court or sheriff may order the property to which the application relates to be released to the applicant if it appears to the court or sheriff that –

(a)   the applicant was deprived of the property to which the application relates, or of property which it represents, by unlawful conduct,
(b)   the property the applicant was deprived of was not, immediately before the applicant was deprived of it, recoverable property, and
(c)   the property belongs to the applicant.

(5)   If subsection (6) applies, the court or sheriff may order the property to which the application relates to be released to the applicant or to the person from whom it was seized.

(6)   This subsection applies where –

(a)   the applicant is not the person from whom the property to which the application relates was seized,
(b)   it appears to the court or sheriff that that property belongs to the applicant,
(c)   the court or sheriff is satisfied that the release condition is met in relation to that property, and
(d)   no objection to the making of an order under subsection (5) has been made by the person from whom that property was seized.

(7)   The release condition is met –

(a)   in relation to property detained under section 303K or 303L, if the conditions in section 303K or (as the case may be) 303L for the detention of the property are no longer met, and
(b)   in relation to property detained under section 303O, if the court or sheriff decides not to make an order under that section in relation to the property.

303W   Compensation

(1)   If no order under section 303O, 303Q or 303R is made in respect of any property detained under this Chapter, the person to whom the property belongs or from whom it was seized may make an application for compensation.

(2)   An application under subsection (1) is to be made –

(a)   in England and Wales or Northern Ireland, to a magistrates' court;

(b)   in Scotland, to the sheriff.

(3)   If the court or sheriff is satisfied that the applicant has suffered loss as a result of the detention of the property and that the circumstances are exceptional, the court or sheriff may order compensation to be paid to the applicant.

(4)   The amount of compensation to be paid is the amount the court or sheriff thinks reasonable, having regard to the loss suffered and any other relevant circumstances.

(5)   If the property was seized by an officer of Revenue and Customs, the compensation is to be paid by the Commissioners for Her Majesty's Revenue and Customs.

(6)   If the property was seized by a constable, the compensation is to be paid as follows –

(a)   in the case of a constable of a police force in England and Wales, it is to be paid out of the police fund from which the expenses of the police force are met;

(b)   in the case of a constable of the Police Service of Scotland, it is to be paid by the Scottish Police Authority;

(c)   in the case of a police officer within the meaning of the Police (Northern Ireland) Act 2000, it is to be paid out of money provided by the Chief Constable of the Police Service of Northern Ireland.

(7)   If the property was seized by an SFO officer, the compensation is to be paid by the Director of the Serious Fraud Office.

(8)   If the property was seized by a National Crime Agency officer, the compensation is to be paid by the National Crime Agency.

(9)   If the property was seized by an accredited financial investigator who was not an officer of Revenue and Customs, a constable, an SFO officer or a National Crime Agency officer, the compensation is to be paid as follows –

(a)   in the case of an investigator who was –

(i)   a member of the civilian staff of a police force (including the metropolitan police force), within the meaning of Part 1 of the Police Reform and Social Responsibility Act 2011, or

(ii)   a member of staff of the City of London police force,

it is to be paid out of the police fund from which the expenses of the police force are met,

(b)   in the case of an investigator who was a member of staff of the Police Service of Northern Ireland, it is to be paid out of money provided by the Chief Constable of the Police Service of Northern Ireland,

(c)   in the case of an investigator who was a member of staff of a department of the Government of the United Kingdom, it is to be paid by the Minister of the Crown in charge of the department or by the department,

(d)   in the case of an investigator who was a member of staff of a Northern Ireland department, it is to be paid by the department,

(e)   in the case of an investigator who was exercising a function of the Welsh Revenue Authority, it is to be paid by the Welsh Revenue Authority, and

(f)   in any other case, it is to be paid by the employer of the investigator.

(10)   The Secretary of State may by regulations amend subsection (9).

(11)   The power in subsection (10) is exercisable by the Department of Justice

(and not by the Secretary of State) so far as it may be used to make provision which could be made by an Act of the Northern Ireland Assembly without the consent of the Secretary of State (see sections 6 to 8 of the Northern Ireland Act 1998.)

(12)   If an order under section 303O, 303Q or 303R is made in respect only of a part of any property detained under this Chapter, this section has effect in relation to the other part.

303X   Powers for prosecutors to appear in proceedings

(1)   The Director of Public Prosecutions or the Director of Public Prosecutions for Northern Ireland may appear for a constable or an accredited financial investigator in proceedings under this Chapter if the Director –

(a)   is asked by, or on behalf of, a constable or (as the case may be) an accredited financial investigator to do so, and

(b)   considers it appropriate to do so.

(2)   The Director of Public Prosecutions may appear for the Commissioners for Her Majesty's Revenue and Customs or an officer of Revenue and Customs in proceedings under this Chapter if the Director –

(a)   is asked by, or on behalf of, the Commissioners for Her Majesty's Revenue and Customs or (as the case may be) an officer of Revenue and Customs to do so, and

(b)   considers it appropriate to do so.

(3)   The Directors may charge fees for the provision of services under this section.

(4)   The references in subsection (1) to an accredited financial investigator do not include an accredited financial investigator who is an officer of Revenue and Customs but the references in subsection (2) to an officer of Revenue and Customs do include an accredited financial investigator who is an officer of Revenue and Customs.

303Y   "The minimum value"

(1)   For the purposes of this Chapter, "the minimum value" is £1,000.

(2)   The Secretary of State may by regulations amend the amount for the time being specified in subsection (1).

(3)   The Secretary of State must consult the Scottish Ministers and the Department of Justice before making regulations under subsection (2).

303Z   Financial investigators

Where an accredited financial investigator of a particular description –

(a)   applies for an order under section 303L,

(b)   applies for forfeiture under section 303O, or

(c)   brings an appeal under, or relating to, this Chapter,

any subsequent step in the application or appeal, or any further application or appeal relating to the same matter, may be taken, made or brought by a different accredited financial investigator of the same description.'

16   Forfeiture of money held in bank and building society accounts

In Part 5 of the Proceeds of Crime Act 2002 (civil recovery of the proceeds etc of unlawful conduct), after section 303Z (inserted by section 15 above) insert –

'CHAPTER 3B   FORFEITURE OF MONEY HELD IN BANK AND BUILDING
                SOCIETY ACCOUNTS

Freezing of bank and building society accounts

303Z1   Application for account freezing order

(1)   This section applies if an enforcement officer has reasonable grounds for
        suspecting that money held in an account maintained with a bank or
        building society –

        (a)   is recoverable property, or
        (b)   is intended by any person for use in unlawful conduct.

(2)   Where this section applies (but subject to section 303Z2) the enforcement
        officer may apply to the relevant court for an account freezing order in
        relation to the account in which the money is held.

(3)   For the purposes of this Chapter –

        (a)   an account freezing order is an order that, subject to any exclusions
                (see section 303Z5), prohibits each person by or for whom the
                account to which the order applies is operated from making with-
                drawals or payments from the account;
        (b)   an account is operated by or for a person if the person is an account
                holder or a signatory or identified as a beneficiary in relation to the
                account.

(4)   An application for an account freezing order may be made without notice if
        the circumstances of the case are such that notice of the application would
        prejudice the taking of any steps under this Chapter to forfeit money that is
        recoverable property or intended by any person for use in unlawful conduct.

(5)   The money referred to in subsection (1) may be all or part of the credit
        balance of the account.

(6)   In this Chapter –

        "bank" has the meaning given by section 303Z7;

        "building society" has the same meaning as in the Building Societies Act
                1986;

        "enforcement officer" means –

        (a)   an officer of Revenue and Customs,
        (b)   a constable,
        (c)   an SFO officer, or
        (d)   an accredited financial investigator who falls within a description
                specified in an order made for the purposes of this Chapter by the
                Secretary of State under section 453;

        "the minimum amount" has the meaning given by section 303Z8;

        "relevant court" –

        (a)   in England and Wales and Northern Ireland, means a magistrates'
                court, and
        (b)   in Scotland, means the sheriff.

303Z2   Restrictions on making of application under section 303Z1

(1)   The power to apply for an account freezing order is not exercisable if the
        money in relation to which the enforcement officer's suspicion exists is less
        in amount than the minimum amount.

(2)   An enforcement officer may not apply for an account freezing order unless the officer is a senior officer or is authorised to do so by a senior officer.

(3)   The power to apply for an account freezing order is not exercisable by an SFO officer, or by an accredited financial investigator, in relation to an account maintained with a branch of a bank or building society that is in Scotland.

(4)   For the purposes of this Chapter, a "senior officer" is –

    (a)   an officer of Revenue and Customs of a rank designated by the Commissioners for Her Majesty's Revenue and Customs as equivalent to that of a senior police officer,

    (b)   a senior police officer,

    (c)   the Director of the Serious Fraud Office,

    (d)   the Director General of the National Crime Agency or any other National Crime Agency officer authorised by the Director General (whether generally or specifically) for this purpose, or

    (e)   an accredited financial investigator who falls within a description specified in an order made for the purposes of this Chapter by the Secretary of State under section 453.

(5)   In subsection (4), a "senior police officer" means a police officer of at least the rank of inspector.

303Z3   Making of account freezing order

(1)   This section applies where an application for an account freezing order is made under section 303Z1 in relation to an account.

(2)   The relevant court may make the order if satisfied that there are reasonable grounds for suspecting that money held in the account (whether all or part of the credit balance of the account) –

    (a)   is recoverable property, or

    (b)   is intended by any person for use in unlawful conduct.

(3)   An account freezing order ceases to have effect at the end of the period specified in the order (which may be varied under section 303Z4) unless it ceases to have effect at an earlier or later time in accordance with the provision made by sections 303Z9(6)(c), 303Z11(2) to (7), 303Z14(6) to (8) and 303Z15.

(4)   The period specified by the relevant court for the purposes of subsection (3) (whether when the order is first made or on a variation under section 303Z4) may not exceed the period of 2 years, starting with the day on which the account freezing order is (or was) made.

(5)   An account freezing order must provide for notice to be given to persons affected by the order.

303Z4   Variation and setting aside of account freezing order

(1)   The relevant court may at any time vary or set aside an account freezing order on an application made by –

    (a)   an enforcement officer, or

    (b)   any person affected by the order.

(2)   But an enforcement officer may not make an application under subsection (1) unless the officer is a senior officer or is authorised to do so by a senior officer.

(3)   Before varying or setting aside an account freezing order the court must (as well as giving the parties to the proceedings an opportunity to be heard) give such an opportunity to any person who may be affected by its decision.

(4)   In relation to Scotland, the references in this section to setting aside an order are to be read as references to recalling it.

303Z5   Exclusions

(1)   The power to vary an account freezing order includes (amongst other things) power to make exclusions from the prohibition on making withdrawals or payments from the account to which the order applies.

(2)   Exclusions from the prohibition may also be made when the order is made.

(3)   An exclusion may (amongst other things) make provision for the purpose of enabling a person by or for whom the account is operated –

(a)   to meet the person's reasonable living expenses, or

(b)   to carry on any trade, business, profession or occupation.

(4)   An exclusion may be made subject to conditions.

(5)   Where a magistrates' court exercises the power to make an exclusion for the purpose of enabling a person to meet legal expenses that the person has incurred, or may incur, in respect of proceedings under this Part, it must ensure that the exclusion –

(a)   is limited to reasonable legal expenses that the person has reasonably incurred or that the person reasonably incurs,

(b)   specifies the total amount that may be released for legal expenses in pursuance of the exclusion, and

(c)   is made subject to the same conditions as would be the required conditions (see section 286A) if the order had been made under section 245A (in addition to any conditions imposed under subsection (4)).

(6)   A magistrates' court, in deciding whether to make an exclusion for the purpose of enabling a person to meet legal expenses in respect of proceedings under this Part –

(a)   must have regard to the desirability of the person being represented in any proceedings under this Part in which the person is a participant, and

(b)   must disregard the possibility that legal representation of the person in any such proceedings might, were an exclusion not made –

(i)   be made available under arrangements made for the purposes of Part 1 of the Legal Aid, Sentencing and Punishment of Offenders Act 2012, or

(ii)   be funded by the Northern Ireland Legal Services Commission.

(7)   The sheriff's power to make exclusions may not be exercised for the purpose of enabling any person to meet any legal expenses in respect of proceedings under this Part.

(8)   The power to make exclusions must, subject to subsection (6), be exercised with a view to ensuring, so far as practicable, that there is not undue prejudice to the taking of any steps under this Chapter to forfeit money that is recoverable property or intended by any person for use in unlawful conduct.

303Z6   Restriction on proceedings and remedies

(1)   If a court in which proceedings are pending in respect of an account maintained with a bank or building society is satisfied that an account

freezing order has been applied for or made in respect of the account, it may either stay the proceedings or allow them to continue on any terms it thinks fit.

(2) Before exercising the power conferred by subsection (1), the court must (as well as giving the parties to any of the proceedings concerned an opportunity to be heard) give such an opportunity to any person who may be affected by the court's decision.

(3) In relation to Scotland, the reference in subsection (1) to staying the proceedings is to be read as a reference to sisting the proceedings.

303Z7   "Bank"

(1) "Bank" means an authorised deposit-taker, other than a building society, that has its head office or a branch in the United Kingdom.

(2) In subsection (1), "authorised deposit-taker" means –

(a) a person who has permission under Part 4A of the Financial Services and Markets Act 2000 to accept deposits;

(b) a person who –

(i) is specified, or is within a class of persons specified, by an order under section 38 of that Act (exemption orders), and

(ii) accepts deposits;

(c) an EEA firm of the kind mentioned in paragraph 5(b) of Schedule 3 to that Act that has permission under paragraph 15 of that Schedule (as a result of qualifying for authorisation under paragraph 12(1) of that Schedule) to accept deposits.

(3) A reference in subsection (2) to a person or firm with permission to accept deposits does not include a person or firm with permission to do so only for the purposes of, or in the course of, an activity other than accepting deposits.

303Z8   "The minimum amount"

(1) "The minimum amount" is £1,000.

(2) The Secretary of State may by regulations amend the amount for the time being specified in subsection (1).

(3) The Secretary of State must consult the Scottish Ministers and the Department of Justice before making regulations under subsection (2).

(4) For the purposes of this Chapter the amount of any money held in an account maintained with a bank or building society in a currency other than sterling must be taken to be its sterling equivalent, calculated in accordance with the prevailing rate of exchange.

Account forfeiture notices (England and Wales and Northern Ireland)

303Z9   Account forfeiture notice

(1) This section applies while an account freezing order made by a magistrates' court has effect.

In this section the account to which the order applies is "the frozen account".

(2) A senior officer may give a notice for the purpose of forfeiting money held in the frozen account (whether all or part of the credit balance of the account) if satisfied that the money –

(a) is recoverable property, or

(b) is intended by any person for use in unlawful conduct.

(3)   A notice given under subsection (2) is referred to in this Chapter as an account forfeiture notice.

(4)   An account forfeiture notice must –

    (a)   state the amount of money held in the frozen account which it is proposed be forfeited,

    (b)   confirm that the senior officer is satisfied as mentioned in subsection (2),

    (c)   specify a period for objecting to the proposed forfeiture and an address to which any objections must be sent, and

    (d)   explain that the money will be forfeited unless an objection is received at that address within the period for objecting.

(5)   The period for objecting must be at least 30 days starting with the day after the notice is given.

(6)   If no objection is made within the period for objecting, and the notice has not lapsed under section 303Z11 –

    (a)   the amount of money stated in the notice is forfeited (subject to section 303Z12),

    (b)   the bank or building society with which the frozen account is maintained must transfer that amount of money into an interest-bearing account nominated by an enforcement officer, and

    (c)   immediately after the transfer has been made, the account freezing order made in relation to the frozen account ceases to have effect.

(7)   An objection may be made by anyone (whether a recipient of the notice or not).

(8)   An objection means a written objection sent to the address specified in the notice; and an objection is made when it is received at the address.

(9)   An objection does not prevent forfeiture of the money held in the frozen account under section 303Z14.

303Z10   Giving of account forfeiture notice

(1)   The Secretary of State must make regulations about how an account forfeiture notice is to be given.

(2)   The regulations may (amongst other things) provide –

    (a)   for an account forfeiture notice to be given to such person or persons, and in such manner, as may be prescribed;

    (b)   for circumstances in which, and the time at which, an account forfeiture notice is to be treated as having been given.

(3)   The regulations must ensure that where an account forfeiture notice is given it is, if possible, given to every person to whom notice of the account freezing order was given.

303Z11   Lapse of account forfeiture notice

(1)   An account forfeiture notice lapses if –

    (a)   an objection is made within the period for objecting specified in the notice under section 303Z9(4)(c),

    (b)   an application is made under section 303Z14 for the forfeiture of money held in the frozen account, or

    (c)   an order is made under section 303Z4 setting aside the relevant account freezing order.

(2)   If an account forfeiture notice lapses under subsection (1)(a), the relevant

account freezing order ceases to have effect at the end of the period of 48 hours starting with the making of the objection ("the 48-hour period").

This is subject to subsections (3) and (7).

(3)   If within the 48-hour period an application is made –

(a)   for a variation of the relevant account freezing order under section 303Z4 so as to extend the period specified in the order, or

(b)   for forfeiture of money held in the frozen account under section 303Z14,

the order continues to have effect until the relevant time (and then ceases to have effect).

(4)   In the case of an application of the kind mentioned in subsection (3)(a), the relevant time means –

(a)   if an extension is granted, the time determined in accordance with section 303Z3(3), or

(b)   if an extension is not granted, the time when the application is determined or otherwise disposed of.

(5)   In the case of an application of the kind mentioned in subsection (3)(b), the relevant time is the time determined in accordance with section 303Z14(6).

(6)   If within the 48-hour period it is decided that no application of the kind mentioned in subsection (3)(a) or (b) is to be made, an enforcement officer must, as soon as possible, notify the bank or building society with which the frozen account is maintained of that decision.

(7)   If the bank or building society is notified in accordance with subsection (6) before the expiry of the 48-hour period, the relevant account freezing order ceases to have effect on the bank or building society being so notified.

(8)   In relation to an account forfeiture notice –

(a)   "the frozen account" is the account in which the money to which the account forfeiture notice relates is held;

(b)   "the relevant account freezing order" is the account freezing order made in relation to the frozen account.

(9)   In calculating a period of 48 hours for the purposes of this section no account is to be taken of –

(a)   any Saturday or Sunday,

(b)   Christmas Day,

(c)   Good Friday, or

(d)   any day that is a bank holiday under the Banking and Financial Dealings Act 1971 in the part of the United Kingdom in which the account freezing order was made.

303Z12   Application to set aside forfeiture

(1)   A person aggrieved by the forfeiture of money in pursuance of section 303Z9(6)(a) may apply to a magistrates' court for an order setting aside the forfeiture of the money or any part of it.

(2)   The application must be made before the end of the period of 30 days starting with the day on which the period for objecting ended ("the 30-day period").

(3)   But the court may give permission for an application to be made after the 30-day period has ended if it thinks that there are exceptional circumstances to explain why the applicant –

(a)   failed to object to the forfeiture within the period for objecting, and

(b)   failed to make an application within the 30-day period.

(4)   On an application under this section the court must consider whether the money to which the application relates could be forfeited under section 303Z14 (ignoring the forfeiture mentioned in subsection (1)).

(5)   If the court is satisfied that the money to which the application relates or any part of it could not be forfeited under that section it must set aside the forfeiture of that money or part.

(6)   Where the court sets aside the forfeiture of any money –

(a)   it must order the release of that money, and
(b)   the money is to be treated as never having been forfeited.

(7)   Where money is released by virtue of subsection (6)(a), there must be added to the money on its release any interest accrued on it whilst in the account referred to in section 303Z9(6)(b).

303Z13   Application of money forfeited under account forfeiture notice

(1)   Money forfeited in pursuance of section 303Z9(6)(a), and any interest accrued on it whilst in the account referred to in section 303Z9(6)(b), is to be paid into the Consolidated Fund.

(2)   But it is not to be paid in –

(a)   before the end of the period within which an application under section 303Z12 may be made (ignoring the possibility of an application by virtue of section 303Z12(3)), or
(b)   if an application is made within that period, before the application is determined or otherwise disposed of.

Forfeiture orders

303Z14   Forfeiture order

(1)   This section applies while an account freezing order has effect.

In this section the account to which the account freezing order applies is "the frozen account".

(2)   An application for the forfeiture of money held in the frozen account (whether all or part of the credit balance of the account) may be made –

(a)   to a magistrates' court by a person specified in subsection (3), or
(b)   to the sheriff by the Scottish Ministers.

(3)   The persons referred to in subsection (2)(a) are –

(a)   the Commissioners for Her Majesty's Revenue and Customs,
(b)   a constable,
(c)   an SFO officer, or
(d)   an accredited financial investigator who falls within a description specified in an order made for the purposes of this Chapter by the Secretary of State under section 453.

(4)   The court or sheriff may order the forfeiture of the money or any part of it if satisfied that the money or part –

(a)   is recoverable property, or
(b)   is intended by any person for use in unlawful conduct.

(5)   But in the case of recoverable property which belongs to joint tenants, one of whom is an excepted joint owner, an order by a magistrates' court may not apply to so much of it as the court thinks is attributable to the excepted joint owner's share.

(6)   Where an application is made under subsection (2), the account freezing order is to continue to have effect until the time referred to in subsection (7)(b) or (8).

But subsections (7)(b) and (8) are subject to section 303Z15.

(7)   Where money held in a frozen account is ordered to be forfeited under subsection (4) –

(a)   the bank or building society with which the frozen account is maintained must transfer that amount of money into an interest-bearing account nominated by an enforcement officer, and

(b)   immediately after the transfer has been made the account freezing order made in relation to the frozen account ceases to have effect.

(8)   Where, other than by the making of an order under subsection (4), an application under subsection (2) is determined or otherwise disposed of, the account freezing order ceases to have effect immediately after that determination or other disposal.

303Z15   Continuation of account freezing order pending appeal

(1)   This section applies where, on an application under subsection (2) of section 303Z14 in relation to an account to which an account freezing order applies, the court or sheriff decides –

(a)   to make an order under subsection (4) of that section in relation to part only of the money to which the application related, or

(b)   not to make an order under subsection (4) of that section.

(2)   The person who made the application under section 303Z14(2) may apply without notice to the court or sheriff that made the decision referred to in subsection (1)(a) or (b) for an order that the account freezing order is to continue to have effect.

(3)   Where the court or sheriff makes an order under subsection (2) the account freezing order is to continue to have effect until –

(a)   the end of the period of 48 hours starting with the making of the order under subsection (2), or

(b)   if within that period of 48 hours an appeal is brought under section 303Z16 against the decision referred to in subsection (1)(a) or (b), the time when the appeal is determined or otherwise disposed of.

(4)   Subsection (9) of section 303Z11 applies for the purposes of subsection (3) as it applies for the purposes of that section.

303Z16   Appeal against decision under section 303Z14

(1)   Any party to proceedings for an order for the forfeiture of money under section 303Z14 who is aggrieved by an order under that section or by the decision of the court not to make such an order may appeal –

(a)   from an order or decision of a magistrates' court in England and Wales, to the Crown Court;

(b)   from an order or decision of the sheriff, to the Sheriff Appeal Court;

(c)   from an order or decision of a magistrates' court in Northern Ireland, to a county court.

(2)   An appeal under subsection (1) must be made before the end of the period of 30 days starting with the day on which the court makes the order or decision.

(3)   The court hearing the appeal may make any order it thinks appropriate.

(4)   If the court upholds an appeal against an order forfeiting the money, it may order the release of the whole or any part of the money.

(5)   Where money is released by virtue of subsection (4), there must be added to the money on its release any interest accrued on it whilst in the account referred to in section 303Z14(7)(a).

303Z17   Application of money forfeited under account forfeiture order

(1)   Money forfeited by an order under section 303Z14, and any interest accrued on it whilst in the account referred to in subsection (7)(a) of that section –

   (a)   if forfeited by a magistrates' court, is to be paid into the Consolidated Fund, and

   (b)   if forfeited by the sheriff, is to be paid into the Scottish Consolidated Fund.

(2)   But it is not to be paid in –

   (a)   before the end of the period within which an appeal under section 303Z16 may be made, or

   (b)   if a person appeals under that section, before the appeal is determined or otherwise disposed of.

Supplementary

303Z18   Compensation

(1)   This section applies if –

   (a)   an account freezing order is made, and

   (b)   none of the money held in the account to which the order applies is forfeited in pursuance of an account forfeiture notice or by an order under section 303Z14.

(2)   Where this section applies a person by or for whom the account to which the account freezing order applies is operated may make an application to the relevant court for compensation.

(3)   If the relevant court is satisfied that the applicant has suffered loss as a result of the making of the account freezing order and that the circumstances are exceptional, the relevant court may order compensation to be paid to the applicant.

(4)   The amount of compensation to be paid is the amount the relevant court thinks reasonable, having regard to the loss suffered and any other relevant circumstances.

(5)   If the account freezing order was applied for by an officer of Revenue and Customs, the compensation is to be paid by the Commissioners for Her Majesty's Revenue and Customs.

(6)   If the account freezing order was applied for by a constable, the compensation is to be paid as follows –

   (a)   in the case of a constable of a police force in England and Wales, it is to be paid out of the police fund from which the expenses of the police force are met;

   (b)   in the case of a constable of the Police Service of Scotland, it is to be paid by the Scottish Police Authority;

   (c)   in the case of a police officer within the meaning of the Police (Northern Ireland) Act 2000, it is to be paid out of money provided by the Chief Constable of the Police Service of Northern Ireland.

(7)   If the account freezing order was applied for by an SFO officer, the compensation is to be paid by the Director of the Serious Fraud Office.

(8)   If the account freezing order was applied for by a National Crime Agency officer, the compensation is to be paid by the National Crime Agency.

(9)   If the account freezing order was applied for by an accredited financial investigator who was not an officer of Revenue and Customs, a constable, an SFO officer or a National Crime Agency officer, the compensation is to be paid as follows –

   (a)   in the case of an investigator who was –

      (i)   a member of the civilian staff of a police force (including the metropolitan police force), within the meaning of Part 1 of the Police Reform and Social Responsibility Act 2011, or

      (ii)   a member of staff of the City of London police force,

   it is to be paid out of the police fund from which the expenses of the police force are met,

   (b)   in the case of an investigator who was a member of staff of the Police Service of Northern Ireland, it is to be paid out of money provided by the Chief Constable of the Police Service of Northern Ireland,

   (c)   in the case of an investigator who was a member of staff of a department of the Government of the United Kingdom, it is to be paid by the Minister of the Crown in charge of the department or by the department,

   (d)   in the case of an investigator who was a member of staff of a Northern Ireland department, it is to be paid by the department,

   (e)   in the case of an investigator who was exercising a function of the Welsh Revenue Authority, it is to be paid by the Welsh Revenue Authority, and

   (f)   in any other case, it is to be paid by the employer of the investigator.

(10)   The Secretary of State may by regulations amend subsection (9).

(11)   The power in subsection (10) is exercisable by the Department of Justice (and not by the Secretary of State) so far as it may be used to make provision which could be made by an Act of the Northern Ireland Assembly without the consent of the Secretary of State (see sections 6 to 8 of the Northern Ireland Act 1998.)

303Z19   Powers for prosecutors to appear in proceedings

(1)   The Director of Public Prosecutions or the Director of Public Prosecutions for Northern Ireland may appear for a constable or an accredited financial investigator in proceedings under this Chapter if the Director –

   (a)   is asked by, or on behalf of, a constable or (as the case may be) an accredited financial investigator to do so, and

   (b)   considers it appropriate to do so.

(2)   The Director of Public Prosecutions may appear for the Commissioners for Her Majesty's Revenue and Customs or an officer of Revenue and Customs in proceedings under this Chapter if the Director –

   (a)   is asked by, or on behalf of, the Commissioners for Her Majesty's Revenue and Customs or (as the case may be) an officer of Revenue and Customs to do so, and

   (b)   considers it appropriate to do so.

(3)   The Directors may charge fees for the provision of services under this section.

(4)   The references in subsection (1) to an accredited financial investigator do not include an accredited financial investigator who is an officer of Revenue

and Customs but the references in subsection (2) to an officer of Revenue and Customs do include an accredited financial investigator who is an officer of Revenue and Customs.'

CHAPTER 4   ENFORCEMENT POWERS AND RELATED OFFENCES

Extension of powers

17   Serious Fraud Office

Schedule 1 contains amendments conferring certain powers under the Proceeds of Crime Act 2002 on members of staff of the Serious Fraud Office.

18   Her Majesty's Revenue and Customs: removal of restrictions

(1)   The following provisions, which impose restrictions on the exercise of certain powers conferred on officers of Revenue and Customs, are amended as follows.

(2)   In section 23A of the Criminal Law (Consolidation) (Scotland) Act 1995 (investigation of offences by Her Majesty's Revenue and Customs), omit the following –

    (a)   in subsection (2), the words 'Subject to subsection (3) below,' and the words from 'other than' to the end of the subsection;

    (b)   subsection (3).

(3)   In section 307 of the Criminal Procedure (Scotland) Act 1995 (interpretation), omit the following –

    (a)   in subsection (1), in paragraph (ba) of the definition of 'officer of law', the words 'subject to subsection (1A) below,';

    (b)   subsection (1A).

(4)   In the Proceeds of Crime Act 2002 omit the following –

    (a)   in section 289 (searches), subsections (5)(ba) and (5A);

    (b)   in section 294 (seizure of cash), subsections (2A), (2B) and (2C);

    (c)   section 375C (restriction on exercise of certain powers conferred on officers of Revenue and Customs);

    (d)   section 408C (restriction on exercise of certain powers conferred on officers of Revenue and Customs).

(5)   In the Finance Act 2007, in section 84 (sections 82 and 83: supplementary), omit subsection (3).

19   Her Majesty's Revenue and Customs: new powers

(1)   The Proceeds of Crime Act 2002 is amended as follows.

(2)   In section 316 (civil recovery of the proceeds etc of unlawful conduct: general interpretation), in the definition of 'enforcement authority' in subsection (1) –

    (a)   in paragraph (a), before 'the National Crime Agency,' insert 'Her Majesty's Revenue and Customs,';

    (b)   in paragraph (c), before 'the National Crime Agency,' insert 'Her Majesty's Revenue and Customs,'.

(3)   In section 378 (appropriate officers and senior appropriate officers for purposes of investigations under Part 8), for subsection (3) substitute –

    '(3)   In relation to a civil recovery investigation these are appropriate officers –

        (a)   a National Crime Agency officer;

        (b)   the relevant Director;

        (c)   an officer of Revenue and Customs.

(3ZA) In relation to a civil recovery investigation these are senior appropriate officers –

    (a)   a senior National Crime Agency officer;

    (b)   the Commissioners for Her Majesty's Revenue and Customs or an officer of Revenue and Customs authorised by the Commissioners (whether generally or specifically) for this purpose.'

20   Financial Conduct Authority

(1) The Proceeds of Crime Act 2002 is amended as follows.

(2) In section 316 (civil recovery of the proceeds etc of unlawful conduct: general interpretation), in the definition of 'enforcement authority' in subsection (1) –

    (a)   in paragraph (a), after 'means' insert 'the Financial Conduct Authority,';

    (b)   in paragraph (c), after 'means' insert 'the Financial Conduct Authority,'.

(3) Section 378 (appropriate officers and senior appropriate officers for purposes of investigations under Part 8) is amended in accordance with subsections (4) to (6).

(4) In subsection (3) (as substituted by section 19 above), after paragraph (c) insert –

    '(d)   a Financial Conduct Authority officer.'

(5) In subsection (3ZA) (as inserted by that section), after paragraph (b) insert –
    '(c)   a senior Financial Conduct Authority officer.'

(6) After subsection (8) insert –

    '(9)   For the purposes of this Part –

        (a)   "Financial Conduct Authority officer" means a member of staff of the Financial Conduct Authority;

        (b)   "senior Financial Conduct Authority officer" means a Financial Conduct Authority officer who is not below such grade as is designated by the Treasury for those purposes.'

21   Immigration officers

(1) Section 24 of the UK Borders Act 2007 (seizure of cash) is amended as follows.

(2) For the heading substitute 'Exercise of civil recovery powers by immigration officers'.

(3) For subsection (1) substitute –

    '(1)   Chapters 3 to 3B of Part 5 of the Proceeds of Crime Act 2002 (civil recovery) apply in relation to an immigration officer as they apply in relation to a constable.'

(4) In subsection (2)(a), for 'section 289' substitute 'sections 289 and 303C and Chapter 3B'.

(5) In subsection (2)(c), for 'and 297A' substitute ', 297A and 303E and in Chapter 3B (see section 303Z2(4))'.

(6) In subsection (2)(d), for 'section 292' substitute 'sections 292 and 303G'.

(7) In subsection (2)(e), for 'and 293A' substitute ', 293A, 303H and 303I'.

(8) In subsection (2)(f), in the words before sub-paragraph (i), after '295(2)' insert 'or 303L(1)'.

(9) In subsection (2)(f)(ii), after '298' insert 'or (as the case may be) 303O'.

(10) In subsection (2)(g), after '298' insert ', 303O or 303Z14'.

(11) In subsection (2)(h), after '302' insert ', 303W or 303Z18'.

Assault and obstruction offences

22   Search and seizure warrants: assault and obstruction offences

After section 356 of the Proceeds of Crime Act 2002 (and before the italic heading before section 357) insert –

'356A   Certain offences in relation to execution of search and seizure warrants

(1)   A person commits an offence if the person assaults an appropriate person who is acting in the exercise of a power conferred by a search and seizure warrant issued under section 352.

(2)   A person commits an offence if the person resists or wilfully obstructs an appropriate person who is acting in the exercise of a power conferred by a search and seizure warrant issued under section 352.

(3)   A person guilty of an offence under subsection (1) is liable –

(a)   on summary conviction in England and Wales, to imprisonment for a term not exceeding 51 weeks, or to a fine, or to both;

(b)   on summary conviction in Northern Ireland, to imprisonment for a term not exceeding 6 months, or to a fine not exceeding level 5 on the standard scale, or to both.

(4)   A person guilty of an offence under subsection (2) is liable –

(a)   on summary conviction in England and Wales, to imprisonment for a term not exceeding 51 weeks, or to a fine not exceeding level 3 on the standard scale, or to both;

(b)   on summary conviction in Northern Ireland, to imprisonment for a term not exceeding 1 month, or to a fine not exceeding level 3 on the standard scale, or to both.

(5)   An appropriate person is –

(a)   a National Crime Agency officer, a Financial Conduct Authority officer or a member of the staff of the relevant Director, if the warrant was issued for the purposes of a civil recovery investigation;

(b)   a National Crime Agency officer, if the warrant was issued for the purposes of an exploitation proceeds investigation.

(6)   In relation to an offence committed before the coming into force of section 281(5) of the Criminal Justice Act 2003 (alteration of penalties for certain summary offences: England and Wales) –

(a)   the reference in subsection (3)(a) to 51 weeks is to be read as a reference to 6 months;

(b)   the reference in subsection (4)(a) to 51 weeks is to be read as a reference to 1 month.'

23   Assault and obstruction offence in relation to SFO officers

After section 453A of the Proceeds of Crime Act 2002 insert –

'453B   Certain offences in relation to SFO officers

(1)   A person commits an offence if the person assaults an SFO officer who is acting in the exercise of a relevant power.

(2)   A person commits an offence if the person resists or wilfully obstructs an SFO officer who is acting in the exercise of a relevant power.

(3)   A person guilty of an offence under subsection (1) is liable –

(a)   on summary conviction in England and Wales, to imprisonment for a term not exceeding 51 weeks, or to a fine, or to both;

(b)   on summary conviction in Northern Ireland, to imprisonment for a term not exceeding 6 months, or to a fine not exceeding level 5 on the standard scale, or to both.

(4)   A person guilty of an offence under subsection (2) is liable –

(a)   on summary conviction in England and Wales, to imprisonment for a term not exceeding 51 weeks, or to a fine not exceeding level 3 on the standard scale, or to both;

(b)   on summary conviction in Northern Ireland, to imprisonment for a term not exceeding 1 month, or to a fine not exceeding level 3 on the standard scale, or to both.

(5)   In this section "relevant power" means a power exercisable under any of the following –

(a)   sections 47C to 47F or 195C to 195F (powers to seize and search for realisable property);
(b)   section 289 (powers to search for cash);
(c)   section 294 (power to seize cash);
(d)   section 295(1) (power to detain seized cash);
(e)   section 303C (powers to search for a listed asset);
(f)   section 303J (powers to seize property);
(g)   section 303K (powers to detain seized property);
(h)   a search and seizure warrant issued under section 352.

(6)   In relation to an offence committed before the coming into force of section 281(5) of the Criminal Justice Act 2003 (alteration of penalties for certain summary offences: England and Wales) –

(a)   the reference in subsection (3)(a) to 51 weeks is to be read as a reference to 6 months;
(b)   the reference in subsection (4)(a) to 51 weeks is to be read as a reference to 1 month.'

24   External requests, orders and investigations

(1)   Part 11 of the Proceeds of Crime Act 2002 (co-operation) is amended as follows.
(2)   In section 444 (external requests and orders), in subsection (3), after paragraph (a) insert –
'(aa)   provision creating offences in relation to external requests and orders which are equivalent to the offences created by section 453B;'
(3)   In section 445 (external investigations), in subsection (1)(b), after 'Part 8' insert 'and section 453B'.

25   Obstruction offence in relation to immigration officers

After section 453B of the Proceeds of Crime Act 2002 (inserted by section 23 above) insert –

'453C   Obstruction offence in relation to immigration officers

(1)   A person commits an offence if the person resists or wilfully obstructs an immigration officer who is acting in the exercise of a relevant power.
(2)   A person guilty of an offence under this section is liable –

(a)   on summary conviction in England and Wales, to imprisonment for a term not exceeding 51 weeks, to a fine not exceeding level 3 on the standard scale, or to both;
(b)   on summary conviction in Scotland, to imprisonment for a term not exceeding 12 months, to a fine not exceeding level 3 on the standard scale, or to both;
(c)   on summary conviction in Northern Ireland, to imprisonment for a term not exceeding 1 month, to a fine not exceeding level 3 on the standard scale, or to both.

(3)   In this section "relevant power" means a power exercisable under –

(a)   sections 47C to 47F, 127C to 127F or 195C to 195F (powers to seize and search for realisable property);

(b)   section 289 as applied by section 24 of the UK Borders Act 2007 (powers to search for cash);

(c)   section 294 as so applied (powers to seize cash);

(d)   section 295(1) as so applied (power to detain seized cash);

(e)   section 303C as so applied (powers to search for a listed asset);

(f)   section 303J as so applied (powers to seize property);

(g)   section 303K as so applied (powers to detain seized property);

(h)   a search and seizure warrant issued under section 352; or

(i)   a search and seizure warrant issued under section 387.

(4)   The power conferred by subsection (5) of section 28A of the Immigration Act 1971 (arrest without warrant) applies in relation to an offence under this section as it applies in relation to an offence under section 26(1)(g) of that Act (and subsections (6) to (9), (10) and (11) of section 28A of that Act apply accordingly).

(5)   In relation to an offence committed before the coming into force of section 281(5) of the Criminal Justice Act 2003 (alteration of penalties for certain summary offences: England and Wales) the reference in subsection (2)(a) to 51 weeks is to be read as a reference to 1 month.'

CHAPTER 5   MISCELLANEOUS

Seized money: England and Wales and Northern Ireland

26   Seized money: England and Wales

(1)   Section 67 of the Proceeds of Crime Act 2002 (seized money) is amended as follows.

(2)   In subsection (2), for paragraphs (a) and (b) substitute –

'(a)   has been seized under a relevant seizure power by a constable or another person lawfully exercising the power, and

(b)   is being detained in connection with a criminal investigation or prosecution or with an investigation of a kind mentioned in section 341.'

(3)   After subsection (2) insert –

'(2A)   But this section applies to money only so far as the money is free property.'

(4)   Omit subsection (3).

(5)   In subsection (5), for 'bank or building society' substitute 'appropriate person'.

(6)   In subsection (5A), at the beginning insert 'Where this section applies to money which is held in an account maintained with a bank or building society,'.

(7)   In subsection (7A), after 'applies' insert 'by virtue of subsection (1)'.

(8)   For subsection (8) substitute –

'(8)   In this section –

"appropriate person" means –

(a)   in a case where the money is held in an account maintained with a bank or building society, the bank or building society;

(b)   in any other case, the person on whose authority the money is detained;

"bank" means an authorised deposit-taker, other than a building society, that has its head office or a branch in the United Kingdom;

"building society" has the same meaning as in the Building Societies Act 1986;

"relevant seizure power" means a power to seize money conferred by or by virtue of –

(a)   a warrant granted under any enactment or rule of law, or

(b)   any enactment, or rule of law, under which the authority of a warrant is not required.'

(9)   After subsection (8) insert –

'(9)   In the definition of "bank" in subsection (8), "authorised deposit-taker" means –

(a)   a person who has permission under Part 4A of the Financial Services and Markets Act 2000 to accept deposits;

(b)   a person who –

(i)   is specified, or is within a class of persons specified, by an order under section 38 of that Act (exemption orders), and

(ii)   accepts deposits;

(c)   an EEA firm of the kind mentioned in paragraph 5(b) of Schedule 3 to that Act that has permission under paragraph 15 of that Schedule (as a result of qualifying for authorisation under paragraph 12(1) of that Schedule) to accept deposits.

(10)   A reference in subsection (9) to a person or firm with permission to accept deposits does not include a person or firm with permission to do so only for the purposes of, or in the course of, an activity other than accepting deposits.'

27   Seized money: Northern Ireland

(1)   Section 215 of the Proceeds of Crime Act 2002 (seized money) is amended as follows.

(2)   In subsection (2), for paragraphs (a) and (b) substitute –

'(a)   has been seized under a relevant seizure power by a constable or another person lawfully exercising the power, and

(b)   is being detained in connection with a criminal investigation or prosecution or with an investigation of a kind mentioned in section 341.'

(3)   After subsection (2) insert –

'(2A)   But this section applies to money only so far as the money is free property.'

(4)   Omit subsection (3).

(5)   In subsection (5) (as it has effect before and after its amendment by section 36 of the Serious Crime Act 2015), for 'bank or building society' substitute 'appropriate person'.

(6)   In subsection (5A), at the beginning insert 'Where this section applies to money which is held in an account maintained with a bank or building society,'.

(7)   In subsection (7A), after 'applies' insert 'by virtue of subsection (1)'.

(8)   For subsection (8) substitute –

'(8)   In this section –

"appropriate chief clerk" has the same meaning as in section 202(7);

"appropriate person" means –

(a)   in a case where the money is held in an account maintained with a bank or building society, the bank or building society;

    (b)   in any other case, the person on whose authority the money is detained;

"bank" means an authorised deposit-taker, other than a building society, that has its head office or a branch in the United Kingdom;

"building society" has the same meaning as in the Building Societies Act 1986;

"relevant seizure power" means a power to seize money conferred by or by virtue of –

    (a)   a warrant granted under any enactment or rule of law, or

    (b)   any enactment, or rule of law, under which the authority of a warrant is not required.'

(9)   After subsection (8) insert –

    '(9)   In the definition of "bank" in subsection (8), "authorised deposit-taker" means –

        (a)   a person who has permission under Part 4A of the Financial Services and Markets Act 2000 to accept deposits;

        (b)   a person who –

            (i)   is specified, or is within a class of persons specified, by an order under section 38 of that Act (exemption orders), and

            (ii)   accepts deposits;

        (c)   an EEA firm of the kind mentioned in paragraph 5(b) of Schedule 3 to that Act that has permission under paragraph 15 of that Schedule (as a result of qualifying for authorisation under paragraph 12(1) of that Schedule) to accept deposits.

    (10)   A reference in subsection (9) to a person or firm with permission to accept deposits does not include a person or firm with permission to do so only for the purposes of, or in the course of, an activity other than accepting deposits.'

Miscellaneous provisions relating to Scotland

28   Seized money

After section 131 of the Proceeds of Crime Act 2002 insert –

'Seized money

131ZA   Seized money

(1)   This section applies to money which –

    (a)   is held by a person, and

    (b)   is held in an account maintained by the person with a bank or building society.

(2)   This section also applies to money which is held by a person and which –

    (a)   has been seized under a relevant seizure power by a constable or another person lawfully exercising the power, and

    (b)   is being detained in connection with a criminal investigation or prosecution or with an investigation of a kind mentioned in section 341.

(3)   But this section applies to money only so far as the money is free property.

(4)   Subsection (5) applies if –

    (a)   a confiscation order is made against a person holding money to which this section applies, and

    (b)   an administrator has not been appointed under section 128 in relation to the money.

(5)   The relevant court may order the appropriate person to pay, within such period as the court may specify, the money or a portion of it specified by the court to the appropriate clerk of court on account of the amount payable under the confiscation order.

(6)   An order under subsection (5) may be made –

    (a)   on the application of the prosecutor, or

    (b)   by the relevant court of its own accord.

(7)   The Scottish Ministers may by regulations amend this section so that it applies by virtue of subsection (1) not only to money held in an account maintained with a bank or building society but also to –

    (a)   money held in an account maintained with a financial institution of a specified kind, or

    (b)   money that is represented by, or may be obtained from, a financial instrument or product of a specified kind.

(8)   Regulations under subsection (7) may amend this section so that it makes provision about realising an instrument or product within subsection (7)(b) or otherwise obtaining money from it.

(9)   In this section –

"appropriate clerk of court", in relation to a confiscation order, means the sheriff clerk of the sheriff court responsible for enforcing the confiscation order under section 211 of the Procedure Act as applied by section 118(1);

"appropriate person" means –

    (a)   in a case where the money is held in an account maintained with a bank or building society, the bank or building society;

    (b)   in any other case, the person on whose authority the money is detained;

"bank" means an authorised deposit-taker, other than a building society, that has its head office or a branch in the United Kingdom;

"building society" has the same meaning as in the Building Societies Act 1986;

"relevant court", in relation to a confiscation order, means –

    (a)   the court which makes the confiscation order, or

    (b)   the sheriff court responsible for enforcing the confiscation order under section 211 of the Procedure Act as applied by section 118(1);

"relevant seizure power" means a power to seize money conferred by or by virtue of –

    (a)   a warrant granted under any enactment or rule of law, or

    (b)   any enactment, or rule of law, under which the authority of a warrant is not required.

(10)   In the definition of "bank" in subsection (9), "authorised deposit-taker" means –

   (a)   a person who has permission under Part 4A of the Financial Services and Markets Act 2000 to accept deposits;

   (b)   a person who –

      (i)   is specified, or is within a class of persons specified, by an order under section 38 of that Act (exemption orders), and

      (ii)   accepts deposits;

   (c)   an EEA firm of the kind mentioned in paragraph 5(b) of Schedule 3 to that Act that has permission under paragraph 15 of that Schedule (as a result of qualifying for authorisation under paragraph 12(1) of that Schedule) to accept deposits.

(11)   A reference in subsection (10) to a person or firm with permission to accept deposits does not include a person or firm with permission to do so only for the purposes of, or in the course of, an activity other than accepting deposits.'

29   Recovery orders relating to heritable property

(1)   The Proceeds of Crime Act 2002 is amended as follows.

(2)   After section 245 insert –

'245ZA   Notice to local authority: Scotland

(1)   This section applies if, in proceedings under this Chapter for a recovery order, the enforcement authority applies under section 266(8ZA) for decree of removing and warrant for ejection in relation to heritable property which consists of or includes a dwellinghouse.

(2)   The enforcement authority must give notice of the application to the local authority in whose area the dwellinghouse is situated.

(3)   Notice under subsection (2) must be given in the form and manner prescribed under section 11(3) of the Homelessness etc. (Scotland) Act 2003.

(4)   In this section –

"dwellinghouse" has the meaning given by section 11(8) of the Homelessness etc. (Scotland) Act 2003;

"local authority" means a council constituted under section 2 of the Local Government etc. (Scotland) Act 1994; and "area", in relation to a local authority, means the local government area for which the authority is constituted.'

(3)   In section 266 (recovery orders), after subsection (8) insert –

'(8ZA)   If the recoverable property in respect of which the Court of Session makes a recovery order includes heritable property, the Court of Session must, on the application of the enforcement authority, also grant decree of removing and warrant for ejection, enforceable by the trustee for civil recovery, in relation to any persons occupying the heritable property.'

(4)   In section 267(3) (functions of trustee for civil recovery), after paragraph (b) insert –

'(ba)   if decree of removing and warrant for ejection is granted by the Court of Session under section 266(8ZA), to enforce the decree and warrant,'

(5)   After section 269 insert –

'269A   Leases and occupancy rights: Scotland

(1)   This section applies where, in making a recovery order, the Court of Session also grants decree of removing and warrant for ejection under section 266(8ZA) in relation to any persons occupying the heritable property.

(2)   Any lease under which a person has the right to occupy the heritable property (or part of it) for residential or commercial purposes is terminated on the granting of decree of removing and warrant for ejection.

(3)   Any other right to occupy the heritable property (or part of it) which subsists immediately before the granting of decree of removing and warrant for ejection is extinguished on the granting of the decree and warrant.

(4)   Subsection (3) does not apply in relation to a right under a lease to occupy or use the property other than those mentioned in subsection (2).

(5)   Where the heritable property is vested in the trustee for civil recovery under the recovery order, the following enactments do not apply in relation to the heritable property –

    (a)   sections 34 to 38A of the Sheriff Courts (Scotland) Act 1907 (removings, notice of termination of tenancy and notice of removal);

    (b)   the Tenancy of Shops (Scotland) Act 1949;

    (c)   the Matrimonial Homes (Family Protection) (Scotland) Act 1981;

    (d)   Parts 2 and 3 of the Rent (Scotland) Act 1984 (security of tenure and protection against harassment and unlawful eviction);

    (e)   sections 4 to 7 of the Law Reform (Miscellaneous Provisions) (Scotland) Act 1985 (termination of certain leases);

    (f)   Part 2 of the Housing (Scotland) Act 1988 (rented accommodation: security of tenure etc.);

    (g)   Chapter 3 of Part 3 of the Civil Partnership Act 2004 (occupancy rights and tenancies);

    (h)   Part 5 of the Private Housing (Tenancies) (Scotland) Act 2016 (security of tenure, termination of tenancy and eviction).'

30   Money received by administrators

(1)   Paragraph 6 of Schedule 3 to the Proceeds of Crime Act 2002 (money received by administrator) is amended as follows.

(2)   In sub-paragraph (1) for 'an appropriate bank or institution' substitute 'a bank or building society'.

(3)   For sub-paragraph (3) substitute –

    '(3)   In sub-paragraph (1) –

        (a)   "bank" means an authorised deposit-taker, other than a building society, that has its head office or a branch in the United Kingdom;

        (b)   "building society" has the same meaning as in the Building Societies Act 1986.

    (4)   In sub-paragraph (3)(a) "authorised deposit-taker" means –

        (a)   a person who has permission under Part 4A of the Financial Services and Markets Act 2000 to accept deposits;

        (b)   a person who –

            (i)   is specified, or is within a class of persons specified, by an order under section 38 of that Act (exemption orders), and

            (ii)   accepts deposits;

        (c)   an EEA firm of the kind mentioned in paragraph 5(b) of Schedule 3 to that Act that has permission under paragraph 15 of that Schedule (as a result of qualifying for authorisation under paragraph 12(1) of that Schedule) to accept deposits.

(5)   A reference in sub-paragraph (4) to a person or firm with permission to accept deposits does not include a person or firm with permission to do so only for the purposes of, or in the course of, an activity other than accepting deposits.'

Other miscellaneous provisions

31   Accredited financial investigators

(1) The Proceeds of Crime Act 2002 is amended as follows.

(2) In section 47G (appropriate approval for exercise of search and seizure powers in England and Wales), in subsection (3), after paragraph (b) insert –

'(ba)   in relation to the exercise of a power by an accredited financial investigator who is –

(i)   a member of the civilian staff of a police force in England and Wales (including the metropolitan police force), within the meaning of Part 1 of the Police Reform and Social Responsibility Act 2011, or

(ii)   a member of staff of the City of London police force, a senior police officer,'

(3) In section 195G (appropriate approval for exercise of search and seizure powers in Northern Ireland), in subsection (3), after paragraph (b) insert –

'(ba)   in relation to the exercise of a power by an accredited financial investigator who is a member of staff of the Police Service of Northern Ireland, a senior police officer,'

(4) In section 290 (prior approval for exercise of search powers in relation to cash), in subsection (4), after paragraph (b) insert –

'(ba)   in relation to the exercise of a power by an accredited financial investigator who is –

(i)   a member of the civilian staff of a police force in England and Wales (including the metropolitan police force), within the meaning of Part 1 of the Police Reform and Social Responsibility Act 2011,

(ii)   a member of staff of the City of London police force, or

(iii)   a member of staff of the Police Service of Northern Ireland, a senior police officer,'

32   Reconsideration of discharged orders

(1) The Proceeds of Crime Act 2002 is amended as follows.

(2) In section 24 (inadequacy of available amount: discharge of order made under Part 2), after subsection (5) insert –

'(6)   The discharge of a confiscation order under this section does not prevent the making of an application in respect of the order under section 21(1)(d) or 22(1)(c).

(7)   Where on such an application the court determines that the order should be varied under section 21(7) or (as the case may be) 22(4), the court may provide that its discharge under this section is revoked.'

(3) In section 25 (small amount outstanding: discharge of order made under Part 2), after subsection (3) insert –

'(4)   The discharge of a confiscation order under this section does not prevent the making of an application in respect of the order under section 21(1)(d) or 22(1)(c).

(5)   Where on such an application the court determines that the order should be varied under section 21(7) or (as the case may be) 22(4), the court may provide that its discharge under this section is revoked.'

(4)   In section 109 (inadequacy of available amount: discharge of order made under Part 3), after subsection (5) insert –

'(6)   The discharge of a confiscation order under this section does not prevent the making of an application in respect of the order under section 106(1)(d) or 107(1)(c).

(7)   Where on such an application the court determines that the order should be varied under section 106(6) or (as the case may be) 107(3), the court may provide that its discharge under this section is revoked.'

(5)   In section 174 (inadequacy of available amount: discharge of order made under Part 4), after subsection (5) insert –

'(6)   The discharge of a confiscation order under this section does not prevent the making of an application in respect of the order under section 171(1)(d) or 172(1)(c).

(7)   Where on such an application the court determines that the order should be varied under section 171(7) or (as the case may be) 172(4), the court may provide that its discharge under this section is revoked.'

(6)   In section 175 (small amount outstanding: discharge of order made under Part 4), after subsection (3) insert –

'(4)   The discharge of a confiscation order under this section does not prevent the making of an application in respect of the order under section 171(1)(d) or 172(1)(c).

(5)   Where on such an application the court determines that the order should be varied under section 171(7) or (as the case may be) 172(4), the court may provide that its discharge under this section is revoked.'

(7)   The amendments made by this section apply in relation to a confiscation order whether made before or after the day on which this section comes into force but do so only where the discharge of the order occurs after that day.

33   Confiscation investigations: determination of the available amount

In section 341(1) of the Proceeds of Crime Act 2002 (confiscation investigations), at the beginning of paragraph (c) insert 'the available amount in respect of the person or'.

34   Confiscation orders and civil recovery: minor amendments

(1)   The Proceeds of Crime Act 2002 is amended in accordance with subsections (2) to (10).

(2)   In section 82 (free property: England and Wales) –

(a)   in subsection (2), after paragraph (e) insert –

'(ea)   paragraph 3(2), 6(2), 10D(1), 10G(2), 10J(3), 10S(2) or 10Z2(3) of Schedule 1 to the Anti-terrorism, Crime and Security Act 2001;'

(b)   in subsection (3)(b) for 'or 297D' substitute ', 297D or 298(4)';

(c)   after subsection (3)(c) (as inserted by paragraph 22 of Schedule 5) insert –

'(d)   it has been forfeited in pursuance of a cash forfeiture notice under paragraph 5A of Schedule 1 to the Anti-terrorism, Crime and Security Act 2001 or an account forfeiture notice under paragraph 10W of that Schedule;

(e)   it is detained under paragraph 5B, 5C, 9A or 10G(7) of that Schedule;

(f)   it is the forfeitable property in relation to an order under paragraph 10I(1) of that Schedule.'

(3) In section 148 (free property: Scotland) –

(a)   in subsection (2) –

(i)   omit 'or' at the end of paragraph (e);

(ii)   after that paragraph insert –

'(ea)   paragraph 3(2), 6(2), 10D(1), 10G(2), 10J(3), 10S(2) or 10Z2(3) of Schedule 1 to the Anti-terrorism, Crime and Security Act 2001, or'

(b)   in subsection (3)(b) for 'or 297D' substitute ', 297D or 298(4)';

(c)   after subsection (3)(c) (as inserted by paragraph 24 of Schedule 5) insert –

'(d)   it has been forfeited in pursuance of a cash forfeiture notice under paragraph 5A of Schedule 1 to the Anti-terrorism, Crime and Security Act 2001 or an account forfeiture notice under paragraph 10W of that Schedule;

(e)   it is detained under paragraph 5B, 5C, 9A or 10G(7) of that Schedule;

(f)   it is the forfeitable property in relation to an order under paragraph 10I(1) of that Schedule.'

(4) In section 230 (free property: Northern Ireland) –

(a)   in subsection (2), after paragraph (e) insert –

'(ea)   paragraph 3(2), 6(2), 10D(1), 10G(2), 10J(3), 10S(2) or 10Z2(3) of Schedule 1 to the Anti-terrorism, Crime and Security Act 2001;'

(b)   in subsection (3)(b) for 'or 297D' substitute ', 297D or 298(4)';

(c)   after subsection (3)(c) (as inserted by paragraph 27 of Schedule 5) insert –

'(d)   it has been forfeited in pursuance of a cash forfeiture notice under paragraph 5A of Schedule 1 to the Anti-terrorism, Crime and Security Act 2001 or an account forfeiture notice under paragraph 10W of that Schedule;

(e)   it is detained under paragraph 5B, 5C, 9A or 10G(7) of that Schedule;

(f)   it is the forfeitable property in relation to an order under paragraph 10I(1) of that Schedule.'

(5) In section 245D (restriction on proceedings and remedies), in subsection (1)(b) after 'levied' insert ', and no power to use the procedure in Schedule 12 to the Tribunals, Courts and Enforcement Act 2007 (taking control of goods) may be exercised,'.

(6) In section 290 (prior approval to exercise of section 289 search powers), in subsection (4), after paragraph (aa) (inserted by Schedule 1 to this Act) insert –

'(ab)   in relation to the exercise of a power by a National Crime Agency officer, the Director General of the National Crime Agency or any other National Crime Agency officer authorised by the Director General (whether generally or specifically) for this purpose,'

(7) In section 297A (forfeiture notice), in subsection (6), after paragraph (ba) (inserted by Schedule 1 to this Act, but before the 'or' at the end of that paragraph) insert –

'(bb)   the Director General of the National Crime Agency or any other National Crime Agency officer authorised by the Director General (whether generally or specifically) for this purpose,'

(8) In section 302 (compensation), after subsection (7ZA) (inserted by Schedule 1 to this Act) insert –

'(7ZB)   If the cash was seized by a National Crime Agency officer, the compensation is to be paid by the National Crime Agency.'

(9)   In that section, in subsection (7A)(a)(i), for 'that Part of that Act' substitute 'Part 1 of the Police Reform and Social Responsibility Act 2011'.

(10)   In section 306 (mixing property), in subsection (3) after paragraph (c) insert –

'(ca)   for the discharge (in whole or in part) of a mortgage, charge or other security,'

(11)   In section 8 of the Serious Crime Act 2015 (variation or discharge of confiscation orders), in subsection (3) before paragraph (a) insert –

'(za)   a confiscation order made under the Drug Trafficking Offences Act 1986,'

PART 2   TERRORIST PROPERTY

Disclosures of information

35   Disclosure orders

Schedule 2 contains amendments to the Terrorism Act 2000 which enable the making of disclosure orders in connection with investigations into terrorist financing offences.

36   Sharing of information within the regulated sector

After section 21C of the Terrorism Act 2000 insert –

'21CA   Voluntary disclosures within the regulated sector

(1)   A person (A) may disclose information to one or more other persons if –

(a)   conditions 1 to 4 are met, and
(b)   where applicable, condition 5 is also met.

(2)   Condition 1 is that –

(a)   A is carrying on a business in the regulated sector as a relevant undertaking,
(b)   the information on which the disclosure is based came to A in the course of carrying on that business, and
(c)   the person to whom the information is to be disclosed (or each of them, where the disclosure is to more than one person) is also carrying on a business in the regulated sector as a relevant undertaking (whether or not of the same kind as A).

(3)   Condition 2 is that –

(a)   a constable has requested A to make the disclosure, or
(b)   the person to whom the information is to be disclosed (or at least one of them, where the disclosure is to more than one person) has requested A to do so.

(4)   Condition 3 is that, before A makes the disclosure, the required notification has been made to a constable (see section 21CB(5) to (7)).

(5)   Condition 4 is that A is satisfied that the disclosure of the information will or may assist in determining any matter in connection with –

(a)   a suspicion that a person is involved in the commission of a terrorist financing offence, or
(b)   the identification of terrorist property or of its movement or use.

(6)   Condition 5 is that, before making the disclosure request, the person

making the request (or at least one of them, where the request is made by more than one person) has notified a constable that the request is to be made.

(7) Condition 5 does not apply where the disclosure request concerned is made by a constable.

(8) A person may disclose information to A for the purposes of making a disclosure request if, and to the extent that, the person has reason to believe that A has in A's possession information that will or may assist in determining any matter of the kind mentioned in paragraph (a) or (b) of subsection (5).

21CB Section 21CA: disclosure requests and notifications

(1) A disclosure request must –

    (a) state that it is made in connection with –

        (i) a suspicion that a person is involved in the commission of a terrorist financing offence, or

        (ii) the identification of terrorist property or of its movement or use,

    (b) identify the person or property (so far as known),

    (c) describe the information that is sought from A, and

    (d) specify the person or persons to whom it is requested that the information is disclosed.

(2) Subsections (3) and (4) apply where the disclosure request is made by a person mentioned in section 21CA(3)(b).

(3) If the request states that it is made in connection with a suspicion that a person is involved in the commission of a terrorist financing offence, the request must also –

    (a) set out the grounds for the suspicion, or

    (b) provide such other information as the person making the request thinks appropriate for the purposes of enabling A to determine whether the information requested ought to be disclosed under section 21CA.

(4) If the request states that it is made in connection with the identification of terrorist property or of its movement or use, the request must also provide such other information as the person making the request thinks appropriate for the purposes of enabling A to determine whether the information requested ought to be disclosed under section 21CA.

(5) A required notification for the purposes of section 21CA(4) must be made –

    (a) in the case of a disclosure request made by a constable, by the person who is to disclose information under section 21CA as a result of the request;

    (b) in the case of a disclosure request made by a person mentioned in section 21CA(3)(b), by the person who made the request.

(6) In a case within subsection (5)(a), the required notification must state that information is to be disclosed under section 21CA.

(7) In a case within subsection (5)(b), the required notification must –

    (a) state that a disclosure request has been made;

    (b) specify the person to whom the request was made;

    (c) where the disclosure request to which the notification relates is made in connection with a suspicion of a person's involvement in the commission of a terrorist financing offence, identify the person (so far as known);

(d)   where the disclosure request to which the notification relates is made in connection with the identification of terrorist property or of its movement or use, identify the property and the person who holds it (if known).

(8)   A notification for the purposes of condition 5 in subsection (6) of section 21CA must –

(a)   state that a disclosure request is to be made;
(b)   specify the person to whom it is to be made;
(c)   describe the information to be sought in the request;
(d)   explain why the request is being made.

21CC   Section 21CA: effect on disclosures under section 21A

(1)   This section applies if in any proceedings a question arises as to whether the required disclosure has been made –

(a)   by a person (A) who discloses information under section 21CA(1) as a result of a disclosure request,
(b)   by a person (B) who makes a required notification in accordance with section 21CB(5)(b), or
(c)   by any other person (C) to whom A discloses information under section 21CA(1) as a result of that request.

(2)   The making of a required notification in good faith is to be treated as satisfying any requirement to make the required disclosure on the part of A, B and C.

This is subject to section 21CD(1) to (8).

(3)   The making of a joint disclosure report in good faith is to be treated as satisfying any requirement to make the required disclosure on the part of the persons who jointly make the report.

This is subject to section 21CD(10).

(4)   A joint disclosure report is a report to a constable that –

(a)   is made jointly by A and B (whether or not also jointly with other persons to whom A discloses information under section 21CA(1)),
(b)   satisfies the requirements as to content mentioned in subsection (5) or (as the case may be) subsection (6),
(c)   is prepared after the making of a disclosure by A to B under section 21CA(1) in connection with –

(i)   a suspicion of a person's involvement in the commission of a terrorist financing offence, or
(ii)   the identification of terrorist property or of its movement or use, and

(d)   is sent to the constable before the end of the applicable period.

(5)   In the case of a joint disclosure report prepared in connection with a suspicion of a person's involvement in the commission of a terrorist financing offence, the requirements as to content are that the report must –

(a)   explain the extent to which there are continuing grounds to suspect that the person is involved in the commission of the offence,
(b)   identify the person (if known),

 (c) set out the grounds for the suspicion, and

 (d) provide any other information relevant to the matter.

(6) In the case of a joint disclosure report prepared in connection with the identification of terrorist property or of its movement or use, the requirements as to content are that the report must –

 (a) explain the extent to which there are continuing grounds to suspect that the property is terrorist property,

 (b) identify the property and the person who holds it (if known),

 (c) provide details of its movement or use (if known), and

 (d) provide any other information relevant to the matter.

(7) The applicable period is –

 (a) in a case where the disclosure under section 21CA was made as a result of a request from a constable by virtue of subsection (3)(a) of that section, whatever period may be specified by the constable when making the request;

 (b) in a case where the disclosure was made as a result of a request from another person by virtue of subsection (3)(b) of that section, the period of 28 days beginning with the day on which the notification is made for the purposes of condition 3 in section 21CA(4).

(8) A constable may vary the period of 28 days (whether by lengthening or shortening it) by giving written notice to the person who made the required notification.

(9) A joint disclosure report must be –

 (a) approved by the nominated officer of each person that jointly makes the report, and

 (b) signed by the nominated officer on behalf of each such person.

If there is no nominated officer the report must be approved and signed by another senior officer.

(10) References in this section to A, B or C include –

 (a) a nominated officer acting on behalf of A, B or C, and

 (b) any other person who is an employee, officer or partner of A, B or C.

21CD Limitations on application of section 21CC(2) and (3)

(1) Subsections (2) and (3) apply in a case where the required notification is made by A (notification made as a result of disclosure request received from a constable).

(2) Section 21CC(2) has effect in the case of A, B or C only so far as relating to –

 (a) the suspicion in connection with which the required notification is made, and

 (b) matters known, suspected or believed as a result of the making of the disclosure request concerned.

(3) Accordingly, section 21CC(2) does not remove any requirement to make the required disclosure in relation to anything known, suspected or believed that does not result only from the making of the disclosure request.

(4) Subsections (5) to (8) apply in a case where the required notification is made by B (notification made as a result of disclosure request received from another undertaking in the regulated sector).

(5) Section 21CC(2) has effect in the case of A or C only so far as relating to –

(a)   the suspicion in connection with which the notification by B is made, and

(b)   matters known, suspected or believed by A or C as a result of the making of that notification.

(6)   Accordingly, section 21CC(2) does not remove any requirement to make the required disclosure in relation to anything known, suspected or believed that does not result only from the making of the notification.

(7)   Section 21CC(2) has effect in the case of B only so far as relating to –

(a)   the suspicion in connection with which the notification is made, and

(b)   matters known, suspected or believed by B at the time of the making of the notification.

(8)   If a joint disclosure report is not made before the end of the applicable period (whether the required notification was made by A or B), section 21CC(2) –

(a)   has effect only so far as relating to any requirement to make the required disclosure that would have otherwise arisen within that period, and

(b)   does not remove a requirement to make the required disclosure so far as arising after the end of that period on the part of any person in respect of matters that may become known, suspected or believed by the person after the time when the required notification was made.

(9)   If a joint disclosure report is not made before the end of the applicable period, the person who made the required notification must notify a constable that a report is not being made as soon as reasonably practicable after the period ends.

(10)   Section 21CC(3) has effect only so far as relating to –

(a)   the suspicion in connection with which the report is made, and

(b)   matters known, suspected or believed at the time of the making of the report.

(11)   Terms used in this section have the same meanings as in section 21CC.

21CE   Section 21CA: supplementary

(1)   A relevant disclosure made in good faith does not breach –

(a)   an obligation of confidence owed by the person making the disclosure, or

(b)   any other restriction on the disclosure of information, however imposed.

(2)   But a relevant disclosure may not include information obtained from a UK law enforcement agency unless that agency consents to the disclosure.

(3)   In a case where a person is acting on behalf of another ("the undertaking") as a nominated officer –

(a)   a relevant disclosure by the undertaking must be made by the nominated officer on behalf of the undertaking, and

(b)   a relevant disclosure to the undertaking must be made to that officer.

(4)   Subsection (1) applies whether or not the conditions in section 21CA were met in respect of the disclosure if the person making the disclosure did so in the reasonable belief that the conditions were met.

(5)   In this section –

"relevant disclosure" means any disclosure made in compliance, or intended compliance, with section 21CA;

"UK law enforcement agency" means –

(a)   the National Crime Agency;
(b)   a police force in England, Scotland, Northern Ireland or Wales;
(c)   any other person operating in England, Scotland, Northern Ireland or Wales charged with the duty of preventing, detecting, investigating or prosecuting offences.

21CF   Sections 21CA to 21CE: interpretation

(1)   This section applies for the purposes of sections 21CA to 21CE.
(2)   References to a constable include references to a National Crime Agency officer authorised for those purposes by the Director General of that Agency.
(3)   References to a business in the regulated sector are to be construed in accordance with Schedule 3A.
(4)   "Disclosure request" means a request made for the purposes of condition 2 in section 21CA(3).
(5)   "Nominated officer" means a person nominated to receive disclosures under section 21A.
(6)   "Relevant undertaking" means any of the following –

(a)   a credit institution;
(b)   a financial institution;
(c)   a professional legal adviser;
(d)   a relevant professional adviser;
(e)   other persons (not within paragraphs (a) to (d)) whose business consists of activities listed in paragraph 1(1) of Schedule 3A.

(7)   "Required disclosure" means a disclosure that is made –

(a)   to a constable in connection with a suspicion that a person is involved in the commission of a terrorist financing offence, and
(b)   for the purposes of avoiding the commission of an offence under section 21A by virtue of not satisfying the third condition in subsection (4) of that section.

(8)   "Required notification" means a notification made for the purposes of condition 3 in section 21CA(4).
(9)   For the purposes of subsection (6) –

(a)   "credit institution" has the same meaning as in Schedule 3A;
(b)   "financial institution" means an undertaking that carries on a business in the regulated sector by virtue of any of paragraphs (b) to (i) of paragraph 1(1) of that Schedule;
(c)   "relevant professional adviser" has the meaning given by section 21H(5).

(10)   "Terrorist financing offence" means an offence under any of sections 15 to 18.'

37   Further information orders

After section 22A of the Terrorism Act 2000 insert –

'*Further information orders*

22B   Further information orders

(1)   A magistrates' court or (in Scotland) the sheriff may, on an application made by a law enforcement officer, make a further information order if satisfied that either condition 1 or condition 2 is met.

(2)   The application must –

    (a)   specify or describe the information sought under the order, and

    (b)   specify the person from whom the information is sought ("the respondent").

(3)   A further information order is an order requiring the respondent to provide –

    (a)   the information specified or described in the application for the order, or

    (b)   such other information as the court or sheriff making the order thinks appropriate,

so far as the information is in the possession, or under the control, of the respondent.

(4)   Condition 1 for the making of a further information order is met if –

    (a)   the information required to be given under the order would relate to a matter arising from a disclosure made under section 21A,

    (b)   the respondent is the person who made the disclosure or is otherwise carrying on a business in the regulated sector,

    (c)   the information would assist in –

        (i)   investigating whether a person is involved in the commission of an offence under any of sections 15 to 18 or in determining whether an investigation of that kind should be started, or

        (ii)   identifying terrorist property or its movement or use, and

    (d)   it is reasonable in all the circumstances for the information to be provided.

(5)   Condition 2 for the making of a further information order is met if –

    (a)   the information required to be given under the order would relate to a matter arising from a disclosure made under a corresponding disclosure requirement,

    (b)   an external request has been made to the National Crime Agency for the provision of information in connection with that disclosure,

    (c)   the respondent is carrying on a business in the regulated sector,

    (d)   the information is likely to be of substantial value to the authority that made the external request in determining any matter in connection with the disclosure, and

    (e)   it is reasonable in all the circumstances for the information to be provided.

(6)   For the purposes of subsection (5), "external request" means a request made by an authority of a foreign country which has responsibility in that country for carrying out investigations into whether a corresponding terrorist financing offence has been committed.

(7)   A further information order must specify –

    (a)   how the information required under the order is to be provided, and

    (b)   the date by which it is to be provided.

(8)   If a person fails to comply with a further information order made by a magistrates' court, the magistrates' court may order the person to pay an amount not exceeding £5,000.

(9)   The sum mentioned in subsection (8) is to be treated as adjudged to be paid by a conviction of the court for the purposes of the Magistrates' Courts Act

1980 or (as the case may be) the Magistrates' Courts (Northern Ireland) Order 1981 (S.I. 1981/1675 (N.I. 26)).

(10)   In order to take account of changes in the value of money the Secretary of State may by regulations made by statutory instrument substitute another sum for the sum for the time being specified in subsection (8).

(11)   A statutory instrument containing regulations under subsection (10) is subject to annulment in pursuance of a resolution of either House of Parliament.

(12)   A law enforcement officer who is a constable, a National Crime Agency officer or a counter-terrorism financial investigator may not make an application under this section unless the officer is a senior law enforcement officer or is authorised to do so by a senior law enforcement officer.

(13)   Schedule 3A has effect for the purposes of this section in determining what is a business in the regulated sector.

(14)   In this section –

"corresponding disclosure requirement" means a requirement to make a disclosure under the law of the foreign country concerned that corresponds to a requirement imposed by virtue of this Part;

"corresponding terrorist financing offence" means an offence under the law of the foreign country concerned that would, if done in the United Kingdom, constitute an offence under any of sections 15 to 18;

"foreign country" means a country or territory outside the United Kingdom;

"law enforcement officer" means –

(a)   a constable,
(b)   a National Crime Agency officer authorised for the purposes of this section by the Director General of that Agency,
(c)   a counter-terrorism financial investigator, or
(d)   a procurator fiscal;

"senior law enforcement officer" means –

(a)   a police officer of at least the rank of superintendent;
(b)   the Director General of the National Crime Agency;
(c)   any other National Crime Agency officer authorised by the Director General (whether generally or specifically) for this purpose.

22C   Statements

(1)   A statement made by a person in response to a further information order may not be used in evidence against the person in criminal proceedings.

(2)   Subsection (1) does not apply –

(a)   in the case of proceedings under this Part,
(b)   on a prosecution for perjury, or
(c)   on a prosecution for some other offence where, in giving evidence, the person makes a statement inconsistent with the statement mentioned in subsection (1).

(3)   A statement may not be used by virtue of subsection (2)(c) unless –

(a)   evidence relating to it is adduced, or
(b)   a question relating to it is asked,

by or on behalf of the person in the proceedings arising out of the prosecution.

(4)   In subsection (2)(b) the reference to a prosecution for perjury is –

(a)   in the case of England and Wales, a reference to a prosecution for an offence under section 5 of the Perjury Act 1911;

(b)   in the case of Northern Ireland, a reference to a prosecution for an offence under Article 10 of the Perjury (Northern Ireland) Order 1979 (S.I. 1979/1714 (N.I. 19)).

22D   Appeals

(1)   An appeal from a decision on an application for a further information order lies to the relevant appeal court.

(2)   An appeal under this section lies at the instance of any person who was a party to the proceedings on the application.

(3)   The "relevant appeal court" is –

(a)   the Crown Court, in the case of a decision made by a magistrates' court in England and Wales;

(b)   a county court, in the case of a decision made by a magistrates' court in Northern Ireland;

(c)   the Sheriff Appeal Court, in the case of a decision made by the sheriff.

(4)   On an appeal under this section the relevant appeal court may –

(a)   make or (as the case may be) discharge a further information order, or

(b)   vary the order.

22E   Supplementary

(1)   A further information order does not confer the right to require a person to provide privileged information.

(2)   "Privileged information" is information which a person would be entitled to refuse to provide on grounds of legal professional privilege in proceedings in the High Court or, in Scotland, legal privilege as defined by section 412 of the Proceeds of Crime Act 2002.

(3)   Information provided in pursuance of a further information order is not to be taken to breach any restriction on the disclosure of information (however imposed).

(4)   An application for a further information order may be heard and determined in private.

(5)   Rules of court may make provision as to the practice and procedure to be followed in connection with proceedings relating to further information orders.'

Civil recovery

38   Forfeiture of terrorist cash

(1)   Schedule 1 to the Anti-terrorism, Crime and Security Act 2001 (forfeiture of terrorist cash) is amended as follows.

(2)   In paragraph 1 (meaning of terrorist cash) –

(a)   after sub-paragraph (2)(e) insert –

'(f)   gaming vouchers,
(g)   fixed-value casino tokens,
(h)   betting receipts,'

(b)   after sub-paragraph (4) insert –

'(5)   For the purposes of sub-paragraph (2) –

(a)   "gaming voucher" means a voucher in physical form issued by a gaming machine that represents a right to be paid the amount stated on it;

(b)   "fixed-value casino token" means a casino token that represents a right to be paid the amount stated on it;

(c)   "betting receipt" means a receipt in physical form that represents a right to be paid an amount in respect of a bet placed with a person holding a betting licence.

(6)   In sub-paragraph (5) –

"bet" –

(a)   in relation to England and Wales and Scotland, has the same meaning as in section 9(1) of the Gambling Act 2005;

(b)   in relation to Northern Ireland, has the same meaning as in the Betting, Gaming, Lotteries and Amusements (Northern Ireland) Order 1985 (S.I. 1985/1204 (N.I. 11)) (see Article 2 of that Order);

"betting licence" –

(a)   in relation to England and Wales and Scotland, means a general betting operating licence issued under Part 5 of the Gambling Act 2005;

(b)   in relation to Northern Ireland, means a bookmaker's licence as defined in Article 2 of the Betting, Gaming, Lotteries and Amusements (Northern Ireland) Order 1985;

"gaming machine" –

(a)   in relation to England and Wales and Scotland, has the same meaning as in the Gambling Act 2005 (see section 235 of that Act);

(b)   in relation to Northern Ireland, has the same meaning as in the Betting, Gaming, Lotteries and Amusements (Northern Ireland) Order 1985 (see Article 2 of that Order).

(7)   In the application of sub-paragraph (5) to Northern Ireland references to a right to be paid an amount are to be read as references to the right that would exist but for Article 170 of the Betting, Gaming, Lotteries and Amusements (Northern Ireland) Order 1985 (gaming and wagering contracts void).'

(3)   In paragraph 3 (detention of seized cash) –

(a)   in sub-paragraph (2)(a), for 'three' substitute '6';

(b)   after sub-paragraph (8) insert –

'(9)   Where an application for an order under sub-paragraph (2) relates to cash seized under paragraph 2(2), the court, sheriff or justice may make the order if satisfied that –

(a)   the condition in sub-paragraph (6), (7) or (8) is met in respect of part of the cash, and

(b)   it is not reasonably practicable to detain only that part.'

(4)   After paragraph 5 insert –

'PART 2A   FORFEITURE OF TERRORIST CASH WITHOUT COURT ORDER

Cash forfeiture notice

5A   (1)   This paragraph applies while any cash is detained in pursuance of an order under paragraph 3(2).

(2)   A senior officer may give a notice for the purpose of forfeiting the cash or any part of it if satisfied that the cash or part is terrorist cash.

(3)   A notice given under sub-paragraph (2) is referred to in this Schedule as a cash forfeiture notice.

(4)   A cash forfeiture notice must –

(a)   state the amount of cash in respect of which it is given,

(b)   state when and where the cash was seized,

(c)   confirm that the senior officer is satisfied as mentioned in sub-paragraph (2),

(d)   specify a period for objecting to the proposed forfeiture and an address to which any objections must be sent, and

(e)   explain that the cash will be forfeited unless an objection is received at that address within the period for objecting.

(5)   The period for objecting must be at least 30 days starting with the day after the notice is given.

(6)   The Secretary of State must by regulations made by statutory instrument make provision about how a cash forfeiture notice is to be given.

(7)   The regulations may (amongst other things) provide –

(a)   for a cash forfeiture notice to be given to such person or persons, and in such manner, as may be prescribed;

(b)   for a cash forfeiture notice to be given by publication in such manner as may be prescribed;

(c)   for circumstances in which, and the time at which, a cash forfeiture notice is to be treated as having been given.

(8)   The regulations must ensure that where a cash forfeiture notice is given it is, if possible, given to every person to whom notice of an order under paragraph 3(2) in respect of the cash has been given.

(9)   A statutory instrument containing regulations under this paragraph is subject to annulment in pursuance of a resolution of either House of Parliament.

(10)   In this Part of this Schedule –

"senior officer" means –

(a)   a senior police officer;

(b)   an officer of Revenue and Customs of a rank designated by the Commissioners for Her Majesty's Revenue and Customs as equivalent to that of a senior police officer;

(c)   an immigration officer of a rank designated by the Secretary of State as equivalent to that of a senior police officer;

"senior police officer" means a police officer of at least the rank of superintendent.

Effect of cash forfeiture notice

5B   (1)   This paragraph applies if a cash forfeiture notice is given in respect of any cash.

(2)   The cash is to be detained until –

(a)   the cash is forfeited under this paragraph,

(b)   the notice lapses under this paragraph, or

(c)   the cash is released under a power conferred by this Schedule.

(3)   If no objection is made within the period for objecting specified in the

notice under paragraph 5A(4)(d), and the notice has not lapsed, the cash is forfeited (subject to paragraph 5D).

(4) If an objection is made within the period for objecting, the notice lapses.

(5) If an application is made for the forfeiture of the whole or any part of the cash under paragraph 6, the notice lapses.

(6) If the cash or any part of it is released under a power conferred by this Schedule, the notice lapses or (as the case may be) lapses in relation to that part.

(7) An objection may be made by anyone (whether a recipient of the notice or not).

(8) An objection means a written objection sent to the address specified in the notice; and an objection is made when it is received at the address.

(9) An objection does not prevent forfeiture of the cash under paragraph 6.

(10) Nothing in this paragraph affects the validity of an order under paragraph 3(2).

Detention following lapse of cash forfeiture notice

5C (1) This paragraph applies if –

(a) a cash forfeiture notice is given in respect of any cash,
(b) the notice lapses under paragraph 5B(4), and
(c) the period for which detention of the cash was authorised under paragraph 3(2) has expired.

(2) The cash may be detained for a further period of up to 48 hours (calculated in accordance with paragraph 3(1A)).

(3) But if within that period it is decided that neither of the applications mentioned in sub-paragraph (4) is to be made, the cash must be released.

(4) The applications are –

(a) an application for a further order under paragraph 3(2);
(b) an application for forfeiture of the cash under paragraph 6.

(5) If within that period an application is made for a further order under paragraph 3(2), the cash may be detained until the application is determined or otherwise disposed of.

Application to set aside forfeiture

5D (1) A person aggrieved by the forfeiture of cash in pursuance of paragraph 5B(3) may apply to a magistrates' court or (in Scotland) the sheriff for an order setting aside the forfeiture of the cash or any part of it.

(2) The application must be made before the end of the period of 30 days starting with the day on which the period for objecting ended ("the 30-day period").

(3) But the court or sheriff may give permission for an application to be made after the 30-day period has ended if the court or sheriff thinks that there are exceptional circumstances to explain why the applicant –

(a) failed to object to the forfeiture within the period for objecting, and
(b) failed to make an application within the 30-day period.

(4)   On an application under this paragraph the court or sheriff must consider whether the cash to which the application relates could be forfeited under paragraph 6 (ignoring the forfeiture mentioned in sub-paragraph (1)).

(5)   If the court or sheriff is satisfied that the cash to which the application relates or any part of it could not be forfeited under that paragraph the court or sheriff must set aside the forfeiture of that cash or part.

(6)   Where the court or sheriff sets aside the forfeiture of any cash –

(a)   the court or sheriff must order the release of that cash, and
(b)   the cash is to be treated as never having been forfeited.

Release of cash subject to cash forfeiture notice

5E   (1)   This paragraph applies while any cash is detained under paragraph 5B or 5C.

(2)   The person from whom the cash was seized may apply to a magistrates' court or (in Scotland) the sheriff for the cash to be released.

(3)   On an application under sub-paragraph (2), the court or sheriff may direct the release of the cash or any part of it if not satisfied that the cash to be released is terrorist cash.

(4)   An authorised officer may release the cash or any part of it if satisfied that the detention of the cash to be released is no longer justified.

Application of cash forfeited under cash forfeiture notice

5F   (1)   Cash forfeited in pursuance of paragraph 5B(3), and any accrued interest on it –

(a)   if first detained in pursuance of an order under paragraph 3(2) made by a magistrates' court or a justice of the peace, is to be paid into the Consolidated Fund;
(b)   if first detained in pursuance of an order under paragraph 3(2) made by the sheriff, is to be paid into the Scottish Consolidated Fund.

(2)   But it is not to be paid in –

(a)   before the end of the period within which an application under paragraph 5D may be made (ignoring the possibility of an application by virtue of paragraph 5D(3)), or
(b)   if an application is made within that period, before the application is determined or otherwise disposed of.'

(5)   In paragraph 7(4) (release of cash on appeal against decision in forfeiture proceedings), after 'of' insert 'the whole or any part of'.

(6)   In paragraph 9 (victims), after sub-paragraph (3) insert –

'(4)   If sub-paragraph (5) applies, the court or sheriff may order the cash to be released to the applicant or to the person from whom it was seized.

(5)   This sub-paragraph applies where –

(a)   the applicant is not the person from whom the cash claimed was seized,
(b)   it appears to the court or sheriff that the cash belongs to the applicant,
(c)   the court or sheriff is satisfied that the release condition is met in relation to the cash, and
(d)   no objection to the making of an order under sub-paragraph (4) has been made by the person from whom the cash was seized.

(6)   The release condition is met –

    (a)   in relation to cash detained under paragraph 3, if the conditions in that paragraph for the detention of the cash are no longer met,

    (b)   in relation to cash detained under paragraph 5B or 5C, if the cash is not terrorist cash, and

    (c)   in relation to cash detained pending the conclusion of proceedings in pursuance of an application under paragraph 6, if the court or sheriff decides not to make an order under that paragraph in relation to the cash.'

(7)   In paragraph 19 (general interpretation), in sub-paragraph (1), at the appropriate places insert –

     '"cash forfeiture notice" has the meaning given by paragraph 5A(3),

     "senior officer" (in Part 2A) has the meaning given by paragraph 5A(10),'

39   Forfeiture of certain personal (or moveable) property

Schedule 3 contains amendments to the Anti-terrorism, Crime and Security Act 2001 which enable the forfeiture of certain personal (or moveable) property which –

(a)   is intended to be used for the purposes of terrorism,

(b)   consists of resources of a proscribed organisation, or

(c)   is, or represents, property obtained through terrorism.

40   Forfeiture of money held in bank and building society accounts

Schedule 4 contains amendments to the Anti-terrorism, Crime and Security Act 2001 which enable the forfeiture of money held in a bank or building society account which –

(a)   is intended to be used for the purposes of terrorism,

(b)   consists of resources of a proscribed organisation, or

(c)   is, or represents, property obtained through terrorism.

Counter-terrorism financial investigators

41   Extension of powers to financial investigators

(1)   The Terrorism Act 2000 is amended in accordance with subsections (2) to (5).

(2)   After section 63E insert –

   'Counter-terrorism financial investigators

63F   Counter-terrorism financial investigators

(1)   The metropolitan police force must provide a system for the accreditation of financial investigators ("counter-terrorism financial investigators").

(2)   The system of accreditation must include provision for –

    (a)   the monitoring of the performance of counter-terrorism financial investigators,

    (b)   the withdrawal of accreditation from any person who contravenes or fails to comply with any condition subject to which he or she was accredited, and

    (c)   securing that decisions under that system which concern –

        (i)   the grant or withdrawal of accreditations, or

        (ii)   the monitoring of the performance of counter-terrorism financial investigators,

    are taken without regard to their effect on operations by the metropolitan police force or any other person.

(3)   A person may be accredited if he or she is –

    (a)   a member of the civilian staff of a police force in England and Wales (including the metropolitan police force), within the meaning of Part 1 of the Police Reform and Social Responsibility Act 2011;

    (b)   a member of staff of the City of London police force;

    (c)   a member of staff of the Police Service of Northern Ireland.

(4)   A person may be accredited –

    (a)   in relation to this Act;

    (b)   in relation to the Anti-terrorism, Crime and Security Act 2001;

    (c)   in relation to particular provisions of this Act or of the Anti-terrorism, Crime and Security Act 2001.

(5)   But the accreditation may be limited to specified purposes.

(6)   A reference in this Act or in the Anti-terrorism, Crime and Security Act 2001 to a counter-terrorism financial investigator is to be construed accordingly.

(7)   The metropolitan police force must make provision for the training of persons in –

    (a)   financial investigation,

    (b)   the operation of this Act, and

    (c)   the operation of the Anti-terrorism, Crime and Security Act 2001.'

(3) In Part 1 of Schedule 5 (terrorist investigations: information: England and Wales and Northern Ireland) –

  (a)   in paragraph 5 –

    (i)   in sub-paragraph (1) for 'A constable' substitute 'An appropriate officer';

    (ii)   after sub-paragraph (1) insert –

      '(1A) Where the appropriate officer is a counter-terrorism financial investigator, the officer may apply for an order under this paragraph only for the purposes of a terrorist investigation so far as relating to terrorist property.'

    (iii)   in sub-paragraph (3)(a) for 'a constable' substitute 'an appropriate officer';

    (iv)   in sub-paragraph (3)(b) for 'a constable' substitute 'an appropriate officer';

    (v)   after sub-paragraph (5) insert –

      '(6)   "Appropriate officer" means –

        (a)   a constable, or

        (b)   a counter-terrorism financial investigator.'

  (b)   in paragraph 6 after sub-paragraph (3) insert –

    '(4)   In the case of an order sought by a counter-terrorism financial investigator, the first condition is satisfied only to the extent that the terrorist investigation mentioned in sub-paragraph (2)(a) and (b) relates to terrorist property.'

  (c)   in paragraph 7(2)(a) for 'constable' substitute 'appropriate officer (as defined in paragraph 5(6))';

  (d)   in paragraph 13 after sub-paragraph (1) insert –

    '(1A) A counter-terrorism financial investigator may apply to a Circuit Judge or a District Judge (Magistrates' Courts) for an order under this paragraph requiring any person specified in the order to provide an explanation of any material produced or made available to a counter-terrorism financial investigator under paragraph 5.'

(4) In paragraph 1 of Schedule 6 (financial information orders) –

   (a)   in sub-paragraph (1) after 'constable' insert 'or counter-terrorism financial investigator';

   (b)   in sub-paragraph (2)(a) after 'constable' insert 'or counter-terrorism financial investigator'.

(5) In Schedule 6A (account monitoring orders) –

   (a)   in paragraph 1 after sub-paragraph (4)(a) insert –

      '(aa) a counter-terrorism financial investigator, in England and Wales or Northern Ireland;'

   (b)   after paragraph 3(3) insert –

      '(4)   If the application was made by a counter-terrorism financial investigator, the description of information specified in it may be varied by a different counter-terrorism financial investigator.'

   (c)   after paragraph 4(2) insert –

      '(2A) If the application for the account monitoring order was made by a counter-terrorism financial investigator, an application to discharge or vary the order may be made by a different counter-terrorism financial investigator.'

(6) In Schedule 1 to the Anti-terrorism, Crime and Security Act 2001 (forfeiture of terrorist cash) –

   (a)   after paragraph 10(7) insert –

      '(7A) If the cash was seized by a counter-terrorism financial investigator, the compensation is to be paid as follows –

         (a)   in the case of a counter-terrorism financial investigator who was –

            (i)   a member of the civilian staff of a police force (including the metropolitan police force), within the meaning of Part 1 of the Police Reform and Social Responsibility Act 2011, or

            (ii) a member of staff of the City of London police force, it is to be paid out of the police fund from which the expenses of the police force are met,

         (b)   in the case of a counter-terrorism financial investigator who was a member of staff of the Police Service of Northern Ireland, it is to be paid out of money provided by the Chief Constable of the Police Service of Northern Ireland.'

   (b)   in paragraph 19(1) –

      (i)   in the definition of 'authorised officer', after 'constable' insert ', a counter-terrorism financial investigator';

      (ii) at the appropriate place insert –

      '"counter-terrorism financial investigator" is to be read in accordance with section 63F of the Terrorism Act 2000,'

42   Offences in relation to counter-terrorism financial investigators

(1) After section 120A of the Terrorism Act 2000 insert –

'**120B   Offences in relation to counter-terrorism financial investigators**

(1)   A person commits an offence if the person assaults a counter-terrorism financial investigator who is acting in the exercise of a relevant power.

(2)   A person commits an offence if the person resists or wilfully obstructs a counter-terrorism financial investigator who is acting in the exercise of a relevant power.

(3)   A person guilty of an offence under subsection (1) is liable –

    (a)   on summary conviction in England and Wales, to imprisonment for a term not exceeding 51 weeks, or to a fine, or to both;

    (b)   on summary conviction in Northern Ireland, to imprisonment for a term not exceeding 6 months, or to a fine not exceeding level 5 on the standard scale, or to both.

(4)   A person guilty of an offence under subsection (2) is liable –

    (a)   on summary conviction in England and Wales, to imprisonment for a term not exceeding 51 weeks, or to a fine not exceeding level 3 on the standard scale, or to both;

    (b)   on summary conviction in Northern Ireland, to imprisonment for a term not exceeding 1 month, or to a fine not exceeding level 3 on the standard scale, or to both.

(5)   In this section "relevant power" means a power exercisable under Schedule 5 (terrorist investigations: information) or Part 1 of Schedule 5A (terrorist financing investigations in England and Wales and Northern Ireland: disclosure orders).

(6)   In relation to an offence committed before the coming into force of section 281(5) of the Criminal Justice Act 2003 (alteration of penalties for certain summary offences: England and Wales) –

    (a)   the reference to 51 weeks in subsection (3)(a) is to be read as a reference to 6 months;

    (b)   the reference to 51 weeks in subsection (4)(a) is to be read as a reference to 1 month.'

(2)   After paragraph 10Z7 of Schedule 1 to the Anti-terrorism, Crime and Security Act 2001 (inserted by Schedule 4 to this Act) insert –

'**PART 4C   OFFENCES**

Offences in relation to counter-terrorism financial investigators

10Z8   (1)   A person commits an offence if the person assaults a counter-terrorism financial investigator who is acting in the exercise of a power under this Schedule.

    (2)   A person commits an offence if the person resists or wilfully obstructs a counter-terrorism financial investigator who is acting in the exercise of a power under this Schedule.

    (3)   A person guilty of an offence under sub-paragraph (1) is liable –

        (a)   on summary conviction in England and Wales, to imprisonment for a term not exceeding 51 weeks, or to a fine, or to both;

        (b)   on summary conviction in Northern Ireland, to imprisonment for a term not exceeding 6 months, or to a fine not exceeding level 5 on the standard scale, or to both.

    (4)   A person guilty of an offence under sub-paragraph (2) is liable –

(a)   on summary conviction in England and Wales, to imprisonment for a term not exceeding 51 weeks, or to a fine not
exceeding level 3 on the standard scale, or to both;

(b)   on summary conviction in Northern Ireland, to imprisonment
for a term not exceeding 1 month, or to a fine not exceeding
level 3 on the standard scale, or to both.

(5)   In relation to an offence committed before the coming into force of
section 281(5) of the Criminal Justice Act 2003 (alteration of penalties for certain summary offences: England and Wales) –

(a)   the reference to 51 weeks in sub-paragraph (3)(a) is to be read
as a reference to 6 months;

(b)   the reference to 51 weeks in sub-paragraph (4)(a) is to be read
as a reference to 1 month.'

Enforcement in other parts of United Kingdom

43   Enforcement in other parts of United Kingdom

After section 120B of the Terrorism Act 2000 (inserted by section 42 above) insert –

'120C   Enforcement of orders in other parts of United Kingdom

(1)   Her Majesty may by Order in Council make provision for an investigatory
order made in one part of the United Kingdom to be enforced in another
part.

(2)   In subsection (1) "investigatory order" means any of the following kinds of
order –

(a)   an order under section 22B (further information orders);

(b)   an order under paragraph 5 of Schedule 5 (production orders: England and Wales and Northern Ireland) that is made in connection
with a terrorist investigation in relation to terrorist property;

(c)   an order under paragraph 13(1)(b) of that Schedule that is made in
connection with material produced or made available as a result of an
order within paragraph (b) of this subsection;

(d)   an order under paragraph 22 of Schedule 5 (production orders:
Scotland) that is made in connection with a terrorist investigation in
relation to terrorist property;

(e)   an order under paragraph 30(1)(b) of that Schedule that is made in
connection with material produced or made available as a result of an
order within paragraph (d) of this subsection;

(f)   an order under paragraph 9 of Schedule 5A (disclosure orders:
England and Wales and Northern Ireland);

(g)   an order under paragraph 19 of that Schedule (disclosure orders:
Scotland);

(h)   an order under paragraph 1 of Schedule 6 (financial information
orders);

(i)   an order under paragraph 2 of Schedule 6A (account monitoring
orders).

(3)   An Order under this section may apply (with or without modifications) any
provision of or made under –

(a)   an Act (including this Act),

(b)   an Act of the Scottish Parliament, or

(c)   Northern Ireland legislation.

(4)   An Order under this section –

(a)   may make different provision for different purposes;
(b)   may include supplementary, incidental, saving or transitional provisions.

(5)   Rules of court may make whatever provision is necessary or expedient to give effect to an Order under this section.

(6)   A statutory instrument containing an Order under this section is subject to annulment in pursuance of a resolution of either House of Parliament.'

PART 3   CORPORATE OFFENCES OF FAILURE TO PREVENT FACILITATION OF TAX EVASION

Preliminary

44   Meaning of relevant body and acting in the capacity of an associated person

(1)   This section defines expressions used in this Part.

(2)   'Relevant body' means a body corporate or partnership (wherever incorporated or formed).

(3)   'Partnership' means –

(a)   a partnership within the meaning of the Partnership Act 1890, or
(b)   a limited partnership registered under the Limited Partnerships Act 1907,

or a firm or entity of a similar character formed under the law of a foreign country.

(4)   A person (P) acts in the capacity of a person associated with a relevant body (B) if P is –

(a)   an employee of B who is acting in the capacity of an employee,
(b)   an agent of B (other than an employee) who is acting in the capacity of an agent, or
(c)   any other person who performs services for or on behalf of B who is acting in the capacity of a person performing such services.

(5)   For the purposes of subsection (4)(c) the question whether or not P is a person who provides services for or on behalf of B is to be determined by reference to all the relevant circumstances and not merely by reference to the nature of the relationship between P and B.

Failure of relevant bodies to prevent tax evasion facilitation offences by associated persons

45   Failure to prevent facilitation of UK tax evasion offences

(1)   A relevant body (B) is guilty of an offence if a person commits a UK tax evasion facilitation offence when acting in the capacity of a person associated with B.

(2)   It is a defence for B to prove that, when the UK tax evasion facilitation offence was committed –

(a)   B had in place such prevention procedures as it was reasonable in all the circumstances to expect B to have in place, or
(b)   it was not reasonable in all the circumstances to expect B to have any prevention procedures in place.

(3)   In subsection (2) 'prevention procedures' means procedures designed to prevent persons acting in the capacity of a person associated with B from committing UK tax evasion facilitation offences.

(4)   In this Part 'UK tax evasion offence' means –

(a)   an offence of cheating the public revenue, or

(b)   an offence under the law of any part of the United Kingdom consisting of being knowingly concerned in, or in taking steps with a view to, the fraudulent evasion of a tax.

(5)   In this Part 'UK tax evasion facilitation offence' means an offence under the law of any part of the United Kingdom consisting of –

(a)   being knowingly concerned in, or in taking steps with a view to, the fraudulent evasion of a tax by another person,

(b)   aiding, abetting, counselling or procuring the commission of a UK tax evasion offence, or

(c)   being involved art and part in the commission of an offence consisting of being knowingly concerned in, or in taking steps with a view to, the fraudulent evasion of a tax.

(6)   Conduct carried out with a view to the fraudulent evasion of tax by another person is not to be regarded as a UK tax evasion facilitation offence by virtue of subsection (5)(a) unless the other person has committed a UK tax evasion offence facilitated by that conduct.

(7)   For the purposes of this section 'tax' means a tax imposed under the law of any part of the United Kingdom, including national insurance contributions under –

(a)   Part 1 of the Social Security Contributions and Benefits Act 1992, or

(b)   Part 1 of the Social Security Contributions and Benefits (Northern Ireland) Act 1992.

(8)   A relevant body guilty of an offence under this section is liable –

(a)   on conviction on indictment, to a fine;

(b)   on summary conviction in England and Wales, to a fine;

(c)   on summary conviction in Scotland or Northern Ireland, to a fine not exceeding the statutory maximum.

46   Failure to prevent facilitation of foreign tax evasion offences

(1)   A relevant body (B) is guilty of an offence if at any time –

(a)   a person commits a foreign tax evasion facilitation offence when acting in the capacity of a person associated with B, and

(b)   any of the conditions in subsection (2) is satisfied.

(2)   The conditions are –

(a)   that B is a body incorporated, or a partnership formed, under the law of any part of the United Kingdom;

(b)   that B carries on business or part of a business in the United Kingdom;

(c)   that any conduct constituting part of the foreign tax evasion facilitation offence takes place in the United Kingdom;

and in paragraph (b) 'business' includes an undertaking.

(3)   It is a defence for B to prove that, when the foreign tax evasion facilitation offence was committed –

(a)   B had in place such prevention procedures as it was reasonable in all the circumstances to expect B to have in place, or

(b)   it was not reasonable in all the circumstances to expect B to have any prevention procedures in place.

(4)   In subsection (3) 'prevention procedures' means procedures designed to prevent persons acting in the capacity of a person associated with B from committing foreign tax evasion facilitation offences under the law of the foreign country concerned.

(5)   In this Part 'foreign tax evasion offence' means conduct which –

(a)   amounts to an offence under the law of a foreign country,

(b)   relates to a breach of a duty relating to a tax imposed under the law of that country, and

(c)   would be regarded by the courts of any part of the United Kingdom as amounting to being knowingly concerned in, or in taking steps with a view to, the fraudulent evasion of that tax.

(6)   In this Part 'foreign tax evasion facilitation offence' means conduct which –

(a)   amounts to an offence under the law of a foreign country,

(b)   relates to the commission by another person of a foreign tax evasion offence under that law, and

(c)   would, if the foreign tax evasion offence were a UK tax evasion offence, amount to a UK tax evasion facilitation offence (see section 45(5) and (6)).

(7)   A relevant body guilty of an offence under this section is liable –

(a)   on conviction on indictment, to a fine;

(b)   on summary conviction in England and Wales, to a fine;

(c)   on summary conviction in Scotland or Northern Ireland, to a fine not exceeding the statutory maximum.

Guidance about prevention procedures

47   Guidance about preventing facilitation of tax evasion offences

(1)   The Chancellor of the Exchequer ('the Chancellor') must prepare and publish guidance about procedures that relevant bodies can put in place to prevent persons acting in the capacity of an associated person from committing UK tax evasion facilitation offences or foreign tax evasion facilitation offences.

(2)   The Chancellor may from time to time prepare and publish new or revised guidance to add to or replace existing guidance published by the Chancellor under this section.

(3)   The Chancellor must consult the Scottish Ministers, the Welsh Ministers and the Department of Justice in Northern Ireland when preparing any guidance to be published under this section.

(4)   Guidance prepared and published under this section does not come into operation except in accordance with regulations made by the Chancellor by statutory instrument.

(5)   A statutory instrument containing such regulations is subject to annulment in pursuance of a resolution of either House of Parliament.

(6)   Where for the purposes of subsection (5) a copy of a statutory instrument containing such regulations is laid before Parliament the Chancellor must also lay a copy of the guidance to which the regulations relate.

(7)   The Chancellor may approve guidance prepared by any other person if it relates to any matters within the scope of subsection (1).

(8)   Approval under subsection (7) –

(a)   must be given in writing, and

(b)   may only be given on the condition that the person who prepared it publishes the approved guidance while it remains in operation as approved guidance.

(9)   The Chancellor may withdraw approval under subsection (7) by a notice given to the person who prepared the guidance.

Offences: general and supplementary provision

48   Offences: extra-territorial application and jurisdiction

(1)   It is immaterial for the purposes of section 45 or 46 (except to the extent provided by section 46(2)) whether –

(a)   any relevant conduct of a relevant body, or

(b)   any conduct which constitutes part of a relevant UK tax evasion facilitation offence or foreign tax evasion facilitation offence, or

(c)   any conduct which constitutes part of a relevant UK tax evasion offence or foreign tax evasion offence,

takes place in the United Kingdom or elsewhere.

(2)   Proceedings for an offence under section 45 or 46 may be taken in any place in the United Kingdom.

(3)   If by virtue of subsection (2) proceedings for an offence are to be taken in Scotland, they may be taken in such sheriff court district as the Lord Advocate may determine.

(4)   In subsection (3) 'sheriff court district' is to be read in accordance with section 307(1) of the Criminal Procedure (Scotland) Act 1995.

49   Consent to prosecution under section 46

(1)   In this section 'proceedings' means proceedings for an offence under section 46.

(2)   No proceedings may be instituted in England and Wales except by or with the consent of the Director of Public Prosecutions or the Director of the Serious Fraud Office.

(3)   No proceedings may be instituted in Northern Ireland except by or with the consent of the Director of Public Prosecutions for Northern Ireland or the Director of the Serious Fraud Office.

(4)   The Director of Public Prosecutions and the Director of the Serious Fraud Office must each exercise any function of giving consent under subsection (2) or (3) personally unless –

(a)   the Director concerned is unavailable, and

(b)   there is another person designated in writing by the Director concerned acting personally as the person who is authorised to exercise the function when the Director is unavailable.

(5)   In that case the other person may exercise the function but must do so personally.

(6)   No proceedings may be instituted in Northern Ireland by virtue of section 36 of the Justice (Northern Ireland) Act 2002 (delegation of functions of the DPP for Northern Ireland to persons other than the Deputy Director) except with the consent of the Director of Public Prosecutions for Northern Ireland to the institution of the proceedings.

(7)   The Director of Public Prosecutions for Northern Ireland must exercise personally any function of giving consent under subsection (3) or (6) unless the function is exercised personally by the Deputy Director of Public Prosecutions for Northern Ireland by virtue of section 30(4) or (7) of that Act.

50   Offences by partnerships: supplementary

(1)   Proceedings for an offence under section 45 or 46 alleged to have been committed by a partnership must be brought in the name of the partnership (and not in the name of any of the partners).

(2)   For the purposes of such proceedings –

(a)   rules of court relating to the service of documents have effect as if the partnership were a body corporate, and

(b)   the following provisions (which concern procedure in relation to offences by bodies corporate) apply as they apply to a body corporate –

(i)   section 33 of the Criminal Justice Act 1925 and Schedule 3 to the Magistrates' Courts Act 1980, and

(ii)   section 18 of the Criminal Justice Act (Northern Ireland) 1945 (c. 15 (N.I.)) and Schedule 4 to the Magistrates' Courts (Northern Ireland) Order 1981 (S.I. 1981/1675 (N.I. 26)).

(3) A fine imposed on a partnership on its conviction for an offence under section 45 or 46 is to be paid out of the partnership assets.

Consequential amendments and interpretation

51 Consequential amendments

(1) In section 61(1) of the Serious Organised Crime and Police Act 2005 (offences to which investigatory powers etc apply) after paragraph (h) insert –

> '(i)   any offence under section 45 or 46 of the Criminal Finances Act 2017 (failure to prevent the facilitation of UK tax evasion offences or foreign tax evasion offences).'

(2) In Schedule 1 to the Serious Crime Act 2007 (serious offences) –

(a)   in Part 1 (serious offences in England and Wales), in the heading before paragraph 8 insert 'etc' at the end and in paragraph 8 at the end insert –
> '(6)   An offence under section 45 or 46 of the Criminal Finances Act 2017 (failure to prevent the facilitation of UK tax evasion offences or foreign tax evasion offences).'

(b)   in Part 1A (serious offences in Scotland) in the heading before paragraph 16G insert 'etc' at the end and in paragraph 16G at the end insert –
> '(5) An offence under section 45 or 46 of the Criminal Finances Act 2017 (failure to prevent the facilitation of UK tax evasion offences or foreign tax evasion offences).'

(c)   in Part 2 (serious offences in Northern Ireland) in the heading before paragraph 24 insert 'etc' at the end and in paragraph 24 at the end insert –
> '(6) An offence under section 45 or 46 of the Criminal Finances Act 2017 (failure to prevent the facilitation of UK tax evasion offences or foreign tax evasion offences).'

(3) In Part 2 of Schedule 17 to the Crime and Courts Act 2013 (offences in relation to which a deferred prosecution agreement may be entered into) after paragraph 26 insert –

> '26A   An offence under section 45 or 46 of the Criminal Finances Act 2017 (failure to prevent the facilitation of UK tax evasion offences or foreign tax evasion offences).'

52 Interpretation of Part 3

(1) In this Part –

'conduct' includes acts and omissions;

'foreign country' means a country or territory outside the United Kingdom;

'foreign tax evasion facilitation offence' has the meaning given by section 46(6);

'foreign tax evasion offence' has the meaning given by section 46(5);

'partnership' has the meaning given by section 44(3);

'relevant body' has the meaning given by section 44(2);

'tax' includes duty and any other form of taxation (however described);

'UK tax evasion facilitation offence' has the meaning given by section 45(5) and (6);

'UK tax evasion offence' has the meaning given by section 45(4).

(2) References in this Part to a person acting in the capacity of a person associated with a relevant body are to be construed in accordance with section 44(4).

PART 4   GENERAL

53 Minor and consequential amendments

Schedule 5 contains minor and consequential amendments.

54   Power to make consequential provision

(1) The Secretary of State may by regulations made by statutory instrument make provision in consequence of any provision made by or under Part 1 or 2.

(2) The Scottish Ministers may by regulations make provision in consequence of section 29 or any provision made by or under Part 1 or 2 that extends only to Scotland.

(3) The Department of Justice in Northern Ireland may by regulations make provision in consequence of any provision made by or under Part 1 or 2 that extends only to Northern Ireland.

(4) Regulations under subsections (1) to (3) may include transitional, transitory or saving provision.

(5) Regulations under subsections (1) to (3) may repeal, revoke or otherwise amend any provision of primary or subordinate legislation (including legislation passed or made on or before the last day of the session in which this Act is passed).

(6) Regulations under subsection (2) or (3) may not include provision of the kind mentioned in subsection (5) unless the provision is within legislative competence.

(7) For this purpose, a provision of regulations is within legislative competence if –

    (a)   in the case of regulations made by the Scottish Ministers, it would fall within the legislative competence of the Scottish Parliament if included in an Act of that Parliament;

    (b)   in the case of regulations made by the Department of Justice in Northern Ireland, it deals with a transferred matter.

(8) In this section and in section 55 –

    'primary legislation' means –

    (a)   an Act;

    (b)   an Act of the Scottish Parliament;

    (c)   a Measure or Act of the National Assembly for Wales;

    (d)   Northern Ireland legislation;

    'subordinate legislation' means –

    (a)   subordinate legislation within the meaning of the Interpretation Act 1978;

    (b)   an instrument made under an Act of the Scottish Parliament;

    (c)   an instrument made under a Measure or Act of the National Assembly for Wales;

    (d)   an instrument made under Northern Ireland legislation;

    'transferred matter' has the meaning given by section 4(1) of the Northern Ireland Act 1998.

55   Section 54: procedural requirements

(1) Before making regulations under section 54(1) the Secretary of State must –

    (a)   if the regulations contain provision that would fall within the legislative competence of the Scottish Parliament if included in an Act of that Parliament, consult the Scottish Ministers;

    (b)   if the regulations contain provision that deals with a transferred matter, consult the Department of Justice in Northern Ireland;

    (c)   if the regulations contain provision that would fall within the legislative competence of the National Assembly for Wales if included in an Act of that Assembly, consult the Welsh Ministers.

(2) Before making regulations under section 54(2) the Scottish Ministers must consult the Secretary of State.

(3) Before making regulations under section 54(3) the Department of Justice in Northern Ireland must consult the Secretary of State.

(4) A statutory instrument containing (whether alone or with other provision) regulations

under section 54 made by the Secretary of State that repeal, revoke or otherwise amend any provision of primary legislation is not to be made unless a draft of the instrument has been laid before, and approved by a resolution of, each House of Parliament.

(5) Any other statutory instrument containing regulations under that section made by the Secretary of State is subject to annulment in pursuance of a resolution of either House of Parliament.

(6) Regulations under section 54 made by the Scottish Ministers that repeal, revoke or otherwise amend any provision of primary legislation are subject to the affirmative procedure (see Part 2 of the Interpretation and Legislative Reform (Scotland) Act 2010 (asp 10)).

(7) Any other regulations under that section made by the Scottish Ministers are subject to the negative procedure (see Part 2 of that Act).

(8) Regulations under section 54 made by the Department of Justice in Northern Ireland that repeal, revoke or otherwise amend any provision of primary legislation are not to be made unless a draft of the instrument has been laid before, and approved by a resolution of, the Northern Ireland Assembly.

(9) Any other regulations under that section made by the Department of Justice in Northern Ireland are subject to negative resolution (within the meaning of section 41(6) of the Interpretation Act (Northern Ireland) 1954).

(10) A power of the Department of Justice in Northern Ireland to make regulations under section 54 is exercisable by statutory rule for the purposes of the Statutory Rules (Northern Ireland) Order 1979 (S.I. 1979/1573 (N.I. 12)).

56   Financial provision

The following are to be paid out of money provided by Parliament –

(a) any expenditure incurred under or by virtue of this Act by a Minister of the Crown or a government department, and

(b) any increases attributable to this Act in the sums payable under any other Act out of money so provided.

57   Extent

(1) Except as provided by subsections (2) to (6), this Act extends to England and Wales, Scotland and Northern Ireland.

(2) The following provisions extend to England and Wales only –

    (a)   section 17, so far as relating to paragraphs 3 to 6 of Schedule 1, and those paragraphs;

    (b)   section 26;

    (c)   section 31(2);

    (d)   section 32(2) and (3);

    (e)   section 34(2) and (11);

    (f)   section 51(3).

(3) The following provisions extend to England and Wales and Northern Ireland only –

    (a)   sections 1 to 3;

    (b)   section 7;

    (c)   section 17, so far as relating to paragraphs 24 and 25 of Schedule 1, and those paragraphs;

    (d)   section 18(4)(c);

    (e)   section 19(3);

    (f)   section 20(3) to (6);

    (g)   section 22;

    (h)   section 23;

    (i)   paragraph 3 of Schedule 2;

    (j)   section 41(3);

    (k)   section 42.

(4) The following provisions extend to Scotland only –

    (a)   sections 4 to 6;

    (b)   section 8;

    (c)   section 18(2), (3) and (4)(d);

    (d)   section 28;

    (e)   section 30;

    (f)   section 32(4);

    (g)   section 34(3);

    (h)   paragraph 4 of Schedule 2.

(5) The following provisions extend to Northern Ireland only –

    (a)   section 17, so far as relating to paragraphs 7 to 10 of Schedule 1, and those paragraphs;

    (b)   section 27;

    (c)   section 31(3);

    (d)   section 32(5) and (6);

    (e)   section 34(4).

(6) An amendment made by Schedule 5 has the same extent as the provision amended.

58 Commencement

(1) Except as provided by subsections (2) to (6), this Act comes into force on whatever day or days the Secretary of State appoints by regulations made by statutory instrument.

(2) The following provisions come into force on whatever day or days the Scottish Ministers appoint by regulations after consulting the Secretary of State –

    (a)   section 28;

    (b)   section 30;

    (c)   section 32(4);

    (d)   section 34(3).

(3) The following provisions come into force on whatever day or days the Department of Justice in Northern Ireland appoints by regulations after consulting the Secretary of State –

    (a)   section 27;

    (b)   section 31(3);

    (c)   section 32(5) and (6);

    (d)   section 34(4).

(4) The following provisions come into force two months after the day on which this Act is passed –

    (a)   section 9;

    (b)   section 18;

    (c)   section 41;

    (d)   section 42.

(5) Part 3 comes into force on whatever day or days the Treasury appoints by regulations made by statutory instrument.

(6) The following provisions come into force on the day on which this Act is passed –

    (a)   sections 54 to 57;

    (b)   this section;

    (c)   section 59;

    (d)   any other provision of this Act so far as necessary for enabling the exercise on or after the day on which this Act is passed of any power to make provision by subordinate legislation (within the meaning of the Interpretation Act 1978).

(7) Regulations under subsection (1), (2), (3) or (5) may appoint different days for different purposes or areas.

(8) The Secretary of State may by regulations made by statutory instrument make transitional, transitory or saving provision in connection with the coming into force of any provision of this Act other than –

(a)   the provisions mentioned in subsections (2) and (3), and
(b)   Part 3.

(9) The Scottish Ministers may by regulations make transitional, transitory or saving provision in connection with the coming into force of a provision mentioned in subsection (2).

(10) The Department of Justice in Northern Ireland may by regulations make transitional, transitory or saving provision in connection with the coming into force of a provision mentioned in subsection (3).

(11) The Treasury may by regulations made by statutory instrument make transitional, transitory or saving provision in connection with the coming into force of Part 3.

(12) No regulations may be made under subsection (1) bringing into force any of the following provisions, so far as they extend to Scotland, unless the Secretary of State has consulted the Scottish Ministers –

(a)   sections 4 and 5;
(b)   section 8;
(c)   section 14;
(d)   section 15;
(e)   section 16;
(f)   section 25;
(g)   section 29;
(h)   section 33;
(i)   section 34(10).

(13) No regulations may be made under subsection (1) bringing into force any of the following provisions, so far as they extend to Northern Ireland, unless the Secretary of State has consulted the Department of Justice in Northern Ireland –

(a)   sections 1 and 2;
(b)   section 7;
(c)   section 14;
(d)   section 15;
(e)   section 16;
(f)   section 17 and Schedule 1;
(g)   sections 19 and 20;
(h)   sections 22 to 25;
(i)   section 33;
(j)   section 34(10).

(14) Consultation for the purposes of this section may be, or include, consultation before the day on which this Act is passed.

(15) The power to make regulations under subsections (8) to (11) includes power to make different provision for different purposes.

(16) The power of the Department of Justice in Northern Ireland to make regulations under subsection (3) or (10) is exercisable by statutory rule for the purposes of the Statutory Rules (Northern Ireland) Order 1979 (S.I. 1979/1573 (N.I. 12)).

59   Short title

This Act may be cited as the Criminal Finances Act 2017.

SCHEDULES

SCHEDULE 2   DISCLOSURE ORDERS

(Section 35)

1   The Terrorism Act 2000 is amended as follows.
2   After section 37 insert –

'**37A   Disclosure orders in relation to terrorist financing investigations**

Schedule 5A (terrorist financing investigations: disclosure orders) has effect.'

3   After Schedule 5 insert –

'**Schedule 5A   Terrorist financing investigations: disclosure orders**

Part 1   England and Wales and Northen Ireland

Interpretation

1   This paragraph applies for the purposes of this Part of this Schedule.
2   A disclosure order is an order made under paragraph 9.
3   A judge is –

    (a)   in England and Wales, a judge entitled to exercise the jurisdiction of the Crown Court;
    (b)   in Northern Ireland, a Crown Court judge.

4   A terrorist financing investigation is a terrorist investigation into –

    (a)   the commission, preparation or instigation of an offence under any of sections 15 to 18, or
    (b)   the identification of terrorist property or its movement or use.

5   An appropriate officer is –

    (a)   a constable, or
    (b)   a counter-terrorism financial investigator.

6   A senior police officer is a police officer of at least the rank of superintendent.
7   "Document" means anything in which information of any description is recorded.
8   "Excluded material" –

    (a)   in relation to England and Wales, has the same meaning as in the Police and Criminal Evidence Act 1984;
    (b)   in relation to Northern Ireland, has the same meaning as in the Police and Criminal Evidence (Northern Ireland) Order 1989 (S.I. 1989/1341 (N.I. 12)).

Disclosure orders

9   (1)   A judge may, on the application of an appropriate officer, make a disclosure order if satisfied that each of the requirements for the making of the order is fulfilled.
    (2)   The application must state that a person or property specified in the application is subject to a terrorist financing investigation and the order is sought for the purposes of the investigation.
    (3)   A disclosure order is an order authorising an appropriate officer to give to any person the officer considers has relevant information

notice in writing requiring the person to do any or all of the following with respect to any matter relevant to the terrorist financing investigation concerned –

(a)   answer questions, either at a time specified in the notice or at once, at a place so specified;

(b)   provide information specified in the notice, by a time and in a manner so specified;

(c)   produce documents, or documents of a description, specified in the notice, either at or by a time so specified or at once, and in a manner so specified.

(4)   Relevant information is information (whether or not contained in a document) which the appropriate officer concerned considers to be relevant to the investigation.

(5)   A person is not bound to comply with a requirement imposed by a notice given under a disclosure order unless evidence of authority to give the notice is produced.

(6)   An appropriate officer may not make an application under this paragraph unless the officer is a senior police officer or is authorised to do so by a senior police officer.

Requirements for making of disclosure order

10   (1)   These are the requirements for the making of a disclosure order.

(2)   There must be reasonable grounds for suspecting that a person has committed an offence under any of sections 15 to 18 or that the property specified in the application is terrorist property.

(3)   There must be reasonable grounds for believing that information which may be provided in compliance with a requirement imposed under the order is likely to be of substantial value (whether or not by itself) to the terrorist financing investigation concerned.

(4)   There must be reasonable grounds for believing that it is in the public interest for the information to be provided, having regard to the benefit likely to accrue to the investigation if the information is obtained.

Offences

11   (1)   A person commits an offence if without reasonable excuse the person fails to comply with a requirement imposed under a disclosure order.

(2)   A person guilty of an offence under sub-paragraph (1) is liable –

(a)   on summary conviction in England and Wales, to imprisonment for a term not exceeding 51 weeks, or to a fine, or to both;

(b)   on summary conviction in Northern Ireland, to imprisonment for a term not exceeding 6 months, or to a fine not exceeding level 5 on the standard scale, or to both.

(3)   A person commits an offence if, in purported compliance with a requirement imposed under a disclosure order, the person –

(a)   makes a statement which the person knows to be false or misleading in a material particular, or

(b)   recklessly makes a statement which is false or misleading in a material particular.

(4)   A person guilty of an offence under sub-paragraph (3) is liable –

       (a)   on conviction on indictment, to imprisonment for a term not exceeding 2 years, or to a fine, or to both;

       (b)   on summary conviction in England and Wales, to imprisonment for a term not exceeding 12 months, or to a fine, or to both;

       (c)   on summary conviction in Northern Ireland, to imprisonment for a term not exceeding 6 months, or to a fine not exceeding the statutory maximum, or to both.

(5)   In relation to an offence committed before the coming into force of section 281(5) of the Criminal Justice Act 2003 (alteration of penalties for certain summary offences), the reference in sub-paragraph (2)(a) to 51 weeks is to be read as a reference to 6 months.

(6)   In relation to an offence committed before the coming into force of section 282 of the Criminal Justice Act 2003 (increase in maximum sentence on summary conviction of offence triable either way), the reference in sub-paragraph (4)(b) to 12 months is to be read as a reference to 6 months.

Statements

12   (1)   A statement made by a person in response to a requirement imposed under a disclosure order may not be used in evidence against that person in criminal proceedings.

    (2)   Sub-paragraph (1) does not apply –

       (a)   in the case of proceedings under this Part of this Act (including paragraph 11(1) or (3)),

       (b)   on a prosecution for an offence under section 5 of the Perjury Act 1911 or Article 10 of the Perjury (Northern Ireland) Order 1979 (S.I. 1979/1714 (N.I. 19)) (false statements), or

       (c)   on a prosecution for some other offence where, in giving evidence, the person makes a statement inconsistent with the statement mentioned in sub-paragraph (1).

    (3)   A statement may not be used by virtue of sub-paragraph (2)(c) against a person unless –

       (a)   evidence relating to it is adduced, or

       (b)   a question relating to it is asked,

by or on behalf of the person in the proceedings arising out of the prosecution.

Further provisions

13   (1)   A disclosure order does not confer the right to require a person –

       (a)   to answer any privileged question,

       (b)   to provide any privileged information, or

       (c)   to produce any privileged document or other material,

except that a lawyer may be required to provide the name and address of a client.

    (2)   For the purposes of sub-paragraph (1) –

       (a)   a privileged question is a question which the person would be entitled to refuse to answer on grounds of legal professional privilege in proceedings in the High Court;

       (b)   privileged information is any information which the person would be entitled to refuse to provide on grounds of legal professional privilege in proceedings in the High Court;

(c)   a privileged document or other material is any document or material which the person would be entitled to refuse to produce on grounds of legal professional privilege in proceedings in the High Court.

(3)   A disclosure order does not confer the right to require a person to produce excluded material.

(4)   A disclosure order has effect in spite of any restriction on the disclosure of information (however imposed).

(5)   An appropriate officer may take copies of any documents produced in compliance with a requirement to produce them imposed under a disclosure order.

(6)   The documents may be retained for so long as it is necessary to retain them (as opposed to a copy of them) in connection with the terrorist financing investigation for the purposes of which the order was made.

(7)   But if an appropriate officer has reasonable grounds for believing that –

(a)   the documents may need to be produced for the purposes of any legal proceedings, and

(b)   they might otherwise be unavailable for those purposes,

they may be retained until the proceedings are concluded.

(8)   An appropriate officer may retain documents under sub-paragraph (7) only if the officer is a senior police officer or is authorised to do so by a senior police officer.

Supplementary

14   (1)   An application for a disclosure order may be made without notice to a judge in chambers.

(2)   Rules of court may make provision as to the practice and procedure to be followed in connection with proceedings relating to disclosure orders.

(3)   An application to discharge or vary a disclosure order may be made to the Crown Court by –

(a)   the person who applied for the order;

(b)   any person affected by the order.

(4)   The Crown Court may –

(a)   discharge the order;

(b)   vary the order.

(5)   An application to discharge or vary a disclosure order need not be made by the same appropriate officer that applied for the order.

(6)   References to a person who applied for a disclosure order are to be construed accordingly.

(7)   An appropriate officer may not make an application to discharge or vary a disclosure order unless the officer is a senior police officer or is authorised to do so by a senior police officer.'

4   . . .

SCHEDULE 3   FORFEITURE OF CERTAIN PERSONAL (OR MOVEABLE) PROPERTY

(Section 39)

1   Schedule 1 to the Anti-terrorism, Crime and Security Act 2001 (forfeiture of terrorist cash) is amended as follows.

2   After paragraph 10 insert –

'**Part 4A   Forfeiture of terrorist assets**

Definition of "listed asset"

10A   (1)   In this Part of this Schedule, a "listed asset" means an item of property that falls within one of the following descriptions of property –

(a)   precious metals;
(b)   precious stones;
(c)   watches;
(d)   artistic works;
(e)   face-value vouchers;
(f)   postage stamps.

(2)   The Secretary of State may by regulations made by statutory instrument amend sub-paragraph (1) –

(a)   by removing a description of property;
(b)   by adding a description of tangible personal (or corporeal moveable) property.

(3)   A statutory instrument containing regulations under sub-paragraph (2) may not be made unless a draft of the instrument has been laid before and approved by a resolution of each House of Parliament.

(4)   In this paragraph –

(a)   "precious metal" means gold, silver or platinum (whether in an unmanufactured or a manufactured state);
(b)   "artistic work" means a piece of work falling within section 4(1)(a) of the Copyright, Designs and Patents Act 1988;
(c)   "face-value voucher" means a voucher in physical form that represents a right to receive goods or services to the value of an amount stated on it.

Seizure of listed assets

10B   (1)   An authorised officer may seize any item of property if the authorised officer has reasonable grounds for suspecting that –

(a)   it is a listed asset, and
(b)   it is within subsection (1)(a) or (b) of section 1 or it is property earmarked as terrorist property.

(2)   An authorised officer may also seize any item of property if –

(a)   the authorised officer has reasonable grounds for suspecting the item to be a listed asset,
(b)   the authorised officer has reasonable grounds for suspecting that part of the item is within subsection (1)(a) or (b) of section 1 or is property earmarked as terrorist property, and
(c)   it is not reasonably practicable to seize only that part.

Initial detention of seized property

10C   (1)   Property seized under paragraph 10B may be detained for an initial period of 48 hours.

(2)   Sub-paragraph (1) authorises the detention of property only for so long as an authorised officer continues to have reasonable grounds for suspicion in relation to that property as described in paragraph 10B(1) or (2) (as the case may be).

(3)   In calculating a period of hours for the purposes of this paragraph, no account shall be taken of –

(a)   any Saturday or Sunday,
(b)   Christmas Day,
(c)   Good Friday,
(d)   any day that is a bank holiday under the Banking and Financial Dealings Act 1971 in the part of the United Kingdom within which the property is seized, or
(e)   any day prescribed under section 8(2) of the Criminal Procedure (Scotland) Act 1995 as a court holiday in a sheriff court in the sheriff court district within which the property is seized.

Further detention of seized property

10D   (1)   The period for which property seized under paragraph 10B, or any part of that property, may be detained may be extended by an order made –

(a)   in England and Wales or Northern Ireland, by a magistrates' court;
(b)   in Scotland, by the sheriff.

(2)   An order under sub-paragraph (1) may not authorise the detention of any property –

(a)   beyond the end of the period of 6 months beginning with the date of the order, and
(b)   in the case of any further order under this paragraph, beyond the end of the period of 2 years beginning with the date of the first order.

(3)   A justice of the peace may also exercise the power of a magistrates' court to make the first order under sub-paragraph (1) extending a particular period of detention.

(4)   An application to a magistrates' court, a justice of the peace or the sheriff to make the first order under sub-paragraph (1) extending a particular period of detention –

(a)   may be made and heard without notice of the application or hearing having been given to any of the persons affected by the application or to the legal representatives of such a person, and
(b)   may be heard and determined in private in the absence of persons so affected and of their legal representatives.

(5)   An application for an order under sub-paragraph (1) may be made –

(a)   in relation to England and Wales and Northern Ireland, by the Commissioners for Her Majesty's Revenue and Customs or an authorised officer;
(b)   in relation to Scotland, by a procurator fiscal.

(6)   The court, sheriff or justice may make the order if satisfied, in relation to the item of property to be further detained, that –

(a)   it is a listed asset, and
(b)   condition 1, condition 2 or condition 3 is met.

(7)   Condition 1 is that there are reasonable grounds for suspecting that the property is intended to be used for the purposes of terrorism and that either –

(a)   its continued detention is justified while its intended use is further investigated or consideration is given to bringing (in the United Kingdom or elsewhere) proceedings against any person for an offence with which the property is connected, or
(b)   proceedings against any person for an offence with which the property is connected have been started and have not been concluded.

(8)   Condition 2 is that there are reasonable grounds for suspecting that the property consists of resources of an organisation which is a proscribed organisation and that either –

(a)   its continued detention is justified while investigation is made into whether or not it consists of such resources or consideration is given to bringing (in the United Kingdom or elsewhere) proceedings against any person for an offence with which the property is connected, or
(b)   proceedings against any person for an offence with which the property is connected have been started and have not been concluded.

(9)   Condition 3 is that there are reasonable grounds for suspecting that the property is property earmarked as terrorist property and that either –

(a)   its continued detention is justified while its derivation is further investigated or consideration is given to bringing (in the United Kingdom or elsewhere) proceedings against any person for an offence with which the property is connected, or
(b)   proceedings against any person for an offence with which the property is connected have been started and have not been concluded.

(10)   Where an application for an order under sub-paragraph (1) relates to an item of property seized under paragraph 10B(2), the court, sheriff or justice may make the order if satisfied that –

(11)   An order under sub-paragraph (1) must provide for notice to be given to persons affected by it.

Testing and safekeeping of property seized under paragraph 10B

10E   (1)   An authorised officer may carry out (or arrange for the carrying out of) tests on any item of property seized under paragraph 10B for the purpose of establishing whether it is a listed asset.

(2)   An authorised officer must arrange for any item of property seized under paragraph 10B to be safely stored throughout the period during which it is detained under this Part of this Schedule.

Release of detained property

10F   (1)   This paragraph applies while any property is detained under this Part of this Schedule.

       (2)   A magistrates' court or (in Scotland) the sheriff may direct the release of the whole or any part of the property if satisfied, on an application by the person from whom the property was seized, that the conditions in paragraph 10C or 10D (as the case may be) for the detention of the property are no longer met in relation to the property to be released.

       (3)   An authorised officer or (in Scotland) a procurator fiscal may, after notifying the magistrates' court, sheriff or justice under whose order property is being detained, release the whole or any part of it if satisfied that the detention of the property to be released is no longer justified.

       (4)   But property is not to be released under this paragraph –

              (a)   if an application for its release under paragraph 10O is made, until any proceedings in pursuance of the application (including any proceedings on appeal) are concluded;

              (b)   if (in the United Kingdom or elsewhere) proceedings are started against any person for an offence with which the property is connected, until the proceedings are concluded.

              See also paragraph 10G(7).

Forfeiture

10G   (1)   While property is detained under this Part of this Schedule, an application for the forfeiture of the whole or any part of it may be made –

              (a)   to a magistrates' court, by the Commissioners for Her Majesty's Revenue and Customs or an authorised officer;

              (b)   to the sheriff, by the Scottish Ministers.

       (2)   The court or sheriff may order the forfeiture of the property or any part of it if satisfied that –

              (a)   the property is a listed asset, and

              (b)   what is to be forfeited is within subsection (1)(a) or (b) of section 1 or is property earmarked as terrorist property.

       (3)   An order under sub-paragraph (2) made by a magistrates' court may provide for payment under paragraph 10N of reasonable legal expenses that a person has reasonably incurred, or may reasonably incur, in respect of –

              (a)   the proceedings in which the order is made, or

              (b)   any related proceedings under this Part of this Schedule.

       (4)   A sum in respect of a relevant item of expenditure is not payable under paragraph 10N in pursuance of provision under sub-paragraph (3) unless –

              (a)   the person who applied for the order under sub-paragraph (2) agrees to its payment, or

              (b)   the court has assessed the amount allowed in respect of that item and the sum is paid in respect of the assessed amount.

       (5)   For the purposes of sub-paragraph (4) –

(a)   a "relevant item of expenditure" is an item of expenditure to which regulations under section 286B of the Proceeds of Crime Act 2002 would apply if the order under sub-paragraph (2) had instead been a recovery order made under section 266 of that Act;

(b)   an amount is "allowed" in respect of a relevant item of expenditure if it would have been allowed by those regulations;

(c)   if the person who applied for the order under sub-paragraph (2) was an authorised officer, that person may not agree to the payment of a sum unless the person is a senior officer or is authorised to do so by a senior officer.

(6)   Sub-paragraph (2) ceases to apply on the transfer of an application made under this paragraph in accordance with paragraph 10J(1)(a) or (b).

(7)   Where an application for the forfeiture of any property is made under this paragraph, the property is to be detained (and may not be released under any power conferred by this Part of this Schedule) until any proceedings in pursuance of the application (including any proceedings on appeal) are concluded.

(8)   Where the property to which the application relates is being detained under this Part of this Schedule as part of an item of property, having been seized under paragraph 10B(2), sub-paragraph (7) is to be read as if it required the continued detention of the whole of the item of property.

(9)   For the purposes of sub-paragraph (5)(c), a "senior officer" means –

(a)   in relation to an application made by a constable or a counter-terrorism financial investigator, a senior police officer;

(b)   in relation to an application made by an officer of Revenue and Customs, such an officer of a rank designated by the Commissioners for Her Majesty's Revenue and Customs as equivalent to that of a senior police officer;

(c)   in relation to an application made by an immigration officer, such an officer of a rank designated by the Secretary of State as equivalent to that of a senior police officer.

(10)   In sub-paragraph (9), a "senior police officer" means a police officer of at least the rank of superintendent.

Associated and joint property

10H   (1)   Paragraphs 10I and 10J apply if –

(a)   an application is made under paragraph 10G in respect of property detained under this Part of this Schedule,

(b)   the court or sheriff is satisfied that the property is a listed asset,

(c)   the court or sheriff is satisfied that all or part of the property is within subsection (1)(a) or (b) of section 1 or is property earmarked as terrorist property, and

(d)   there exists property that is associated with the property in relation to which the court or sheriff is satisfied as mentioned in paragraph (c).

(2)   Paragraphs 10I and 10J also apply in England and Wales and Northern Ireland if –

(a)   an application is made under paragraph 10G in respect of property detained under this Part of this Schedule,

(b)   the court is satisfied that the property is a listed asset,

(c)   the court is satisfied that all or part of the property is property earmarked as terrorist property, and

(d)   the property in relation to which the court or sheriff is satisfied as mentioned in paragraph (c) belongs to joint tenants and one of the tenants is an excepted joint owner.

(3)   In this paragraph and paragraphs 10I and 10J "associated property" means property of any of the following descriptions that is not itself the forfeitable property –

(a)   any interest in the forfeitable property;

(b)   any other interest in the property in which the forfeitable property subsists;

(c)   if the forfeitable property is a tenancy in common, the tenancy of the other tenant;

(d)   if (in Scotland) the forfeitable property is owned in common, the interest of the other owner;

(e)   if the forfeitable property is part of a larger property, but not a separate part, the remainder of that property.

References to property being associated with forfeitable property are to be read accordingly.

(4)   In this paragraph and paragraphs 10I and 10J the "forfeitable property" means the property in relation to which the court or sheriff is satisfied as mentioned in sub-paragraph (1)(c) or (2)(c) (as the case may be).

(5)   For the purposes of this paragraph and paragraphs 10I and 10J –

(a)   an excepted joint owner is a joint tenant who obtained the property in circumstances in which it would not (as against him or her) be earmarked, and

(b)   references to the excepted joint owner's share of property are to so much of the property as would have been his or hers if the joint tenancy had been severed.

Agreements about associated and joint property

10I   (1)   Where –

(a)   this paragraph applies, and

(b)   the person who applied for the order under paragraph 10G (on the one hand) and the person who holds the associated property or who is the excepted joint owner (on the other hand) agree,

the magistrates' court or sheriff may, instead of making an order under paragraph 10G(2), make an order requiring the person who holds the associated property or who is the excepted joint owner to make a payment to a person identified in the order.

(2)   The amount of the payment is (subject to sub-paragraph (3)) to be the amount which the persons referred to in sub-paragraph (1)(b) agree represents –

(a)   in a case where this paragraph applies by virtue of paragraph 10H(1), the value of the forfeitable property;

(b)   in a case where this paragraph applies by virtue of paragraph

10H(2), the value of the forfeitable property less the value of the excepted joint owner's share.

(3)   The amount of the payment may be reduced if the person who applied for the order under paragraph 10G agrees that the other party to the agreement has suffered loss as a result of the seizure of the forfeitable property and any associated property under paragraph 10B and its subsequent detention.

(4)   The reduction that is permissible by virtue of sub-paragraph (3) is such amount as the parties to the agreement agree is reasonable, having regard to the loss suffered and any other relevant circumstances.

(5)   An order under sub-paragraph (1) may, so far as required for giving effect to the agreement, include provision for vesting, creating or extinguishing any interest in property.

(6)   An order under sub-paragraph (1) made by a magistrates' court may provide for payment under sub-paragraph (11) of reasonable legal expenses that a person has reasonably incurred, or may reasonably incur, in respect of –

(a)   the proceedings in which the order is made, or
(b)   any related proceedings under this Part of this Schedule.

(7)   A sum in respect of a relevant item of expenditure is not payable under sub-paragraph (11) in pursuance of provision under sub-paragraph (6) unless –

(a)   the person who applied for the order under paragraph 10G agrees to its payment, or
(b)   the court has assessed the amount allowed in respect of that item and the sum is paid in respect of the assessed amount.

(8)   For the purposes of sub-paragraph (7) –

(a)   a "relevant item of expenditure" is an item of expenditure to which regulations under section 286B of the Proceeds of Crime Act 2002 would apply if the order under sub-paragraph (1) had instead been a recovery order made under section 266 of that Act;
(b)   an amount is "allowed" in respect of a relevant item of expenditure if it would have been allowed by those regulations.

(9)   If there is more than one item of associated property or more than one excepted joint owner, the total amount to be paid under sub-paragraph (1), and the part of that amount which is to be provided by each person who holds any such associated property or who is an excepted joint owner, is to be agreed between both (or all) of them and the person who applied for the order under paragraph 10G.

(10)   If the person who applied for the order under paragraph 10G was an authorised officer, that person may enter into an agreement for the purposes of any provision of this paragraph only if the person is a senior officer or is authorised to do so by a senior officer.

"Senior officer" has the same meaning in this sub-paragraph as it has in paragraph 10G(5)(c).

(11)   An amount received under an order under sub-paragraph (1) must be applied as follows –

(a)   first, it must be applied in making any payment of legal expenses which, after giving effect to sub-paragraph (7), are payable under this sub-paragraph in pursuance of provision under sub-paragraph (6);

(b)   second, it must be applied in payment or reimbursement of any reasonable costs incurred in storing or insuring the forfeitable property and any associated property whilst detained under this Part of this Schedule;

(c)   third, it must be paid –

(i)   if the order was made by a magistrates' court, into the Consolidated Fund;

(ii)   if the order was made by the sheriff, into the Scottish Consolidated Fund.

Associated and joint property: default of agreement

10J   (1)   Where this paragraph applies and there is no agreement under paragraph 10I, the magistrates' court or sheriff –

(a)   must transfer the application made under paragraph 10G to the relevant court if satisfied that the value of the forfeitable property and any associated property is £10,000 or more;

(b)   may transfer the application made under paragraph 10G to the relevant court if satisfied that the value of the forfeitable property and any associated property is less than £10,000.

(2)   The "relevant court" is –

(a)   the High Court, where the application under paragraph 10G was made to a magistrates' court;

(b)   the Court of Session, where the application under paragraph 10G was made to the sheriff.

(3)   Where (under sub-paragraph (1)(a) or (b)) an application made under paragraph 10G is transferred to the relevant court, the relevant court may order the forfeiture of the property to which the application relates, or any part of that property, if satisfied that –

(a)   the property is a listed asset, and

(b)   what is to be forfeited is within subsection (1)(a) or (b) of section 1 or is property earmarked as terrorist property.

(4)   An order under sub-paragraph (3) made by the High Court may include provision of the type that may be included in an order under paragraph 10G(2) made by a magistrates' court by virtue of paragraph 10G(3).

(5)   If provision is included in an order of the High Court by virtue of sub-paragraph (4) of this paragraph, paragraph 10G(4) and (5) apply with the necessary modifications.

(6)   The relevant court may, as well as making an order under sub-paragraph (3), make an order –

(a)   providing for the forfeiture of the associated property or (as the case may be) for the excepted joint owner's interest to be extinguished, or

(b)   providing for the excepted joint owner's interest to be severed.

(7)   Where (under sub-paragraph (1)(b)) the magistrates' court or sheriff decides not to transfer an application made under paragraph 10G to

the relevant court, the magistrates' court or sheriff may, as well as making an order under paragraph 10G(2), make an order –

(a) providing for the forfeiture of the associated property or (as the case may be) for the excepted joint owner's interest to be extinguished, or

(b) providing for the excepted joint owner's interest to be severed.

(8) An order under sub-paragraph (6) or (7) may be made only if the relevant court, the magistrates' court or the sheriff (as the case may be) thinks it just and equitable to do so.

(9) An order under sub-paragraph (6) or (7) must provide for the payment of an amount to the person who holds the associated property or who is an excepted joint owner.

(10) In making an order under sub-paragraph (6) or (7), and including provision in it by virtue of sub-paragraph (9), the relevant court, the magistrates' court or the sheriff (as the case may be) must have regard to –

(a) the rights of any person who holds the associated property or who is an excepted joint owner and the value to that person of that property or (as the case may) of that person's share (including any value that cannot be assessed in terms of money), and

(b) the interest of the person who applied for the order under paragraph 10G in realising the value of the forfeitable property.

(11) If the relevant court, the magistrates' court or the sheriff (as the case may be) is satisfied that –

(a) the person who holds the associated property or who is an excepted joint owner has suffered loss as a result of the seizure of the forfeitable property and any associated property under paragraph 10B and its subsequent detention, and

(b) the circumstances are exceptional,

an order under sub-paragraph (6) or (7) may require the payment of compensation to that person.

(12) The amount of compensation to be paid by virtue of sub-paragraph (11) is the amount the relevant court, the magistrates' court or the sheriff (as the case may be) thinks reasonable, having regard to the loss suffered and any other relevant circumstances.

(13) Compensation to be paid by virtue of sub-paragraph (11) is to be paid in the same way that compensation is to be paid under paragraph 10P.

Paragraphs 10G to 10J: appeals

10K (1) Any party to proceedings for an order for the forfeiture of property under paragraph 10G may appeal against –

(a) the making of an order under paragraph 10G;

(b) the making of an order under paragraph 10J(7);

(c) a decision not to make an order under paragraph 10G unless the reason that no order was made is that an order was instead made under paragraph 10I;

(d) a decision not to make an order under paragraph 10J(7).

Paragraphs (c) and (d) do not apply if the application for the order under paragraph 10G was transferred in accordance with paragraph 10J(1)(a) or (b).

(2)   Where an order under paragraph 10I is made by a magistrates' court, any party to the proceedings for the order (including any party to the proceedings under paragraph 10G that preceded the making of the order) may appeal against a decision to include, or not to include, provision in the order under sub-paragraph (6) of paragraph 10I.

(3)   An appeal under this paragraph lies –

(a)   in relation to England and Wales, to the Crown Court;
(b)   in relation to Scotland, to the Sheriff Appeal Court;
(c)   in relation to Northern Ireland, to a county court.

(4)   An appeal under this paragraph must be made before the end of the period of 30 days starting with the day on which the court makes the order or decision.

(5)   Sub-paragraph (4) is subject to paragraph 10L.

(6)   The court hearing the appeal may make any order it thinks appropriate.

(7)   If the court upholds an appeal against an order forfeiting property, it may order the release of the whole or any part of the property.

Extended time for appealing in certain cases where deproscription order made

10L   (1)   This paragraph applies where –

(a)   a successful application for an order under paragraph 10G relies (wholly or partly) on the fact that an organisation is proscribed,
(b)   an application under section 4 of the Terrorism Act 2000 for a deproscription order in respect of the organisation is refused by the Secretary of State,
(c)   the property forfeited by the order under paragraph 10G was seized under this Part of this Schedule on or after the date of the refusal of that application,
(d)   an appeal against that refusal is allowed under section 5 of the Terrorism Act 2000,
(e)   a deproscription order is made accordingly, and
(f)   if the order is made in reliance on section 123(5) of the Terrorism Act 2000, a resolution is passed by each House of Parliament under section 123(5)(b) of that Act.

(2)   Where this paragraph applies, an appeal under paragraph 10K against the making of an order under paragraph 10G, and against the making (in addition) of any order under paragraph 10J(7), may be brought at any time before the end of the period of 30 days beginning with the date on which the deproscription order comes into force.

(3)   In this paragraph a "deproscription order" means an order under section 3(3)(b) or (8) of the Terrorism Act 2000.

Realisation of forfeited property

10M   (1)   If property is forfeited under paragraph 10G or 10J, an authorised officer must realise the property or make arrangements for its realisation.

(2)   But the property is not to be realised –

(a)   before the end of the period within which an appeal may be made (whether under paragraph 10K or otherwise), or

(b)   if an appeal is made within that period, before the appeal is determined or otherwise disposed of.

(3)   The realisation of property under sub-paragraph (1) must be carried out, so far as practicable, in the manner best calculated to maximise the amount obtained for the property.

Proceeds of realisation

10N   (1)   The proceeds of property realised under paragraph 10M must be applied as follows –

(a)   first, they must be applied in making any payment required to be made by virtue of paragraph 10J(9);

(b)   second, they must be applied in making any payment of legal expenses which, after giving effect to paragraph 10G(4) (including as applied by paragraph 10J(5)), are payable under this sub-paragraph in pursuance of provision under paragraph 10G(3) or, as the case may be, 10J(4);

(c)   third, they must be applied in payment or reimbursement of any reasonable costs incurred in storing or insuring the property whilst detained under this Part of this Schedule and in realising the property;

(d)   fourth, they must be paid –

(i)   if the property was forfeited by a magistrates' court or the High Court, into the Consolidated Fund;

(ii)   if the property was forfeited by the sheriff or the Court of Session, into the Scottish Consolidated Fund.

(2)   If what is realised under paragraph 10M represents part only of an item of property seized under paragraph 10B and detained under this Part of this Schedule, the reference in sub-paragraph (1)(c) to costs incurred in storing or insuring the property is to be read as a reference to costs incurred in storing or insuring the whole of the item of property.

Victims

10O   (1)   A person who claims that any property detained under this Part of this Schedule, or any part of it, belongs to him or her may apply for the property or part to be released.

(2)   An application under sub-paragraph (1) is to be made –

(a)   in England and Wales or Northern Ireland, to a magistrates' court;

(b)   in Scotland, to the sheriff.

(3)   The application may be made in the course of proceedings under paragraph 10D or 10G or at any other time.

(4)   The court or sheriff may order the property to which the application relates to be released to the applicant if it appears to the court or sheriff that –

(a)   the applicant was deprived of the property to which the application relates, or of property which it represents, by criminal conduct,

(b)   the property the applicant was deprived of was not, immediately before the applicant was deprived of it, property obtained by or in return for criminal conduct and nor did it then represent such property, and

(c)   the property belongs to the applicant.

(5)   If sub-paragraph (6) applies, the court or sheriff may order the property to which the application relates to be released to the applicant or to the person from whom it was seized.

(6)   This sub-paragraph applies where –

(a)   the applicant is not the person from whom the property to which the application relates was seized,

(b)   it appears to the court or sheriff that the property belongs to the applicant,

(c)   the court or sheriff is satisfied that the release condition is met in relation to the property, and

(d)   no objection to the making of an order under sub-paragraph (5) has been made by the person from whom the property was seized.

(7)   The release condition is met –

(a)   in relation to property detained under paragraph 10C or 10D, if the conditions in paragraph 10C or (as the case may be) 10D for the detention of the property are no longer met, and

(b)   in relation to property detained under paragraph 10G, if the court or sheriff decides not to make an order under that paragraph in relation to the property.

Compensation

10P   (1)   If no order under paragraph 10G, 10I or 10J is made in respect of any property detained under this Part of this Schedule, the person to whom the property belongs or from whom it was seized may make an application for compensation.

(2)   An application under sub-paragraph (1) is to be made –

(a)   in England and Wales or Northern Ireland, to a magistrates' court;

(b)   in Scotland, to the sheriff.

(3)   If the court or sheriff is satisfied that the applicant has suffered loss as a result of the detention of the property and that the circumstances are exceptional, the court or sheriff may order compensation to be paid to the applicant.

(4)   The amount of compensation to be paid is the amount the court or sheriff thinks reasonable, having regard to the loss suffered and any other relevant circumstances.

(5)   If the property was seized by an officer of Revenue and Customs, the compensation is to be paid by the Commissioners for Her Majesty's Revenue and Customs.

(6)   If the property was seized by a constable, the compensation is to be paid as follows –

(a)   in the case of a constable of a police force in England and Wales, it is to be paid out of the police fund from which the expenses of the police force are met;

(b)   in the case of a constable of the Police Service of Scotland, it is to be paid by the Scottish Police Authority;

(c)   in the case of a police officer within the meaning of the Police (Northern Ireland) Act 2000, it is to be paid out of money provided by the Chief Constable of the Police Service of Northern Ireland.

(7)   If the property was seized by a counter-terrorism financial investigator, the compensation is to be paid as follows –

(a)   in the case of a counter-terrorism financial investigator who was –

(i)   a member of the civilian staff of a police force (including the metropolitan police force), within the meaning of Part 1 of the Police Reform and Social Responsibility Act 2011, or

(ii)   a member of staff of the City of London police force,

it is to be paid out of the police fund from which the expenses of the police force are met;

(b)   in the case of a counter-terrorism financial investigator who was a member of staff of the Police Service of Northern Ireland, it is to be paid out of money provided by the Chief Constable of the Police Service of Northern Ireland.

(8)   If the property was seized by an immigration officer, the compensation is to be paid by the Secretary of State.

(9)   If an order under paragraph 10G, 10I or 10J is made in respect only of a part of any property detained under this Part, this paragraph has effect in relation to the other part.

(10) This paragraph does not apply if the court or sheriff makes an order under paragraph 10O.'

3   In paragraph 19 (general interpretation), in sub-paragraph (1), at the appropriate place insert –

'"listed asset" has the meaning given by paragraph 10A,'

SCHEDULE 4   FORFEITURE OF MONEY HELD IN BANK AND BUILDING SOCIETY ACCOUNTS

(Section 40)

1   Schedule 1 to the Anti-terrorism, Crime and Security Act 2001 (forfeiture of terrorist cash) is amended as follows.

2   After paragraph 10P (inserted by Schedule 3 above) insert –

'Part 4B   Forfeiture of terrorist money held in bank and building society accounts

Application for account freezing order

10Q   (1)   This paragraph applies if an enforcement officer has reasonable grounds for suspecting that money held in an account maintained with a bank or building society –

(a)   is within subsection (1)(a) or (b) of section 1, or

(b)   is property earmarked as terrorist property.

(2)   Where this paragraph applies the enforcement officer may apply to

the relevant court for an account freezing order in relation to the account in which the money is held.

(3)   But –

    (a)   an enforcement officer may not apply for an account freezing order unless the officer is a senior officer or is authorised to do so by a senior officer, and

    (b)   the senior officer must consult the Treasury before making the application for the order or (as the case may be) authorising the application to be made, unless in the circumstances it is not reasonably practicable to do so.

(4)   For the purposes of this Part of this Schedule –

    (a)   an account freezing order is an order that, subject to any exclusions (see paragraph 10U), prohibits each person by or for whom the account to which the order applies is operated from making withdrawals or payments from the account;

    (b)   an account is operated by or for a person if the person is an account holder or a signatory or identified as a beneficiary in relation to the account.

(5)   An application for an account freezing order may be made without notice if the circumstances of the case are such that notice of the application would prejudice the taking of any steps under this Part of this Schedule to forfeit money that is within subsection (1)(a) or (b) of section 1 or is property earmarked as terrorist property.

(6)   The money referred to in sub-paragraph (1) may be all or part of the credit balance of the account.

(7)   In this Part of this Schedule –

"bank" has the meaning given by paragraph 10R;

"building society" has the same meaning as in the Building Societies Act 1986;

"enforcement officer" means –

(a)   a constable, or

(b)   a counter-terrorism financial investigator;

"relevant court" –

(a)   in England and Wales and Northern Ireland, means a magistrates' court, and

(b)   in Scotland, means the sheriff;

"senior officer" means a police officer of at least the rank of superintendent.

Meaning of "bank"

10R   (1)   "Bank" means an authorised deposit-taker, other than a building society, that has its head office or a branch in the United Kingdom.

     (2)   In sub-paragraph (1), "authorised deposit-taker" means –

    (a)   a person who has permission under Part 4A of the Financial Services and Markets Act 2000 to accept deposits;

    (b)   a person who –

        (i)   is specified, or is within a class of persons specified, by an order under section 38 of that Act (exemption orders), and

        (ii)   accepts deposits;

    (c)   an EEA firm of the kind mentioned in paragraph 5(b) of Schedule 3 to that Act that has permission under paragraph 15 of that Schedule (as a result of qualifying for authorisation under paragraph 12(1) of that Schedule) to accept deposits.

(3)   A reference in sub-paragraph (2) to a person or firm with permission to accept deposits does not include a person or firm with permission to do so only for the purposes of, or in the course of, an activity other than accepting deposits.

Making of account freezing order

10S   (1)   This paragraph applies where an application for an account freezing order is made under paragraph 10Q in relation to an account.

    (2)   The relevant court may make the order if satisfied that there are reasonable grounds for suspecting that money held in the account (whether all or part of the credit balance of the account) –

    (a)   is within subsection (1)(a) or (b) of section 1, or
    (b)   is property earmarked as terrorist property.

    (3)   An account freezing order ceases to have effect at the end of the period specified in the order (which may be varied under paragraph 10T) unless it ceases to have effect at an earlier or later time in accordance with the provision made by paragraphs 10W(6)(c), 10Y(2) to (7), 10Z2(6) to (8) and 10Z3.

    (4)   The period specified by the relevant court for the purposes of sub-paragraph (3) (whether when the order is first made or on a variation under paragraph 10T) may not exceed the period of 2 years, starting with the day on which the account freezing order is (or was) made.

    (5)   An account freezing order must provide for notice to be given to persons affected by the order.

Variation and setting aside of account freezing order

10T   (1)   The relevant court may at any time vary or set aside an account freezing order on an application made by –

    (a)   an enforcement officer, or
    (b)   any person affected by the order.

    (2)   But an enforcement officer may not make an application under sub-paragraph (1) unless the officer is a senior officer or is authorised to do so by a senior officer.

    (3)   Before varying or setting aside an account freezing order the court must (as well as giving the parties to the proceedings an opportunity to be heard) give such an opportunity to any person who may be affected by its decision.

    (4)   In relation to Scotland, the references in this paragraph to setting aside an order are to be read as references to recalling it.

Exclusions

10U   (1)   The power to vary an account freezing order includes (amongst other things) power to make exclusions from the prohibition on making withdrawals or payments from the account to which the order applies.

(2) Exclusions from the prohibition may also be made when the order is made.

(3) An exclusion may (amongst other things) make provision for the purpose of enabling a person by or for whom the account is operated –

(a)   to meet the person's reasonable living expenses, or

(b)   to carry on any trade, business, profession or occupation.

(4) An exclusion may be made subject to conditions.

(5) Where a magistrates' court exercises the power to make an exclusion for the purpose of enabling a person to meet legal expenses that the person has incurred, or may incur, in respect of proceedings under this Schedule, it must ensure that the exclusion –

(a)   is limited to reasonable legal expenses that the person has reasonably incurred or that the person reasonably incurs,

(b)   specifies the total amount that may be released for legal expenses in pursuance of the exclusion, and

(c)   is made subject to the same conditions as would be the required conditions (see section 286A of the Proceeds of Crime Act 2002) if the order had been made under section 245A of that Act (in addition to any conditions imposed under sub-paragraph (4)).

(6) A magistrates' court, in deciding whether to make an exclusion for the purpose of enabling a person to meet legal expenses in respect of proceedings under this Schedule –

(a)   must have regard to the desirability of the person being represented in any proceedings under this Schedule in which the person is a participant, and

(b)   must disregard the possibility that legal representation of the person in any such proceedings might, were an exclusion not made –

(i)   be made available under arrangements made for the purposes of Part 1 of the Legal Aid, Sentencing and Punishment of Offenders Act 2012, or

(ii)   be funded by the Northern Ireland Legal Services Commission.

(7) The sheriff's power to make exclusions may not be exercised for the purpose of enabling any person to meet any legal expenses in respect of proceedings under this Schedule.

(8) The power to make exclusions must, subject to sub-paragraph (6), be exercised with a view to ensuring, so far as practicable, that there is not undue prejudice to the taking of any steps under this Part of this Schedule to forfeit money that is within subsection (1)(a) or (b) of section 1 or is property earmarked as terrorist property.

Restriction on proceedings and remedies

10V   (1)   If a court in which proceedings are pending in respect of an account maintained with a bank or building society is satisfied that an account freezing order has been applied for or made in respect of the account, it may either stay the proceedings or allow them to continue on any terms it thinks fit.

(2)   Before exercising the power conferred by sub-paragraph (1), the court must (as well as giving the parties to any of the proceedings

concerned an opportunity to be heard) give such an opportunity to any person who may be affected by the court's decision.

(3)   In relation to Scotland, the reference in sub-paragraph (1) to staying the proceedings is to be read as a reference to sisting the proceedings.

Account forfeiture notice

10W   (1)   This paragraph applies while an account freezing order has effect. In this paragraph the account to which the order applies is "the frozen account".

(2)   A senior officer may give a notice for the purpose of forfeiting money held in the frozen account (whether all or part of the credit balance of the account) if satisfied that the money –

(a)   is within subsection (1)(a) or (b) of section 1, or

(b)   is property earmarked as terrorist property.

(3)   A notice given under sub-paragraph (2) is referred to in this Part of this Schedule as an account forfeiture notice.

(4)   An account forfeiture notice must –

(a)   state the amount of money held in the frozen account which it is proposed be forfeited,

(b)   confirm that the senior officer is satisfied as mentioned in sub-paragraph (2),

(c)   specify a period for objecting to the proposed forfeiture and an address to which any objections must be sent, and

(d)   explain that the money will be forfeited unless an objection is received at that address within the period for objecting.

(5)   The period for objecting must be at least 30 days starting with the day after the notice is given.

(6)   If no objection is made within the period for objecting, and the notice has not lapsed under paragraph 10Y –

(a)   the amount of money stated in the notice is forfeited (subject to paragraph 10Z),

(b)   the bank or building society with which the frozen account is maintained must transfer that amount of money into an interest-bearing account nominated by an enforcement officer, and

(c)   immediately after the transfer has been made, the account freezing order made in relation to the frozen account ceases to have effect.

(7)   An objection may be made by anyone (whether a recipient of the notice or not).

(8)   An objection means a written objection sent to the address specified in the notice; and an objection is made when it is received at the address.

(9)   An objection does not prevent forfeiture of the money held in the frozen account under paragraph 10Z2.

Giving of account forfeiture notice

10X   (1)   The Secretary of State must by regulations made by statutory instrument make provision about how an account forfeiture notice is to be given.

(2)   The regulations may (amongst other things) provide –

(a)   for an account forfeiture notice to be given to such person or persons, and in such manner, as may be prescribed;

(b)   for circumstances in which, and the time at which, an account forfeiture notice is to be treated as having been given.

(3)   The regulations must ensure that where an account forfeiture notice is given it is, if possible, given to every person to whom notice of the account freezing order was given.

(4)   A statutory instrument containing regulations under this paragraph is subject to annulment in pursuance of a resolution of either House of Parliament.

Lapse of account forfeiture notice

10Y   (1)   An account forfeiture notice lapses if –

(a)   an objection is made within the period for objecting specified in the notice under paragraph 10W(4)(c),

(b)   an application is made under paragraph 10Z2 for the forfeiture of money held in the frozen account, or

(c)   an order is made under paragraph 10T setting aside (or recalling) the relevant account freezing order.

(2)   If an account forfeiture notice lapses under sub-paragraph (1)(a), the relevant account freezing order ceases to have effect at the end of the period of 48 hours starting with the making of the objection ("the 48-hour period").

This is subject to sub-paragraphs (3) and (7).

(3)   If within the 48-hour period an application is made –

(a)   for a variation of the relevant account freezing order under paragraph 10T so as to extend the period specified in the order, or

(b)   for forfeiture of money held in the frozen account under paragraph 10Z2,

the order continues to have effect until the relevant time (and then ceases to have effect).

(4)   In the case of an application of the kind mentioned in sub-paragraph (3)(a), the relevant time means –

(a)   if an extension is granted, the time determined in accordance with paragraph 10S(3), or

(b)   if an extension is not granted, the time when the application is determined or otherwise disposed of.

(5)   In the case of an application of the kind mentioned in sub-paragraph (3)(b), the relevant time is the time determined in accordance with paragraph 10Z2(6).

(6)   If within the 48-hour period it is decided that no application of the kind mentioned in sub-paragraph (3)(a) or (b) is to be made, an enforcement officer must, as soon as possible, notify the bank or building society with which the frozen account is maintained of that decision.

(7)   If the bank or building society is notified in accordance with sub-paragraph (6) before the expiry of the 48-hour period, the relevant account freezing order ceases to have effect on the bank or building society being so notified.

(8)   In relation to an account forfeiture notice –

    (a)   "the frozen account" is the account in which the money to which the account forfeiture notice relates is held;

    (b)   "the relevant account freezing order" is the account freezing order made in relation to the frozen account.

(9)   In calculating a period of 48 hours for the purposes of this paragraph no account is to be taken of –

    (a)   any Saturday or Sunday,

    (b)   Christmas Day,

    (c)   Good Friday, or

    (d)   any day that is a bank holiday under the Banking and Financial Dealings Act 1971 in the part of the United Kingdom in which the account freezing order was made.

Application to set aside forfeiture

10Z   (1)   A person aggrieved by the forfeiture of money in pursuance of paragraph 10W(6)(a) may apply to the relevant court for an order setting aside the forfeiture of the money or any part of it.

    (2)   The application must be made before the end of the period of 30 days starting with the day on which the period for objecting ended ("the 30-day period").

    (3)   But the relevant court may give permission for an application to be made after the 30-day period has ended if it thinks that there are exceptional circumstances to explain why the applicant –

        (a)   failed to object to the forfeiture within the period for objecting, and

        (b)   failed to make an application within the 30-day period.

    (4)   On an application under this paragraph the relevant court must consider whether the money to which the application relates could be forfeited under paragraph 10Z2 (ignoring the forfeiture mentioned in sub-paragraph (1)).

    (5)   If the relevant court is satisfied that the money to which the application relates or any part of it could not be forfeited under that paragraph it must set aside the forfeiture of that money or part.

    (6)   Where the relevant court sets aside the forfeiture of any money –

        (a)   it must order the release of that money, and

        (b)   the money is to be treated as never having been forfeited.

    (7)   Where money is released by virtue of sub-paragraph (6)(a), there must be added to the money on its release any interest accrued on it whilst in the account referred to in paragraph 10W(6)(b).

Application of money forfeited under account forfeiture notice

10Z1   (1)   Money forfeited in pursuance of paragraph 10W(6)(a), and any interest accrued on it whilst in the account referred to in paragraph 10W(6)(b) –

    (a)   if, before being forfeited, the money was held in an account in relation to which an account freezing order made by a magistrates' court had effect, is to be paid into the Consolidated Fund;

    (b)   if, before being forfeited, the money was held in an account in relation to which an account freezing order made by the sheriff had effect, is to be paid into the Scottish Consolidated Fund.

(2)   But it is not to be paid in –

(a)   before the end of the period within which an application under paragraph 10Z may be made (ignoring the possibility of an application by virtue of paragraph 10Z(3)), or

(b)   if an application is made within that period, before the application is determined or otherwise disposed of.

Forfeiture order

10Z2   (1)   This paragraph applies while an account freezing order has effect. In this paragraph the account to which the account freezing order applies is "the frozen account".

(2)   An application for the forfeiture of money held in the frozen account (whether all or part of the credit balance of the account) may be made –

(a)   to a magistrates' court, by an enforcement officer, or

(b)   to the sheriff, by the Scottish Ministers.

(3)   The court or sheriff may order the forfeiture of the money or any part of it if satisfied that the money or part –

(a)   is within subsection (1)(a) or (b) of section 1, or

(b)   is property earmarked as terrorist property.

(4)   But in the case of property earmarked as terrorist property which belongs to joint tenants, one of whom is an excepted joint owner, an order by a magistrates' court may not apply to so much of it as the court thinks is attributable to the excepted joint owner's share.

(5)   For the purposes of sub-paragraph (4) –

(a)   an excepted joint owner is a joint tenant who obtained the property in circumstances in which it would not (as against him or her) be earmarked, and

(b)   references to the excepted joint owner's share of property are to so much of the property as would have been his or hers if the joint tenancy had been severed.

(6)   Where an application is made under sub-paragraph (2), the account freezing order is to continue to have effect until the time referred to in sub-paragraph (7)(b) or (8).

But sub-paragraphs (7)(b) and (8) are subject to paragraph 10Z3.

(7)   Where money held in a frozen account is ordered to be forfeited under sub-paragraph (3) –

(a)   the bank or building society with which the frozen account is maintained must transfer that amount of money into an interest-bearing account nominated by an enforcement officer, and

(b)   immediately after the transfer has been made the account freezing order made in relation to the frozen account ceases to have effect.

(8)   Where, other than by the making of an order under sub-paragraph

(3), an application under sub-paragraph (2) is determined or otherwise disposed of, the account freezing order ceases to have effect immediately after that determination or other disposal.

Continuation of account freezing order pending appeal

10Z3 (1)   This paragraph applies where, on an application under sub-paragraph (2) of paragraph 10Z2 in relation to an account to which an account freezing order applies, the court or sheriff decides –

   (a)   to make an order under sub-paragraph (3) of that paragraph in relation to part only of the money to which the application related, or

   (b)   not to make an order under sub-paragraph (3) of that paragraph.

(2)   The person who made the application under paragraph 10Z2(2) may apply without notice to the court or sheriff that made the decision referred to in sub-paragraph (1)(a) or (b) for an order that the account freezing order is to continue to have effect.

(3)   Where the court or sheriff makes an order under sub-paragraph (2) the account freezing order is to continue to have effect until –

   (a)   the end of the period of 48 hours starting with the making of the order under sub-paragraph (2), or

   (b)   if within that period of 48 hours an appeal is brought under paragraph 10Z4 against the decision referred to in sub-paragraph (1)(a) or (b), the time when the appeal is determined or otherwise disposed of.

(4)   Sub-paragraph (9) of paragraph 10Y applies for the purposes of sub-paragraph (3) as it applies for the purposes of that paragraph.

Appeal against decision under paragraph 10Z2

10Z4 (1)   Any party to proceedings for an order for the forfeiture of money under paragraph 10Z2 who is aggrieved by an order under that paragraph or by the decision of the court not to make such an order may appeal –

   (a)   from an order or decision of a magistrates' court in England and Wales, to the Crown Court;

   (b)   from an order or decision of the sheriff, to the Sheriff Appeal Court;

   (c)   from an order or decision of a magistrates' court in Northern Ireland, to a county court.

(2)   An appeal under sub-paragraph (1) must be made before the end of the period of 30 days starting with the day on which the court makes the order or decision.

(3)   Sub-paragraph (2) is subject to paragraph 10Z5.

(4)   The court hearing the appeal may make any order it thinks appropriate.

(5)   If the court upholds an appeal against an order forfeiting the money, it may order the release of the whole or any part of the money.

(6)   Where money is released by virtue of sub-paragraph (5), there must be added to the money on its release any interest accrued on it whilst in the account referred to in paragraph 10Z2(7)(a).

Extended time for appealing in certain cases where deproscription order made

10Z5   (1)   This paragraph applies where –

(a)   a successful application for an order under paragraph 10Z2 relies (wholly or partly) on the fact that an organisation is proscribed,

(b)   an application under section 4 of the Terrorism Act 2000 for a deproscription order in respect of the organisation is refused by the Secretary of State,

(c)   the money forfeited by the order under paragraph 10Z2 was made subject to an account freezing order on or after the date of the refusal of that application,

(d)   an appeal against that refusal is allowed under section 5 of the Terrorism Act 2000,

(e)   a deproscription order is made accordingly, and

(f)   if the order is made in reliance on section 123(5) of the Terrorism Act 2000, a resolution is passed by each House of Parliament under section 123(5)(b) of that Act.

(2)   Where this paragraph applies, an appeal under paragraph 10Z4 against the making of an order under paragraph 10Z2 may be brought at any time before the end of the period of 30 days beginning with the date on which the deproscription order comes into force.

(3)   In this paragraph a "deproscription order" means an order under section 3(3)(b) or (8) of the Terrorism Act 2000.

Application of money forfeited under account forfeiture order

10Z6   (1)   Money forfeited by an order under paragraph 10Z2, and any interest accrued on it whilst in the account referred to in sub-paragraph (7)(a) of that paragraph –

(a)   if forfeited by a magistrates' court, is to be paid into the Consolidated Fund, and

(b)   if forfeited by the sheriff, is to be paid into the Scottish Consolidated Fund.

(2)   But it is not to be paid in –

(a)   before the end of the period within which an appeal under paragraph 10Z4 may be made, or

(b)   if a person appeals under that paragraph, before the appeal is determined or otherwise disposed of.

Compensation

10Z7   (1)   This paragraph applies if –

(a)   an account freezing order is made, and

(b)   none of the money held in the account to which the order applies is forfeited in pursuance of an account forfeiture notice or by an order under paragraph 10Z2.

(2)   Where this paragraph applies a person by or for whom the account to which the account freezing order applies is operated may make an application to the relevant court for compensation.

(3)   If the relevant court is satisfied that the applicant has suffered loss as a result of the making of the account freezing order and that the

circumstances are exceptional, the relevant court may order compensation to be paid to the applicant.

(4)   The amount of compensation to be paid is the amount the relevant court thinks reasonable, having regard to the loss suffered and any other relevant circumstances.

(5)   If the account freezing order was applied for by a constable, the compensation is to be paid as follows –

(a)   in the case of a constable of a police force in England and Wales, it is to be paid out of the police fund from which the expenses of the police force are met;

(b)   in the case of a constable of the Police Service of Scotland, it is to be paid by the Scottish Police Authority;

(c)   in the case of a police officer within the meaning of the Police (Northern Ireland) Act 2000, it is to be paid out of money provided by the Chief Constable of the Police Service of Northern Ireland.

(6)   If the account freezing order was applied for by a counter-terrorism financial investigator, the compensation is to be paid as follows –

(a)   in the case of an investigator who was –

(i)   a member of the civilian staff of a police force (including the metropolitan police force), within the meaning of Part 1 of the Police Reform and Social Responsibility Act 2011, or

(ii)   a member of staff of the City of London police force,

it is to be paid out of the police fund from which the expenses of the police force are met;

(b)   in the case of an investigator who was a member of staff of the Police Service of Northern Ireland, it is to be paid out of money provided by the Chief Constable of the Police Service of Northern Ireland.'

3   (1)   Paragraph 19 (general interpretation) is amended as follows.

(2)   In sub-paragraph (1), at the appropriate places insert –

'"account forfeiture notice" (in Part 4B) has the meaning given by paragraph 10W(3),

"account freezing order" (in Part 4B) has the meaning given by paragraph 10Q(4)(a),

"bank" (in Part 4B) has the meaning given by paragraph 10R,

"building society" (in Part 4B) has the meaning given by paragraph 10Q(7),

"enforcement officer" (in Part 4B) has the meaning given by paragraph 10Q(7),

"relevant court" (in Part 4B) has the meaning given by paragraph 10Q(7),

"senior officer" (in Part 4B) has the meaning given by paragraph 10Q(7),'

(3)   After sub-paragraph (6) insert –

'(7)   References (in Part 4B) to an account being operated by or for a person are to be read in accordance with paragraph 10Q(4)(b).'

Appendix B
TACKLING TAX EVASION: GOVERNMENT GUIDANCE FOR THE CORPORATE OFFENCE OF FAILURE TO PREVENT THE CRIMINAL FACILITATION OF TAX EVASION (EXTRACTS)[1]

B1   GUIDING PRINCIPLES ON REASONABLE PREVENTATIVE MEASURES

2.   THE 6 GUIDING PRINCIPLES

Principle 1 – Risk assessment

[Principle 1 is dealt with in detail at **Chapter 4**.]

Principle 2 – Proportionality of risk-based prevention procedures

Reasonable procedures will be proportionate to the risk a relevant body faces of persons associated with it committing tax evasion facilitation offences. This will depend on the nature, scale and complexity of the relevant body's activities. We recognise that the reasonableness of prevention procedures should take account of the level of control and supervision the organisation is able to exercise over a particular person acting on its behalf, and the proximity of the person to the relevant body. The new offences do not require relevant bodies to undertake excessively burdensome procedures in order to eradicate all risk, but they do demand more than mere lip-service to preventing the criminal facilitation of tax evasion.

Commentary

The term reasonable 'prevention procedures' within this guidance is used to mean both:

■ formal policies adopted by a relevant body to prevent criminal facilitation of tax evasion by those acting on its behalf, and
■ practical steps taken to implement these policies, enforcement of compliance with the policies, and the monitoring of the policies' effectiveness.

To be 'reasonable', prevention procedures should be proportionate to the risks that the organisation faces. An initial assessment of the risks that a relevant body's associated persons may commit tax evasion facilitation offences is therefore a necessary first step.

The prevention procedures should outline the relevant body's position on involvement in the criminal facilitation of tax evasion, including the provision of services which pose a high risk of being misused to commit a tax crime. The relevant body should also have a plan of how it will implement and review measures to ensure that persons associated with it are not criminally facilitating tax evasion.

---

[1]   HMRC's draft guidance, updated October 2016.

Burdensome procedures designed to perfectly address every conceivable risk, no matter how remote, are *not* required. Procedures need only be reasonable given the risks posed in the circumstances.

A number of factors (see table below) will be relevant when assessing the risk posed to a relevant body by the services it provides and the manner in which it provides them, including the size of the relevant body, the nature and complexity of its business and the jurisdictions in which it operates.

When considering the proportionality of reasonable prevention procedures, some suggested risk factors to consider may include the following:

■ **Opportunity – could someone facilitate tax evasion?**

 – Do any associated persons have the opportunity to facilitate client tax evasion?
 – Is their work subject to monitoring or scrutiny, for example a second pair of eyes?
 – How likely is detection of any facilitation?

■ **Motive – why could it happen?**

 – Does the reward and recognition system and corporate culture (including sanctions and penalties) incentivise or dissuade potential criminal facilitation of tax evasion, or whistle-blowing when tax evasion is uncovered?
 – What are the consequences of wrong-doing?

■ **Means – how could it be done?**

 – What means of criminally facilitating tax fraud do your associated persons have?
 – Are there particular products, services or systems that could be open to abuse and used to criminally facilitate tax evasion?
 – Do those in high risk roles receive regular fraud training and how vigorously is compliance with training evaluated or monitored?

Some organisations may face significant risks, and will need more extensive procedures than their counterparts facing limited risks, for example those providing private wealth management services. However, in general small organisations are unlikely to need procedures that are as extensive as those of a large multi-national organisation.

A very small lower risk business, for example, may be able to rely on oral briefings to communicate its policies while a large business may need to rely on more extensive written communications. Larger organisations may also exercise less day-to-day oversight over those providing services on its behalf, and may therefore need to put in place alternative oversight arrangements.

Procedures to prevent the criminal facilitation of tax evasion by a person associated with the relevant body may be independent, standalone procedures; but so long as they properly address the risk of facilitating tax evasion they may form part of a wider package of procedures, for example internal Anti-Money Laundering, Bribery Act or fraud prevention procedures.

What is considered a proportionate timescale for implementing, reviewing and amending procedures to prevent criminal facilitation of tax evasion will depend on the nature, scale and complexity of the relevant body's activities and the resources available to the relevant body. It is expected that a relevant body's procedures will not be static, but will evolve and develop in line with the relevant body's activities and identified risks.

Procedures

The precise prevention procedures that will be reasonable will differ for each organisation, but they are likely to include common elements. For example:

■　A clearly articulated risk assessment on which the procedures are based
■　A top level commitment to preventing the involvement of those acting on the relevant body's behalf in the criminal facilitation of tax evasion
■　An articulation of the approach to mitigating risks of involvement in the criminal facilitation of tax evasion, such as those arising from the nature of its services and areas of operation
■　An overview of the strategy and timeframe to implement prevention policies. It is expected that what is reasonable will evolve over time. For example, IT systems which form part of a relevant body's due diligence procedures may take time to develop and subsequently review and amend
■　Monitoring and enforcing compliance with procedures
■　Reviewing procedures for effectiveness and refining them
■　A clear pathway for reporting wrongdoing by persons associated with the relevant body
■　Protection for whistle-blowers (with no retribution)
■　A commitment to compliance over profit or bonuses.

The procedures put in place to implement a relevant body's preventative policies should be designed to mitigate identified risks as well as address the risk of criminal conduct on the part of those providing services on behalf of the relevant body.

An organisation does not have to publish policies on an external website, but may wish to summarise key principles within corporate materials. The following list is intended as guidance for the topics that preventative procedures may embrace depending on the nature of the particular risks faced:

■　The involvement of the relevant body's top level management
■　The procedures and methods used to assess the risk to the relevant body posed by its activities
■　Due diligence conducted in relation to persons associated with the relevant body
■　The contractual terms and conditions of persons associated with the relevant body
■　Disciplinary and enforcement action taken against those persons breaching the relevant body's policies
■　How the relevant body will communicate its policies to all persons associated with it
■　Policies around reporting criminal actions by persons associated with the relevant body
■　The process and timeline by which the organisation plans to implement its preventative procedures and training in their application
■　The monitoring, review and evaluation of the relevant body's preventative policy and procedures
■　Disclosure of client information in line with existing legal requirements, for example reporting under the Common Reporting Standard and the Proceeds of Crime Act.

No Procedures

It is also worth noting that in some limited circumstances it may be unreasonable to expect a relevant body to have prevention procedures in place. For example, where a relevant body has fully assessed all the risks and they are considered to be extremely low and the costs of implementing any prevention procedures are disproportionate or cost-prohibitive in relation to the negligible risks faced. However, it will rarely be reasonable to have not even conducted a risk assessment.

It should be noted that a relevant body should keep the risks under review and be able to articulate the outcome of the risk assessment and the active decision not to implement any procedures, should they be challenged at a later stage.

Principle 3 – Top level commitment

The top-level management of a relevant body should be committed to preventing persons associated with it from engaging in criminal facilitation of tax evasion. They should foster a culture within the relevant body in which activity intended to facilitate tax evasion is never acceptable.

Commentary

Those at the most senior levels of the organisation are best placed to foster a culture where actions intended to facilitate tax evasion are considered unacceptable. This principle is intended to encourage the involvement of senior management in the creation and implementation of preventative procedures. It is also intended to encourage senior management involvement in the decision making process in relation to the assessment of risk, where this is appropriate.

Procedures

The level and nature of the involvement of senior management of a relevant body will vary depending on the size and structure of the relevant body, but is likely to include:

■ communication and endorsement of the relevant body's stance on preventing the criminal facilitation of tax evasion, and
■ involvement in the development and review of preventative procedures.

Communication and endorsement of the relevant body's position on preventing the facilitation of tax evasion

The manner and form in which a relevant body chooses to communicate, both internally and externally, its position on ensuring that persons associated with it do not criminally facilitate the evasion of taxes may vary depending on a number of factors including the size of the relevant body, the nature and complexity of its business and the jurisdictions within which it operates.

Communication may vary depending on the target audience, for example communications aimed at the relevant body's clients may be different from those aimed at employees of the relevant body or those to whom it sub-contracts work.

Effective formal statements to demonstrate the commitment by senior managers within the relevant body may include:

■ A commitment to zero tolerance towards the criminal facilitation of tax evasion
■ The consequences for persons associated with the relevant body for breaching the relevant body's policy on the facilitation of tax evasion
■ A commitment not to recommend the services of others who do not have reasonable prevention procedures in place
■ Articulation of the benefits of rejecting the provision of services to enable tax evasion (reputational, customer and business partner confidence)
■ Articulation of the relevant body's main preventative procedures
■ Key individuals and/or departments involved in the development and implementation of the organisation's prevention procedures
■ Reference to any membership of collective action against the facilitation of tax evasion, for example, through initiatives undertaken by representative bodies.

Involvement in developing preventative measures

The level and nature of involvement in the creation and implementation of preventative measures will be bespoke to the relevant body involved. It is expected that the level of involvement will be proportionate to the relevant body's size, management structure and business activities.

In smaller relevant bodies, it may be proportionate for the most senior management to be personally involved in the design and implementation of preventative measures. In a large multinational organisation, personal involvement in the design and implementation of preventative measures may not be proportionate, and senior management may instead take responsibility for preventative measures by providing oversight of work delegated to a committee and the publication with positive endorsement for the preventative measures thereby created.

Regardless of the scale of involvement of senior management, it is likely to reflect the following elements:

■   Members of the senior management of the relevant body having designated responsibility for prevention measures
■   Endorsement of the relevant body's prevention policy and associated publications
■   Leadership and designated responsibility for awareness raising of the relevant body's prevention policies
■   Engagement with relevant associated persons and external bodies to help articulate the organisation's policies
■   Designated responsibility for certifying the assessment of risk
■   Designated responsibility at senior level for disciplinary procedures relating to the breach of the relevant body's policies
■   Senior management's commitment to whistleblowing processes and rejecting profit by way of facilitating tax evasion.

Principle 4 – Due diligence

The organisation applies due diligence procedures, taking an appropriate and risk based approach, in respect of persons who perform or will perform services on behalf of the organisation, in order to mitigate identified risks.

Commentary

Those organisations in the sectors facing the greatest risks (those providing bespoke financial or tax-related services to clients, for example) are likely already to undertake a wide variety of due diligence procedures, both mandatory and due diligence undertaken in response to risks associated with specific transactions, customers or jurisdictions.

It is envisaged that due diligence procedures for this offence will be capable of identifying the risk of criminal facilitation of tax evasion by associated persons. However, it should be noted that merely applying old procedures tailored to a different type of risk (or clients-focused procedures) will not necessarily be an adequate response to tackle the risk of tax evasion facilitation.

Those with exposure to the greatest risk may choose to clearly articulate their due diligence procedures specifically in relation to the corporate offence. In addition, a single relevant body might have differing procedures for different parts of its business reflecting the varying levels of risk across all of its activities.

A relevant body may, upon conducting a risk assessment, decide that services provided to a certain group of its clients pose a higher risk of being misused to perpetrate a tax fraud. As a result they may apply increased scrutiny over those providing services to those clients, or over those who provide those services, to address the specific risks of tax evasion facilitation identified.

Procedures

The due diligence procedures put in place should be proportionate to the identified risk. For example, it may be that the risk identified in given situations is so remote as to justify there being no procedures in place. Alternatively, an organisation may assess the risks as being substantial in relation to a particular associated person, or service, and so apply considerably greater scrutiny in that circumstance.

Organisations may choose to conduct their due diligence internally, or externally, for example by internal audit teams or external consultants.

We recognise that the reasonableness of prevention procedures should take account of the level of control and supervision the organisation is able to exercise over a particular person acting on its behalf and the relevant body's proximity to that person.

It is expected that the effectiveness of the organisation's procedures will be reviewed and where necessary the procedures will be amended.

Principle 5 – Communication (including training)

The organisation seeks to ensure that its prevention policies and procedures are communicated, embedded and understood throughout the organisation, through internal and external communication, including training. This is proportionate to the risk to which the organisation assesses that it is exposed.

Commentary

A clear articulation of an organisation's policy against engaging in activities to help clients commit tax fraud deters those providing services on behalf of the relevant body from engaging in such activities. Communication should be from all levels within an organisation, i.e. it is not enough for the senior management [to] say that staff should not commit fraud, if middle management then actively ignore this and encourage junior members to circumvent the relevant body's prevention procedures.

It is important that the relevant body ensures awareness and understanding of its policies amongst those who provide services for or on its behalf. The organisation may feel that it is necessary to require its representatives to undertake fraud or potentially tax evasion-specific training, depending on the risks it is exposed to. This would be to ensure that they have the skills needed to identify when they and those around them might be at risk of engaging in an illegal act and what whistle-blowing procedures should be followed if this occurs.

Procedures

The nature of internal and external communication may vary depending on the nature of the risk being addressed, the size, business and operation of the organisation in question.

Internal communications should make clear the relevant body's zero tolerance policy for the facilitation of tax evasion by its representatives and the consequences for anyone found to be complicit in illegal activity. Such communication may focus on high risk areas of operation for the relevant bodies and what is expected of representatives who find themselves being asked to provide a service which they believe will be used to facilitate a tax fraud.

An important aspect of internal communication is an established and confidential means for representatives of the relevant body to raise concerns about the provision of services to facilitate tax fraud. It should be clear to those providing services on behalf of the relevant body whom they should contact within if they have questions or concerns about the services they are providing. Relevant bodies may wish these communications to form part of their existing communications, for example on money laundering prevention, or to be a stand-alone communication.

External communication of a relevant body's policy on the provision of services to facilitate tax evasion can act as a strong deterrent to those who would seek to use the relevant body's services to further illegal activity. Relevant bodies may consider it proportionate and appropriate to convey these messages to partner organisations, particularly those to whom it is making referral, or from whom clients are referred.

Training

The training should be proportionate to the risk faced. Some relevant bodies may wish to incorporate training into their existing financial crime prevention training, other organisations may wish to introduce bespoke training to address specific tax fraud facilitation risks.

Consideration should be given to the specific training needs of those in the highest risk posts, and to training required to ensure that the relevant body's representatives understand the process for referring any concerns. The effectiveness of training should be monitored and evaluated.

Relevant bodies may choose either to train third party associated persons, or encourage them to ensure their own arrangements are in place.

SUGGESTED TRAINING REQUIREMENTS:

It is not envisaged that all associated persons will require a detailed understanding of tax rules in any one country, but instead training should equip them to understand the scope of this offence and the associated risks, without needing to understand the underlying tax law.

Suggested content for tax evasion and general fraud training could include the following:

- the organisation's policies and procedures, which include provisions of the Act and any other sector regulatory rules and principles
- an explanation of when and how to seek advice and report any concerns or suspicions of tax evasion or wider financial crime, including whistleblowing procedures
- an explanation of the term 'tax evasion' and associated fraud
- an explanation of an employee's duty under the law
- the penalties, relating to the person and corporate entity, for committing an offence under the act
- the social and economic effects of failing to prevent tax evasion.

Principle 6 – Monitoring and review

The organisation monitors and reviews its prevention procedures and makes improvements where necessary.

Commentary

The nature of the risks faced by an organisation will change and evolve over time. This may be as a natural result of external developments, the failure to prevent an incidence of facilitation of tax evasion by an associated person, or as a result of changes in the organisation's activities. The organisation will therefore need to change its procedures in response to the changes in the risks that it faces.

Procedures

There are a range of approaches which a relevant body may wish to take when reviewing its monitoring mechanisms. A relevant body may wish to have its review conducted by an external party, or may choose to conduct its review internally.

Organisations can review their procedures in a number of ways, for example:

- By seeking internal feedback from staff members and looking to other financial crime prevention procedures
- Through formalised periodic review with documented findings
- Through working with other organisations, such as representative bodies or other organisations facing similar risks.

This is not an exhaustive list and it is expected that organisations will choose the approach most suited to their needs. Relevant bodies may change their review process in light of developments, for example a relevant body may need to take a more formalised and detailed approach to reviewing its procedures, following criminal activity by persons associated with it.

B2   EXAMPLES AND CASE STUDIES

1.   INTRODUCTION

1.3   Overview of the offence and illustrative examples

UK Tax Evasion Facilitation Offence

> Below are some illustrative examples of the different types of procedures which would be relevant for companies of varying sizes, complexity, industry focus and risk profile. For all the examples below it should be noted that the precise scale and nature of the tax evasion taking place would influence any decision to prosecute:
>
> . . .
>
> 2) Higher risk
>
> - As part of a large transaction an employee of a UK-based multinational bank knowingly referred a corporate client to an offshore accounting firm with the express intention of assisting the corporate client to set up a structure allowing the client to evade foreign income tax
> - The bank, which had rigorous prevention procedures for money laundering and bribery procedures, undertook only a light-touch tax evasion risk assessment, nominally including the word 'tax' into existing procedures and processes, but not effectively implementing or enforcing them or reviewing tax fraud risks
> - The bank undertook no tax evasion focussed due diligence assessment of the accounting firm to which the client was referred.
>
> In these circumstances, although the bank could attempt to mount a defence of having reasonable procedures in place on paper for tackling the facilitation of tax evasion, in reality it had relied on unaltered money laundering and bribery procedures. Despite being in a high risk sector, it had also failed to undertake a thorough risk assessment, or follow Government or sector-focused guidance on the types of processes and procedures needed to mitigate risks. It is therefore likely that the bank would be found to have committed the new offence and would be unable to put forward a successful reasonable procedures defence.

Foreign Tax Evasion Facilitation Offence

UK NEXUS

The foreign tax offence can only be committed by a relevant body:

- incorporated under UK law, for example a limited company incorporated under UK law;
- carrying on a business or other undertaking from a permanent establishment within the UK, for example a company incorporated under the law of France but operating from an office in Manchester; or
- whose associated person is located within the UK at the time of the criminal act that facilitates the evasion of the overseas tax, for example a company incorporated under German law whose employee helps another person to commit a foreign tax evasion offence whilst in London.

These bodies, described above, are considered to be sufficiently connected to the UK and therefore should be subject to the new offence in relation to overseas tax. Further guidance and examples of different scenarios are in Section 3.

'DUAL CRIMINALITY'

The legislation also requires that there is 'dual criminality' in order to prosecute a foreign tax evasion facilitation offence.

. . .

Therefore the foreign tax offence cannot be committed by [an] act that would be lawful in relation to a UK tax. Due to the dual criminality requirement, it is only necessary to have an understanding of the foreign criminal law when doing something that would be illegal if done in the UK. If the actions of the associated person would be lawful in the UK then the 'dual-criminality' requirement will not be fulfilled and the new foreign tax offence will not be committed regardless of what the foreign law may be.

The legislation also requires that before proceedings for the foreign offence are issued in England, Wales or Northern Ireland the personal consent of the Director of Public Prosecutions or the Director of the Serious Fraud Office must be gained[2]. Such consent would only be forthcoming where, having weighed up all factors, the prosecution was in the *public interest*.

It is highly unlikely that a prosecution would be taken forward where a foreign tax was in some way incompatible with the UK's legal values, such as respect for human rights. It would also be very unlikely to be in the public interest to bring a prosecution where a foreign tax was discriminatory and applied on the basis of race, religion or gender.

Whilst the preference will normally be for the jurisdiction suffering the tax loss to take the appropriate criminal or civil response, if this is not possible (for example due to lack of resources, corruption, or any other reason) the UK Government believes that it should be open to the UK to hold the relevant body to account, should it be in the public interest to do so.

---

[2] In relation to Scotland, the decision to prosecute is always taken by the Crown Office and Procurator Fiscal Service and so personal consent is not required in the legislation on the corporate offence. As a public body the Crown Office and Procurator Fiscal Service are bound by the Human Rights Act.

3.   COMMON TERMINOLOGY AND ADDITIONAL CASE STUDIES

3.3   Branches and subsidiaries

UK Tax Evasion Facilitation Offence

EXAMPLES

Branches and the overseas fraud offence

Gladstone Bank is a bank incorporated and headquartered in Switzerland. The bank has branches in a number of jurisdictions, including the UK and Germany. Whilst the bank has several branches across the world, the branches are not separate legal entities (they are branches not subsidiaries): the bank is a single legal entity, a company incorporated under Swiss law. All the bank's branches comprise a single legal person.

UK branch

The UK branch consists of a small number of employees whose functions are restricted to:

- attracting and on-boarding clients for Gladstone Bank;
- providing minor administrative services; and
- acting as a first point of contact for UK based customers.

The UK branch attracts and on-boards a number of clients for Gladstone Bank resident in London, including Freya who has UK tax liabilities and Larry who has German tax liabilities. The employees of the UK branch attract the clients in good faith believing that Gladstone Bank is providing routine financial services to its clients. Once the clients have been attracted all financial services are provided by either the bank's headquarters in Switzerland or employees in the German branch.

German branch

Employees of the German branch, deliberately and dishonestly help Larry to evade his German tax liabilities. The employees:

- advise Larry on structures that allow him to hide his assets and income from the German tax authorities;
- provide false certification to hide the true owners of accounts; and
- deliberately fail to comply with the applicable Anti Money Laundering Regulations.

Swiss Head Office

Employees of the Swiss headquarters deliberately and dishonestly help Freya to evade her UK tax liabilities. The employees:

- advise Freya on structures to help her hide overseas income from the UK tax authorities;
- deliberately set up a bank account in Switzerland knowing it is going to be used to hide the overseas income from the UK tax authorities

. . .

B. Liability for the Overseas Fraud Offence

Stage 1: taxpayers

Larry has deliberately and dishonestly failed to declare his taxable income and assets to the German revenue authorities with the intention of not paying the tax that he

---

legally owes. There is 'dual criminality' as there are equivalent offences at the taxpayer level in the UK and Germany.

Stage 2: Associated persons of Gladstone Bank and criminal facilitation

Employees of Gladstone's German branch have deliberately and dishonestly provided services to Larry to help him hide his taxable income and assets in order to help him evade his German tax liability.

The associated person was providing services (advice to clients) for or on behalf of the bank. There is 'dual criminality' at the facilitator level as there are equivalent offences in both the UK and Germany.

Stage 3:

As Gladstone Bank has a UK branch and the bank is a single legal entity it is within scope of the new foreign tax evasion facilitation offence. Gladstone Bank has also failed to prevent its associated person, i.e. employees of its German branch, from criminally facilitating the evasion of German tax by Larry.

Gladstone Bank is unable to put forward a defence of having put in place reasonable procedures to prevent the criminal facilitation of tax evasion because its procedures were not reasonable as it decided to only introduce prevention procedures for staff dealing with UK taxpayers. Claiming that it does not believe that it should have to exercise due diligence over employees of its branches in other countries provides no defence to this.

Further examples of branch structures that would be in scope of the overseas offence as there is sufficient UK nexus:

- Any bank incorporated under UK law with overseas branches
- Any bank incorporated under the law of another country that conducts part of its business from the UK, for example a French bank with a London branch
- Any bank incorporated under the law of another country that conducts none of its business from the UK but where its associated person does the facilitating criminal act from within the UK, for example any bank incorporated under the law of another country that sends someone to the UK to perform a criminal act.

. . .

3.5   Referrals

. . .

EXAMPLES

1) Straight-forward Referral Out

A UK Bank 'B' gets occasional client requests for services in South Africa, where it has neither a branch, nor a subsidiary. It has a relationship with a firm 'F' in that country to which it refers business. This arrangement is a 'pure' or 'vanilla' referral. Once the referral has been made, the client becomes a client of F, and bank B takes no further part in any provision of services in the country in question (although its own separate relationship with the client continues to exist independently). Firm F criminally facilitates the client's tax evasion. It is not a relationship in which services are provided by F for or on behalf of bank B.

Question: Would firm F be an associated person of bank B?

Answer: No. Firm F is not an associated person, as it was not providing services on behalf of bank B; once the client was introduced, bank B stepped back.

2) Inward Referral

A UK bank uses a consultancy firm in India that introduces clients to the bank. The consultancy firm was previously exclusive to the UK bank but now also introduces Indian clients to the UK bank's sister bank in India. The consultancy firm is not used by the UK bank to provide any tax advice to clients of either bank.

The consultancy firm later offers additional services (beyond the contracted services with the banks) and criminally facilitates tax evasion for clients of both the UK and Indian-based banks, including by falsifying documentation. Neither bank was aware of the additional services and illegal activity.

Question: Would the activity of the consultancy firm attract liability for the bank?

Answer: No. The Indian consultancy firm was offering tax services outside of its relationship with the bank. Although the consultancy firm was providing some services on behalf of the bank (introducing clients) the criminal facilitation of tax evasion was outside the contracted service provision and was therefore not provided for or on behalf of the bank.

3) Holistic Service Provision/Sub-contracting

A UK financial services firm instructs a foreign tax advisor on behalf of a client to give advice on tax and estate planning proposals in a foreign jurisdiction. The UK firm controls the ongoing relationship with the client and the advice sought, passing the advice on to the client. The UK firm takes responsibility for the foreign lawyer's fees and includes those fees as a disbursement in the annual bill to their client.

Question: Would the advice of the foreign tax advisor attract liability for the UK firm?

Answer: Yes. The foreign tax advisor is providing a service for or on behalf of the UK firm; it is doing work that the UK firm sub-contracted to the foreign tax advisor having entered into a contract with its client. The foreign tax advisor is therefore an 'associated person' under these circumstances.

3.6   Foreign Tax Evasion Facilitation Offence

Dual Criminality

Below is an example of the dual criminality test to illustrate the types of situation that are in scope of the new offence.

DUAL CRIMINALITY EXAMPLE

Gladstone Bank is a bank incorporated and headquartered in Switzerland. The bank has branches in a number of jurisdictions, including the UK and Germany. Whilst the bank has several branches across the world, the branches are not separate legal entities (they are branches not subsidiaries): the bank is a single legal entity, a company incorporated under Swiss law. All the bank's branches comprise a single legal person.

The German taxpayer, Larry, has committed an offence contrary to section 370 of the German Fiscal Code. He is assisted by an employee of Gladstone Bank who is also based in a branch in Germany.

Section 370 German Fiscal Code

Any person who:

■   Furnishes the revenue authorities or other authorities with incorrect or incomplete particulars concerning matters of substantial significance for taxation.

■   Fails to inform the revenue authorities of facts of substantial significance for taxation when obliged to do so.

There is therefore dual criminality at the taxpayer level as there is an equivalent offence in 106A of the Taxes Management Act 1970 (fraudulent evasion of income tax).

The facilitating acts of the staff of the bank would be an offence if done in the UK and Germany also has the equivalent offence, criminal facilitation of tax evasion, by virtue of sections 26–27 of the German Fiscal Code.

Section 26 Abetting

Any person who intentionally induces another to intentionally commit an unlawful act (abettor) shall be liable to be sentenced as if he were a principal.

Section 27 Aiding

(1) Any person who intentionally assists another in the intentional commission of an unlawful act shall be convicted and sentenced as an aider.

There is therefore dual criminality at the taxpayer (stage 1) and associated person (stage 2) levels.

Stage 3: Liability for Gladstone Bank for failing to prevent the criminal facilitation of tax evasion

Gladstone Bank is within scope of the foreign tax evasion offence as it has an establishment in the UK. The fact that the company is incorporated under Swiss law, and that the facilitating acts of its associated person took place outside the UK, does not take it outside the scope of the new offence. It is a legal person with a business presence in the UK and bound by the new foreign tax offence.

Gladstone Bank will be guilty of the foreign tax evasion offence unless it can establish the defence of having reasonable prevention procedures.

3.7   Further illustrative case studies

Example 1) Acting as a broker/conduit – arranging access to others in the 'supply' chain and providing introductions.

Sarah was introduced to Malus GmbH, a Swiss adviser, to create a tax efficient structure for potential future investment into UK property. Malus was an approved intermediary of a UK high street bank (with the referral made in good faith after they carried out appropriate due diligence on Malus), and Sarah planned to put her post-tax employment earnings into this structure.

Sarah had a relative, Maisie, who was neither resident nor domiciled in the UK. Malus advised Sarah that she should set up a Swiss trust using Maisie as the settlor. This was done, although Maisie was never asked to sign anything and was not aware that a trust was being set up with her named as the settlor. Sarah was advised that she retained beneficial ownership of all the assets despite the trust arrangement.

The trust had bank accounts with Lunar Bank in Monaco. Sarah admitted her actions following initial contact with Malus were deliberate.

Under the new offences: There is no evidence that the UK high-street bank knew that Malus would help Sarah to evade UK tax, and the 'vanilla' referral to Malus was made in good faith. Under these circumstances Malus was not acting as an 'associated person' of the UK high-street bank, so the UK high-street bank is not liable under the new offences.

Malus's staff, however, provided structuring advice which Sarah knew was not legal, as well as professional trustee services to Sarah's trust which they knew was not properly constituted and would be used by Sarah to hide her assets and evade the appropriate level of tax. The staff of Malus are persons associated with it. If Malus had not taken reasonable steps to prevent its staff from facilitating Sarah's tax evasion in the course of their work then Malus would be guilty of the new offence. Its compliance with any applicable published guidance, its contractual terms for its staff, the training it provides, and any steps taken to monitor and ensure compliance would all be relevant to the assessment of whether it had taken reasonable steps.

Lunar Bank's staff have performed acts that facilitated Sarah's tax evasion. However, they did so without being aware of any tax evasion. They may have been negligent and failed to comply with their anti-money laundering obligations, but they lack the requisite guilty state of mind to commit an offence relating to facilitating Sarah's tax evasion. Therefore, there is no tax evasion facilitation offence that Lunar Bank has failed to prevent.

Example 2) Providing planning and advice on the jurisdictions, investments and structures which will enable the taxpayer to hide their money.

John ran a UK business. John opened a Channel Islands bank account in which he could hide untaxed business income from HMRC.

John took his untaxed funds on a regular basis to a business contact, Michael, who travels regularly to the Channel Islands. Michael would take the money in a suitcase to the Channel Islands and deposit it in John's bank account.

In 2004, following unsolicited advice from the Channel Island bank, John transferred the bank accounts to a nominee Foundation in Panama to avoid reporting under the EU Savings Directive and retain secrecy over his funds. The Foundation was operated by Channel Island professionals.

Under the new offences: Michael was knowingly helping John to physically move funds offshore for tax evasion purposes. Michael was happy to do this because it fostered continued good business relations with John. Michael is guilty of a tax evasion facilitation offence by virtue of facilitating John's actions but, as he is an individual and not an associated person of a relevant body, no question of his committing the new offence arises.

The Channel Island bank's staff initially opened the account for John knowing that he wanted his activities to remain hidden from HMRC. Many years later the Channel Island bank staff actively advised John on how he could continue to hide his money. This conduct amounts to the criminal facilitation of tax evasion. The Channel Island bank would be guilty of the new offence unless it had taken reasonable steps to prevent its staff facilitating John's tax evasion. Its compliance with any applicable published guidance, its contractual terms for its staff, the training it provides, and any steps taken to monitor and ensure compliance would all be relevant to the assessment of whether it had taken reasonable steps.

The Channel Island bank professionals helped John to maintain a structure which facilitated his evasion activities. These professionals were asked by the bank to assist others in John's position and knew they were assisting people evading UK tax. This conduct amounts to the criminal facilitation of tax evasion. The bank therefore failed to prevent this conduct occurring and would be guilty of the new offence if it could not show that it had taken reasonable steps to prevent its associated persons from facilitating John's tax evasion.

Example 3) Delivery of infrastructure – e.g. setting up companies, trusts and other vehicles which are used to hide beneficial ownership; opening bank accounts; providing legal services and documentation which underpin the structures used in the evasion such as notary services and powers of attorney.

Manjit was the owner and Director of a UK-based interior design business. He generated false invoices and drew cheques with fictitious payee details logged in the company records, in order to divert proceeds offshore and reduce taxable profits in the UK. These cheques were in fact made payable to an extensive network of offshore discretionary trusts and corporate vehicles in Gibraltar, Belize, Seychelles, and the British Virgin Islands ('BVI').

In particular, the trustees invested the funds in a portfolio of bank accounts and investment properties held in the name of 'off the shelf' corporate vehicles in the Seychelles and BVI. The properties, acquired with the proceeds of tax evasion, were then rented out commercially with UK taxes paid on the rental income under the non-resident landlord scheme ('NRLS') to give the appearance of a genuine offshore ownership arrangement. The NRLS arrangement had been accepted by HMRC, being the only contemporaneous information that was available at the time.

Following an HMRC investigation, Manjit accepted that these transactions were fraudulent. Manjit admitted he deliberately committed offshore tax evasion.

Under the new offences: The trustees claimed that they believed everything they were doing was 'above board' – but they also stated that 'the affairs of their clients were none of their business'. HMRC's view was that the trustees turned a blind eye to the true beneficial ownership of the structure in order to retain Manjit's business. If the trustees in truth had knowledge of, but decided to ignore, Manjit's tax evasion, their conduct would amount to the criminal facilitation of Manjit's tax evasion and any trust company or partnership for which they worked would be guilty of the new offence if it had not taken reasonable steps to prevent the facilitation of Manjit's tax evasion. Their employer's compliance with any applicable published guidance, its contractual terms for its staff, the training it provides, and any steps taken to monitor and ensure compliance would all be relevant to the assessment of whether it had taken reasonable steps.

Of course, if the trustees were truly unaware of the tax evasion (whether out of negligence or otherwise) their assistance would not amount to a tax evasion facilitation offence (as these cannot be committed negligently) and the new offence would not be in point.

Example 4) Maintenance of infrastructure e.g. providing professional trustee or company director services including nominee services; providing virtual offices, IT structures, legal services and documentation which obscures the true nature of the arrangements such as audit certificates.

Paula was domiciled in Australia, but had been resident in the UK since the 1970s. In 2017, Paula wanted to regularise her affairs and disclosed to HMRC that she had been hiding substantial UK taxable income for a prolonged period. She had been using companies in Bermuda and the Bahamas to shelter both business and private assets and to facilitate the movement of funds through a variety of jurisdictions.

The network of companies had been set up by Paula's lawyer, a partner in a Guernsey-based legal partnership, in total secrecy, meaning that Paula had never paid UK taxes for more than 30 years of UK residence.

Under the new offences: The lawyer actively assisted Paula in evading UK taxes, knowing that the structures would enable her to evade UK tax. Any company or partnership for which the lawyer was an associated person would be guilty of the new offence if it had not taken reasonable steps to prevent him facilitating Paula's tax evasion. Its compliance with any applicable published guidance, its contractual terms for its staff, the training it provides, and any steps taken to monitor and ensure compliance would all be relevant to the assessment of whether it had taken reasonable steps.

Example 5) Financial assistance – helping the evader to move their money out of the UK, and/or keep it hidden by providing ongoing banking services and platforms; providing client accounts and escrow services; moving money through financial instruments, currency conversions etc.

Christoph was a wealthy non-domiciled individual who was a long-term UK resident. His job entitled him to significant bonus payments, related to duties performed wholly in the UK, on which he did not want to suffer UK tax. His UK accountant put him in touch with an adviser in Israel. The Israeli adviser set up a number of bank accounts in Singapore in the names of BVI-registered companies, under the control of a discretionary trust. Christoph arranged for his bonus payments to be lodged in the accounts operated in Singapore. As well as evading income tax on his employment income over a number of years, Christoph's settlements also attracted significant Inheritance Tax liabilities.

Under the new offences: The UK accountant understood what Christoph was trying to achieve, and for many years acted as a conduit through which Christoph contacted the Israeli adviser. This amounts to a tax evasion facilitation offence. The company or partnership that the accountant worked for would be guilty of the new offence if it had not taken reasonable steps to prevent him or her facilitating the tax evasion. Its compliance with any applicable published guidance, its contractual terms for its staff, the training it provides, and any steps taken to monitor and ensure compliance would all be relevant to the assessment of whether it had taken reasonable steps.

The Israeli adviser also understood Christoph's aims, and knew that secrecy was key to achieving those aims. He provided advice, and also set up and maintained the structure. This conduct facilitated Christoph's tax evasion. The company or partnership that the adviser worked for would be guilty of the new offence if it had not taken reasonable steps to prevent the adviser facilitating the tax evasion. Its compliance with any applicable published guidance, its contractual terms for its staff, the training it provides, and any steps taken to monitor and ensure compliance would all be relevant to the assessment of whether it had taken reasonable steps.

The Singapore bank's staff were unaware that the structure was being used to evade UK tax. As such they would not have the requisite state of mind to be guilty of facilitating Christoph's tax evasion. Therefore the Singapore bank could not be guilty of failing to prevent its staff from facilitating tax evasion.

Appendix C
CRIMINAL FINANCES ACT 2017 – EXPLANATORY NOTES (EXTRACTS)

C1   POLICY BACKGROUND

OTHER PROVISIONS IN PART 1

Civil recovery of the proceeds of gross human rights abuses or violations

25   This provision expands the definition of 'unlawful conduct' within Part 5 of POCA to include conduct outside the UK by a public official that constitutes gross human rights abuse (defined as torture or inhuman, cruel or degrading treatment) of a person on the grounds that they have been obtaining, exercising, defending or promoting human rights, or have sought to expose gross human rights abuse conducted by a public official. Activity by any person that is connected with such conduct is also caught within the expanded definition. As a result, any property obtained through this conduct will be subject to the existing civil recovery powers within Part 5 of POCA.

Granting civil recovery powers to the Financial Conduct Authority and HMRC

26   POCA contains a set of provisions for the recovery of property in cases where there has not been a conviction, but where it can be shown on the balance of probabilities that that property has been obtained through unlawful conduct. These powers are known as 'civil recovery'. The Act extends powers to the Financial Conduct Authority (FCA) and HMRC to allow proceedings to be taken in the High Court to recover criminal property (with the aid of the supporting investigation powers), without the need for the owner of the property to be convicted of a criminal offence. At present, the NCA, SFO and Crown Prosecution Service (CPS) (or Public Prosecution Service of Northern Ireland) have access to these powers. Only Scottish Ministers can pursue civil recovery in the Scottish courts and the amendments to POCA will not alter that position.

Extending Investigation powers to members of staff at the Serious Fraud Office

27   Staff at the SFO did not previously have direct access to the investigative and ancillary asset recovery powers in POCA, unlike officers of all other national law enforcement agencies. The Act grants them direct access to those powers.

Making it a criminal offence to obstruct/assault law enforcement officers

28   Officers from a range of agencies – Immigration Enforcement, the CPS, the SFO and others – are able to use the various search and seizure powers in POCA. Currently, there are criminal offences of obstruction or assault which apply in respect of some officers who are carrying out duties under POCA, but not all officers are captured. The Act ensures that all officers are afforded the same degree of protection, while exercising powers under POCA. This brings consistency of approach and ensure[s] that all users of POCA powers are protected.

Payment of a defendant's cash in settlement of a confiscation order

29   POCA previously allowed the payment of a defendant's cash which had been seized by the police or HMRC to be paid across by order of the court in settlement of an outstanding confiscation order. The Act extends the circumstances in which this power operates to include cash that has been seized by any law enforcement agency under a warrant or a statutory seizure power and whether it is being held by that agency or paid into an account.

Enabling the use of POCA powers for confiscation order 're-visits'

30   Confiscation orders are made to recover the financial benefit that a criminal obtained from their crimes. They are capped at an amount equivalent to the value of the assets available to the Defendant at the time the order is made. This is to ensure that orders are not made in unrealistic amounts that exceed the sum which is actually recoverable from the offender. However, POCA also contains a provision to enable investigators to 're-visit' any confiscation order that has been paid off but was made for an amount lower than the total criminal benefit figure. This means that, if a criminal pays off an order but goes on to make more money in the future, the court can consider whether it would be proportionate to recover more money or property.

31   At present, the financial investigation powers in POCA – for example, powers to monitor bank accounts, search property, or require the production of evidence – are not available for investigations linked to re-visits. The Act extends these powers to ensure they are available for re-visits.

32   The Act also allows for re-visits on confiscation orders where additional evidence emerges after the order has been discharged. This allows for orders to be increased if evidence satisfies the court that either the defendant's benefit from their crime or amount available to pay an order is more than was identified at the time the confiscation order was made.

Allow the writing-off of orders made under the Drug Trafficking Offences Act 1986

33   The Serious Crime Act 2015 allowed for confiscation orders made against people who have subsequently died, to be written off. This only covered orders made under POCA. There are still some orders made under earlier legislation – the Drug Trafficking Offences Act 1986 – to which the amendment in the Serious Crime Act 2015 did not apply. This Act addresses this gap.

Levels of authorisation needed for the use of POCA search and seizure powers

34   POCA contains search and seizure powers to prevent the dissipation of property that may be used to satisfy a future confiscation order following a conviction. Their use must be authorised by a senior officer. Previously, an Accredited Financial Investigator (AFI) could obtain that authorisation from a senior civilian AFI, working for a police force, but not from a senior police officer. The Act allows for AFIs to receive authorisation from a senior police officer.

Circumstances in which 'mixed property' is recoverable

35   The existing civil recovery provisions within POCA allow for other property to be recovered when the criminal property has been mixed with 'clean property'.

36   POCA contains a non-exhaustive list of situations where so called 'mixed property' (i.e. where 'clean property' is associated with that connected to criminal conduct) can be recovered. The Act adds to that list to include property that has been used to redeem a mortgage, providing greater clarity of the extent of civil recovery powers.

Miscellaneous provisions relating to Scotland

37   Operational agencies in Scotland identified two bespoke amendments to POCA to reflect the nuances of the Scottish legal system. The Act:

    a.   allows, for the first time, the High Court of Justiciary and the Sheriff Court the power to order money in accounts and money held as cash productions to be paid in satisfaction of a confiscation order (note that a similar power already existed and is extended by this Act in relation to England, Wales and Northern Ireland); and

    b.   places a duty on the Court of Session to grant the trustee for civil recovery a decree of removing and a warrant for ejection to recover possession of heritable property in respect of which it makes a recovery order.

Definitions

38   The Act clarifies minor and technical inconsistencies in various definitions in existing legislation – the concept of 'distress', a mechanism for taking control of goods; the definition of a bank (where POCA previously referred to the now-repealed Banking Act 1987); and the definition of 'free property' in POCA.

C2   COMMENTARY ON PROVISIONS OF ACT

Part 1: Proceeds of crime

CHAPTER 4: ENFORCEMENT POWERS AND RELATED OFFENCES

Extension of powers

Section 17: Serious Fraud Office

169 Section 17 introduces Schedule 1, which makes a series of technical amendments to a number of provisions in POCA, in order to allow SFO officers to directly access the asset preservation powers under Parts 2 and 4 of POCA, the civil recovery powers under Part 5 and the investigation powers in Part 8.

170 Schedule 1 contains the consequential amendments to POCA.

171 The inclusion of SFO staff in the 'appropriate officer', 'senior officer' and 'senior appropriate officer' definitions under various provisions grant them direct access to asset preservation powers in confiscation proceedings, recovery of cash and investigatory powers.

Section 18: Her Majesty's Revenue and Customs: removal of restrictions

172 Officers of HMRC currently have various powers to enable them to investigate crimes, such as the power of arrest or the power to apply for a search warrant. However, these powers are unavailable in relation to offences committed against certain functions of HMRC (typically former Inland Revenue functions). Section 18 seeks to remove such restrictions, enabling officers of HMRC to use their existing criminal investigation powers in relation to crimes relating to any of HMRC's functions.

173 Sub-section (2) removes the current restriction within section 23A of the Criminal Law (Consolidation) (Scotland) Act 1995 (CLCSA) that prevents HMRC from using its criminal powers for offences relating to prohibitions and restrictions or the movement of goods. This gives officers of HMRC in Scotland criminal powers in relation to crimes involving prohibitions and restrictions or the movement of goods similar to those currently enjoyed by officers of HMRC in England and Wales and Northern Ireland.

174 Sub-sections (3), (4) and (5) remove restrictions on the use of HMRC's criminal

investigation powers in relation to offences relating to functions of HMRC that are functions previously held by the Inland Revenue.

175 Sub-section (3) amends the definition of 'officer of law' in section 307 of the Criminal Procedure (Scotland) Act [1995].

176 Sub-section (4) amends the Proceeds of Crime Act 2002 to remove the restrictions on the exercise of the powers contained in sections 289, 294, 375C and 408C, so that these powers can be used when investigating crimes related to former inland revenue functions for which they are currently unavailable.

177 Sub-section (5) amends the Finance Act 2007 to remove the specified restriction at section 84, enabling HMRC officers to use their criminal investigatory powers from the Police and Criminal Evidence Act 1984 in relation to certain former revenue functions in relation to which they are not currently available.

Section 19: Her Majesty's Revenue and Customs: new powers

178 Section 19 makes amendments to section 316 of POCA in relation to England, Wales and Northern Ireland to include HMRC in the definition of 'enforcement authority'. This allows a member of staff of HMRC to bring forward civil recovery proceedings under Chapter 2 of Part 5 of POCA against property or any person who they think holds recoverable property. 'Recoverable property' is defined in sections 304 to 310 of POCA and essentially means the proceeds of crime or property that directly represents such. The amendment provides HMRC with the powers to bring civil recovery proceedings (section 243) and to make applications in connection with civil recovery proceedings such as: property freezing orders (section 245A) and interim receiving orders (section 246).

179 The inclusion of HMRC staff in the definition of 'appropriate officer' and 'senior appropriate officer' in section 378 of POCA allows them to apply for the orders and warrants to build a case for civil recovery proceedings. They are officers for the purposes of a 'civil recovery investigation', see section 341 of POCA.

Section 20: Financial Conduct Authority

180 Section 20 makes similar amendments to section 316 of POCA in relation to England, Wales and Northern Ireland, to include the FCA in the definition of 'enforcement authority'.

181 The inclusion of FCA staff in the definition of 'appropriate officer' and 'senior appropriate officer' in section 378 of POCA 2002 allows them to apply for the orders and warrants to build a case for civil recovery proceedings.

Section 21: Immigration Officers

182 Section 21 amends section 24 of the UK Borders Act 2007 (UKBA). That section already provided immigration officers with access to the powers to search for, seize, detain and seek the forfeiture of cash under POCA. Those powers are provided in Chapter 3 of Part 5 of POCA and relate to cash that is either the proceeds of unlawful conduct or intended for use in such. Section 21 provides that immigration officers also have access to the powers in this Act relating to the recovery of listed assets in summary proceedings (see section 14) and the forfeiture of money held in bank and building society accounts (see section 15).

183 The heading of section 24 of UKBA is amended to clarify that the power now extends to items other than cash.

184 Section 24(1) of UKBA is amended to provide the civil recovery powers in Chapter 3 to 3B, which cover cash seizure, forfeiture of moveable property and forfeiture of funds held in bank accounts, to immigration officers. The relevant sub-sections within section 24 are then amended to permit all of the aspects of the powers to be available to those officers.

Assault and obstruction offences

Section 22: Search and seizure warrants: assault and obstruction offences

185 Section 22 inserts new section 356A into POCA, making it an offence to assault or wilfully obstruct an appropriate person who is acting under the authority of a search and seizure warrant issued under section 352 of POCA. The definition of an appropriate person includes a NCA officer discharging a warrant in connection with two specified investigations, namely a civil recovery investigation or an exploitation proceeds investigation. It also includes an officer of the FCA and a member of staff of the CPS or the Public Prosecution Service for Northern Ireland, in relation to civil recovery investigations.

Section 23: Assault and obstruction offence in relation to SFO officers

186 Section 23 inserts new section 453B into POCA. This creates an offence of assaulting or obstructing an officer of the SFO who is exercising a relevant POCA search or seizure power. The 'relevant powers' are detailed in sub-section (5).

Section 24: External requests, orders and investigations

187 Section 24 amends sections 444 and 445 of POCA, which give the Secretary of State the power to make provisions (by way of Orders in Council) in respect of orders made by an overseas court. Section 444 applies to 'external orders', which is defined in section 447 to mean orders by an overseas court for freezing or recovery of property obtained as a result of criminal conduct. Section 445 applies to 'external investigations' which are defined in section 447 of POCA as investigations into whether property has been obtained through unlawful conduct, and the extent or whereabouts of any property so obtained. The principal Orders made under those sections are the Proceeds of Crime Act 2002 (External Requests and Orders) Order 2005 (SI 2005 No. 3181 as amended), The Proceeds of Crime Act 2002 (External Investigations) Order 2013 (SI 2013 No. 2605 as amended) and The Proceeds of Crime Act 2002 (External Investigations) Order 2014 (SI 2014 No. 1893 as amended). Section 444 relates to external (overseas) requests and orders – for example the freezing of property in the United Kingdom which may be needed to satisfy overseas orders – and section 445 makes provision for investigative powers to be made available in respect of overseas investigations.

Section 25: Obstruction offence in relation to immigration officers

188 Section 25 inserts new section 453C into POCA, providing an offence for resisting or wilfully obstructing immigration officers exercising a relevant POCA search and seizure power. The 'relevant powers' are listed in sub-section (3). There is already an offence for assaulting an immigration officer in the course of their duties in section 22 of the UK Borders Act 2007.

CHAPTER 5: MISCELLANEOUS

Seized money: England and Wales and Northern Ireland

Section 26: Seized money: England and Wales

189 Section 26 amends section 67 of POCA. Section 67 of POCA provides the magistrates' court with a power to enforce a confiscation order. In particular, it relates to a defendant's money seized by the police or HMRC under the Police and Criminal Evidence Act 1984 that has to be paid into a bank or building society account. The court can order that money be paid to the court in satisfaction of a confiscation order. This section amends the existing scheme provided in section 67 in three ways. Firstly, it is

extended beyond police and HMRC officers to all law enforcement officers who have the power to seize money. Secondly, section 67 now applies to money that has been seized under any power relating to a criminal investigation or proceeding (not just the Police and Criminal Evidence Act), or under the investigatory powers in POCA. Thirdly, this section amends section 67 so that it applies to money however it is held by law enforcement, and not just in a bank or building society account.

190 There is also a technical amendment to provide a definition of 'bank' following the repeal of the provision in the Banking Act 1987 that previously provided the definition.

Section 27: Seized money: Northern Ireland

191 This section extends the power of the court in Northern Ireland in a similar way to the changes made for England and Wales in section 26. It also makes an equivalent technical amendment to the definition of 'bank' for Northern Ireland.

Miscellaneous provisions relating to Scotland

Section 28: Seized money

192 Section 28 inserts a new section 131ZA into Part 3 of POCA. This largely replicates in Scotland the effect, as amended by this Act, of section 67 for England and Wales, and section 215 for Northern Ireland. See the commentary above on the amendments made by this Act to sections 67 and 215 of POCA.

193 Any wilful failure to comply with an order of the court under this section will be dealt with as contempt of court.

194 The new section confers on the Scottish Ministers the power to amend it, by regulations, so that it applies to money held in an account maintained with other financial institutions or to other realisable cash or cash-like instruments or products, and to make the necessary provision for any such financial instrument or product to be realised into cash. This regulation-making power is subject to the affirmative procedure.

Section 29: Recovery orders relating to heritable property

195 Section 29 amends Part 5 of POCA (civil recovery of the proceeds etc. of unlawful conduct), to provide a more efficient and effective means for the trustee for civil recovery to recover possession of heritable property in Scotland where the Court of Session makes a recovery order in respect of that property under section 266.

196 It amends sections 266 and 267 of POCA to allow for the recovery of possession to be dealt with as part of the civil recovery proceedings in the Court of Session rather than, as at present, require a subsequent and separate action in the Sheriff Court. New section 266(8ZA) requires the Court of Session, on the application of the Scottish Ministers (as the enforcement authority), to grant decree of removing and warrant for ejection in relation to any persons occupying heritable property in respect of which it makes a recovery order. New section 267(3)(ba) confers the function of enforcing such a decree and warrant on the trustee for civil recovery, in whom the property vests by virtue of the recovery order.

197 This section also inserts two new sections into Part 5 of POCA in consequence of these provisions. As part of the regime to safeguard against homelessness, new section 245ZA requires the Scottish Ministers to notify the relevant local authority where they apply for a decree of removing and warrant for ejection in relation to heritable property which consists of or includes a dwellinghouse. New section 269A sets out the effect on leases and occupancy rights where the Court of Session, in making a recovery order, also grants decree of removing and warrant for ejection in relation to any persons occupying the heritable property.

Section 30: Money received by administrators

198 Section 30 is a technical amendment to Paragraph 6 of Schedule 3 to POCA (which deals with money received by an administrator in Scotland) to provide a definition of 'bank' following the repeal of the provision in the Banking Act 1987 that previously provided the definition.

Other miscellaneous provisions

Section 31: Accredited financial investigators

199 Sections 47A–47S of POCA, which provide search and seizure powers in England and Wales, prevent the dissipation of realisable property that may be used to satisfy a future confiscation order. Section 31 amends section 47G of POCA to allow civilian AFIs in a police force to obtain approval to use search and seizure powers from a senior police officer (an inspector). Such approval may be sought in cases where seeking the appropriate approval of a justice of the peace is not practicable. The amendment provided by section 31 enables an AFI to seek the approval of a senior police officer as is the case with a constable.

200 Section 31 makes a similar amendment to section 290 of POCA relating to civilian AFIs in a police force. It provides that they now have the powers to search for cash with the approval of a senior police officer (of at least inspector level). This replaces the need to define by secondary legislation authorising officers for police searches undertaken by civilian staff.

201 Section 31 also makes equivalent amendments for Northern Ireland.

Section 32: Reconsideration of discharged orders

202 Sections 21 and 22 of POCA allow for the reconsideration of a confiscation order already made if new evidence becomes available. They allow for the amount on the confiscation order to be increased either to reflect a higher benefit value (i.e. the amount that the defendant made from their crime) or an increase of the available amount (i.e. the amount they had available to pay a confiscation order). This section amends POCA to allow for this reconsideration approach even in relation to confiscation orders that have been discharged by Court order under sections 24 or 25. Those sections apply respectively where there was either an inadequate amount to settle the order or there was only a small amount outstanding.

Section 33: Confiscation investigations: determination of the available amount

203 Section 33 amends section 341(1) of POCA to extend the definition of a confiscation investigation so as to include the ability to investigate the amount available to a defendant for satisfying a confiscation order. This amount is known as the 'available amount' and is the value of all of the defendant's property, minus certain prior obligations of the defendant's such as earlier fines, plus the value of all tainted gifts made by the defendant (see sections 9 and 77 of POCA). In considering the value of the confiscation order made against a defendant, the court will set an amount equivalent to the defendant's benefit from their crime(s) unless the 'available amount' is shown to be less, and in those cases the defendant is ordered to pay that lesser amount.

204 The extension of investigation powers allows the police and others to test the 'available amount' claimed by a defendant. Under section 7(2) of POCA, the defendant is required to prove to the court that the available amount to settle a confiscation order is less than the benefit figure. The amendment also allows the police and others to investigate the financial position of a defendant in cases of a reconsideration under section 22 of POCA. Section 22 applies where the court made a confiscation order in an amount lower than the defendant's assessed benefit because there was insufficient property at that time to satisfy an order in the full amount. An application can be subsequently made to the

Crown Court for the court to recalculate the available amount in cases where the defendant is known to have obtained further property that could be used to satisfy a confiscation order up to the value, as previously assessed by the court, of the benefit they made from their criminality.

205 When calculating the amount that is available for a confiscation order, a court will take account of the factors in section 9 of POCA and will make a determination of the available amount based on the evidence provided. If a revisit is sought under section 22 of POCA by a relevant applicant, the court must make a new calculation of the available amount by applying section 9 as if it were making a determination at the time of the original order. It is then for the court to determine in all the circumstances whether to vary the confiscation order (see section 22(3)).

206 This amendment has the effect that investigatory powers in Part 8 of POCA can be used to obtain evidence in support of an application under section 22, to enable the court to reapply section 9 as required.

Section 34: Confiscation orders and civil recovery: minor amendments

207 Section 34 makes minor amendments to sections 82, 148, 230, 245D, 290, 297A, 302 and 306 of POCA and section 8 of the Serious Crime Act 2015. The definition of 'free property' in sections 82, 148 and 230 of POCA is extended to include cash which is detained pending the hearing of a forfeiture application. Free property can be taken into account when calculating the 'available amount' for satisfying a confiscation order. It is any property that is not already subject to certain kinds of forfeiture and deprivation orders – property already subject to one of those orders in earlier proceedings cannot then be taken into account for the purposes of confiscation proceedings because it is not 'available' and is accounted for elsewhere.

208 The amendments also update POCA to ensure that it is consistent with legislative changes to the concept of 'distress', and extend the list of situations whereby mixed property – i.e. criminal property mixed with 'clean' property – can be recovered. The non-exhaustive list in section 306 now includes property that has been used to redeem a mortgage.

209 The amendments also extend the provisions in the Serious Crime Act 2015 that allow for the writing-off of orders to include orders made under the Drug Trafficking Offences Act 1986.

Part 2: Terrorist property

Disclosures of information

Section 35: Disclosure orders

210 Section 35 and Schedule 2 introduce a disclosure order regime under TACT. Schedule 2 amends TACT by inserting a new Schedule 5A. Schedule 5A makes provision for the making of disclosure orders in connection with investigations into terrorist financing offences and terrorist property. Part 1 of the Schedule makes provision for England and Wales and Northern Ireland, and Part 2 of the Schedule makes equivalent provision for Scotland. Paragraph numbers below refer to paragraphs in the new Schedule 5A Part 1 of TACT.

211 Paragraphs 1 to 8 of Part 1 provide details of the process for making an application for a disclosure order in England, Wales and Northern Ireland. Paragraph 4 defines a terrorist financing investigation as a terrorist investigation into the commission, preparation or instigation of an offence under any of sections 15 to 18, or the identification of terrorist property or its movement or use.

212 Paragraph 9 allows an appropriate officer to apply to a Crown Court judge for a disclosure order so far as relating to a terrorist financing investigation.

213 Sub-paragraph 9(3) defines a disclosure order as an order authorising an officer to give

anyone he thinks has relevant information a written notice requiring that person to answer questions, provide information or to produce documents on any matter that is relevant to the confiscation investigation.

214 Paragraph 10 sets out the requirements for making a disclosure order, which include that there must be reasonable grounds for suspecting that a person has committed an offence under any of sections 15 to 18, or that the property specified in the application is terrorist property. There must also be reasonable grounds for believing that information which may be provided in compliance with a requirement imposed under the order is likely to be of substantial value to the terrorist financing investigation concerned; and for believing that it is in the public interest for the information to be provided, having regard to the benefit likely to accrue to the investigation if the information is obtained.

215 Paragraph 11 provides for two offences in relation to disclosure orders. An offence is committed under paragraph 11(1) if, without reasonable excuse, a person fails to comply with a requirement imposed under a disclosure order. A person guilty of this offence is liable on summary conviction in (i) England and Wales, to imprisonment for a term not exceeding 51 weeks or a fine, or both and (ii) Northern Ireland, to imprisonment for a term not exceeding six months or a fine not exceeding level 5 on the standard scale, or both. It is also an offence under paragraph 11(3) if a person purports to comply with a requirement imposed under a disclosure order by knowingly or recklessly making a false or misleading statement. A person guilty of this offence is liable on (a) indictment to imprisonment for a term not exceeding two years or a fine, or both; or (b) summary conviction in (i) England and Wales, to imprisonment for a term not exceeding 12 months or a fine, or both; and (ii) Northern Ireland, to imprisonment for a term not exceeding six months or a fine not exceeding level 5 on the standard scale, or both.

216 Paragraph 12 preserves the privilege against self-incrimination by providing that a statement made in response to a disclosure order may not be used in evidence against the statement maker in criminal proceedings. Paragraph 12(2) sets out certain exceptions to this rule. Paragraph 12 does not make any reference to limitations of use of other information or material produced by that person in response to the disclosure order.

217 Sub-paragraph 13(1) provides that a disclosure order does not confer the right to adduce information or material from a person which would come within the scope of legal professional privilege (LPP), save that a lawyer can be required to provide the name and address of a client.

218 Paragraph 14 makes supplementary provisions in relation to disclosure orders. Paragraph 14(1) provides that an application for a disclosure order may be made without notice to a judge in chambers. Paragraph 14(4) makes provision for the court to vary or discharge a disclosure order, whilst paragraph 14(3) provides that an application for variation or discharge can be made either by the person who applied for the order or any person affected by the order.

219 Part 1 of the Schedule makes provision for disclosure orders in England and Wales and Northern Ireland. Part 2 of the Schedule makes equivalent provision for Scotland. The approach in Scotland varies from that in England, Wales and Northern Ireland in some aspects, for example, applications for disclosure orders in Scotland are made to the High Court of Justiciary.

Section 36: Sharing of information within the regulated sector

220 Section 36 inserts, after section 21C of TACT, new sections 21CA–21CF, which make provision for the voluntary sharing of information between relevant undertakings in the regulated sector in connection with suspicions of terrorist financing or the identification of terrorist property or its movement or use.

221 Section 21CA allows a person (A) in a regulated sector business to disclose information, which came to them in the course of their business, with another person in a regulated sector business (in response to a request from them or the police), where (A) is satisfied

that disclosing the information may assist in determining any matter in connection with a suspicion that a person is involved in the commission of a terrorist financing offence or identifying terrorist property. The person making the request must notify a constable that a request is to be made, unless a constable has requested the disclosure.

222 Section 21CB specifies the information to be provided in a disclosure request or the notification to a constable.

223 Section 21CC specifies the effect of section 21CA on required disclosures under section 21A of TACT, in particular that the making of a required notification under section 21CA in good faith or the making of a joint disclosure report in good faith is to be treated as satisfying the requirement to make a required disclosure. Section 21CC also sets out the information to be provided as part of the joint disclosure report, and the timeframe for information sharing to take place before a joint disclosure report must be provided. Where the request is made by a constable, the applicable period will be specified by a constable. Where the request is made by the regulated sector business, the applicable period is 28 days, however a constable may vary the period of 28 days by giving written notice to the person who made the required notification.

224 Section 21CD provides certain limitations on the application of section 21CC, in particular the fact that the provisions in 21CC do not remove the requirement to make a required disclosure under section 21A of TACT on matters which are wider than the disclosure request.

225 Section 21CE provides that a relevant disclosure (one made in compliance with section 21CA) made in good faith does not breach an obligation of confidence or any other restrictions on the disclosure of information (however imposed). This section also clarifies that a relevant disclosure may not include information obtained from a UK law enforcement agency (as defined within the section) unless that agency consents to the disclosure. See also consequential amendments to section 21G (tipping off: other permitted disclosures) of TACT and to the Data Protection Act 1998 which are contained within paragraphs 6 to 10 of Schedule 5.

226 Section 21CF provides interpretation of terms used within this section.

Section 37: Further information orders

227 Section 37 inserts, after section 22A of TACT, new sections 22B–22E, which make provision for a law enforcement officer to apply to the court for a further information order which is an order requiring further information to be provided by the regulated sector in relation to a disclosure under section 21A of TACT or a corresponding disclosure requirement (under the law of a foreign country) which would assist an investigation about the commission of a terrorist financing offence or with identifying terrorist property.

228 Section 22B sets out the conditions for making such an order including that the information sought must relate to a matter arising from a disclosure under TACT or to a corresponding disclosure requirement under the law of a foreign state (where the information is sought by a foreign authority). If a person fails to comply with the further information order in England, Wales or Northern Ireland, then they may be ordered to pay a monetary penalty of up to £5000; in Scotland, contempt proceedings would be the available penalty.

229 Section 22C provides that statements made by a person, in response to a further information order, may not be used in evidence against that person in criminal proceedings, unless the limited exceptions provisions in sub-section (2) apply.

230 Section 22D sets out the process for appeals against a decision on an application for a further information order. The appeal can be made by any person who was a party to the proceedings on the application. On appeal, the relevant court may make, discharge or vary an order.

231 Section 22E provides that a further information order does not oblige the person to

provide legally privileged information. Sub-section (3) also provides that any information provided is given immunity from any restriction on the disclosure of information.

Civil recovery

Section 38: Forfeiture of terrorist cash

232 Section 38 amends Schedule 1 to ATCSA which provides for the forfeiture of terrorist cash. In particular, this section amends the definition of terrorist cash in paragraph 1 of Schedule 1 to include gaming vouchers, fixed-value casino tokens and betting receipts. Gaming vouchers are defined as a voucher in physical form issued by a gaming machine, such as a fixed odds betting terminal, that represents a right to be paid the amount stated on it. Fixed value casino tokens mean a token, issued by a casino that represents a right to be paid the value stated on it. Betting receipt means a receipt in physical form that represents a right to be paid an amount in respect of a bet placed with a person holding a betting licence.

233 This section also amends paragraph 3 of Schedule 1 to extend the length of time that the magistrates' court or (in Scotland) the sheriff may authorise the detention of cash following seizure from three months to six months (subject to an overall cap of two years). Paragraph 9 is amended to make provision for the court to order the release of detained cash to a person to whom the cash belongs but from whom it was not seized, providing certain conditions are met.

234 Section 38(4) inserts after paragraph 5 of Schedule 1 new Part 2A (comprising paragraphs 5A to 5F) which provides for the forfeiture of terrorist cash without a court order, allowing terrorist cash to be administratively forfeited by way of a notice issued by an appropriate law enforcement officer.

235 Paragraph 5A makes provision for a cash forfeiture notice to be given by a senior officer for the purpose of forfeiting terrorist cash which has been detained and specifies the information which such a notice must contain. It also provides a period of 30 days for objections to the proposed forfeiture to be made and requires the Secretary of State to make regulations which detail how a forfeiture notice is to be given.

236 Paragraph 5B sets out what the effect of a cash forfeiture notice is and the circumstances in which such a notice will lapse.

237 Paragraph 5C makes provision for the detention of cash where a cash forfeiture notice has lapsed following an objection being made thereto and the period for detaining the cash authorised by the court under paragraph 3(2) has expired.

238 Paragraph 5D makes provision for a person aggrieved by the forfeiture of cash via a cash forfeiture notice to apply to the magistrates' court or (in Scotland) the sheriff for an order to set aside the forfeiture.

239 In paragraph 5E, provision is made for the release of cash which is detained following the giving or lapse of a cash forfeiture notice. The person from whom the cash was seized may apply for its release to the magistrates' court or (in Scotland) the sheriff, which may direct its release if not satisfied that the cash is terrorist cash. Alternatively, an authorised officer may release the cash if satisfied that the detention is no longer justified.

240 Paragraph 5F deals with the application of cash which has been forfeited under a cash forfeiture notice. Provision is made for cash which is forfeited by this process to be paid into the Consolidated Fund or, if forfeited in Scotland, to be paid in the Scottish Consolidated Fund but not before the end of the period within which an application to set aside the forfeiture can be made or, if such an application is made, until it is determined.

Section 39: Forfeiture of certain personal (or moveable) property

241 Section 39 introduces Schedule 3, which amends Schedule 1 to ATCSA by inserting a

new Part 4A which comprises paragraphs 10A–10P and which makes provision for the seizure, detention and forfeiture of certain personal or moveable property ('listed assets').

242 Paragraph 10A(1) defines a 'listed asset' and paragraph 10A(2) provides that the Secretary of State may by regulations add or remove items from the definition of 'listed asset'.

243 Paragraph 10B(1) provides that an authorised officer may seize any item of property if he has reasonable grounds for suspecting that it is a listed asset and it is property within the meaning of paragraph 10B(1)(b) i.e. it is intended to be used for the purposes of terrorism, or consists of resources of an organisation which is a proscribed organisation, or it is property which is earmarked as terrorist property, as defined in Part 5 of Schedule 1 to ATCSA. Under sub-paragraph 10B(2), an authorised officer may also seize any item of property if he has reasonable grounds for suspecting it is a listed asset, that part of it is property within the meaning of paragraph 10B(1)(b) and it is not reasonably practicable to seize only that part.

244 Paragraph 10C provides for the detention of property seized under paragraph 10B by an authorised officer for an initial period of 48 hours providing there continues to be reasonable grounds for suspecting it is a listed asset or property within the meaning of paragraph 10B(1)(b).

245 Paragraph 10D provides that the period for which property seized under paragraph 10B may be detained can be extended by a judicial authority for a period of up to six months, up to an overall maximum of two years (from the first order). The judicial authority may make this order if satisfied that the property is a listed asset and there are reasonable grounds for suspecting that it is property within the meaning of paragraph 10B(1)(b), and that its continued detention is justified whilst investigations are made into its origin or intended use, or whilst consideration is being given to the bringing of proceedings for an offence with which the property is connected, or whilst such proceedings are ongoing.

246 Paragraph 10D(4) provides that the first application to extend the period of detention may be made and heard without notice, and in private.

247 Paragraph 10E(1) provides that an authorised officer may carry out tests on any item of property seized under paragraph 10B for the purpose of establishing whether it is a listed asset. Paragraph 10E(2) provides that such property must be safely stored throughout the period during which it is detained.

248 Paragraph 10F makes provision for the release of property detained under Part 4A. Where a judicial authority is satisfied, on application by the person from whom the property was seized, that the conditions for detention are no longer met, it may direct the release of the property, or part thereof. An authorised officer or, in Scotland, the procurator fiscal may release all or part of the property if satisfied that the detention can no longer be justified (providing the judicial authority has been notified).

249 Paragraph 10G provides that a judicial authority, on application, may order the forfeiture of property or any part of it if satisfied that the property is a listed asset and what is to be forfeited is within the meaning of paragraph 10B(1)(b) i.e. it is intended for use in terrorism, or that it is the resources of a proscribed organisation, or that it is property earmarked as terrorist property. It also provides that a magistrates' court may provide for the payment of reasonable legal expenses that a person has or may reasonably incur in certain proceedings from the proceeds of realisation.

250 Paragraphs 10H to 10K explain how associated property and joint property are to be dealt with when forfeiture is ordered.

251 Paragraph 10H defines 'associated property' (at sub-paragraph (3)) and defines an 'excepted joint owner' (at sub-paragraph (5)) for the purpose of considering forfeitable property of a joint tenant.

252 Paragraph 10I provides that a judicial authority may order that a person who holds associated property or who is an excepted joint owner may retain the property but must pay the law enforcement agency a sum equivalent to the value of the recoverable share.

This section applies where there is agreement amongst the parties as to the extent of the recoverable portion of the property. The section also provides that a relevant court may provide for the payment of reasonable legal expenses to the person from whom the property was seized from the proceeds of realisation.

253 Paragraph 10J describes how a judicial authority can deal with a person who holds associated property or who is an excepted joint owner but where there is no agreement under Paragraph 10I. If an order for forfeiture of part of the property is made, and the court considers it is 'just and equitable' to do so, it may also order that the excepted joint owner's interest will be extinguished, or that the excepted joint owner's interest will be severed, and it may order that a payment be made to that individual.

254 Paragraph 10K provides for a right of appeal against a forfeiture decision made under Paragraph 10G to 10J.

255 Paragraph 10L sets out how the right of appeal will operate in certain circumstances where an organisation is challenging its status as a proscribed organisation, as defined by section 3 of TACT.

256 Paragraph 10M provides that the relevant law enforcement agency must realise the property or make arrangements for [its] realisation, subject to any appeal rights against the forfeiture being exhausted.

257 Paragraph 10N sets out the order in which the proceeds realised should be applied.

258 Paragraph 10O provides for the true owner of the property to apply for its release.

259 Paragraph 10P provides that where no forfeiture is made, following seizure, the person from whom the property was seized, or the person to whom the cash belongs, may apply to the court for compensation.

Section 40: Forfeiture of money held in bank and building society accounts

260 Section 40 and Paragraph 2 to Schedule 4 insert into Schedule 1 of ATCSA a new Part 4B, which make provision for the freezing and forfeiture of bank and building society accounts, where those accounts contain monies which are: intended to be used for terrorism, the resources of a proscribed organisation or property earmarked as terrorist property.

261 Paragraph 10Q allows a 'senior officer', or an 'enforcement officer' with senior officer approval, (as defined in sub-paragraph 7) to apply for an account freezing order (AFO) in respect of bank and building society accounts, where there are reasonable grounds to suspect that the money held in them are: intended to be used for terrorism, the resources of a proscribed organisation or property earmarked as terrorist property. The AFO can be made without notice, if notice of application would prejudice the taking of any steps to later forfeit such monies.

262 The AFO prohibits each person by or for who the account to which the order applies is operated, from making withdrawals or payments from the account. The AFO must be applied for at a magistrates' court in England, Wales and Northern Ireland, or to the Sheriff in Scotland. The funds within the account remain with the bank or building society.

263 Sub-paragraph 10Q(3)(b) introduces a requirement to consult with HM Treasury into the AFO application process. The requirement to consult will enable the Treasury to consider whether it should be exercising its powers under the Terrorist Asset-Freezing etc. Act 2010 in the particular case.

264 Paragraph 10R defines the term 'bank'.

265 Paragraph 10S provides that the court may make the order, if [it] is satisfied that the funds in the account (whether all or in part) meet the relevant definition in Paragraph 10Q.

266 The court sets the timeframe for the AFO which may not exceed an overall 2-year maximum period, starting on the day it was made.

267 Paragraph 10T allows a court to vary or set aside an account freezing order at any time,

and can also do so upon application by any person affected by such an order. This is at the discretion of the court.

268 Paragraph 10U allows the court to make exclusions from the restriction on activity on the account for the purpose of meeting living expenses or to allow a person to carry on a business or trade. It also permits exclusions for legal expenses.

269 Paragraph 10V provides that a court, in which proceedings relating to a frozen account are pending, can stay those proceedings if satisfied that an AFO order has been applied for or obtained. That court may also order that proceedings can continue on any terms it thinks appropriate.

270 Paragraph 10W allows a senior officer to give an 'account forfeiture notice', which is a notice for the purposes of forfeiting the funds in an account. The funds must be subject to an account freezing order for an account forfeiture notice to be served. This is an administrative procedure.

271 Sub-paragraph 10W(2) provides that a senior officer may give a notice that they intend to seek forfeiture of the balance of the account, provided that they are satisfied that the contents either are intended to be used for the purposes of terrorism, consist of the resources of a proscribed organisation or are property earmarked as terrorist property. Per sub-paragraph 10W(4) the account forfeiture notice (AFN) must set out the amount to be forfeited, the period for objecting to the forfeiture, and the address to which any objections must be sent. The period for objecting must be at least 30 days. An objection may be made by anyone, in writing. If no objection is received, at the end of the period the amount of money stated in the account forfeiture notice will be forfeited, and the bank or building society must transfer that money into the interest bearing account nominated by an enforcement officer. An objection does not prevent forfeiture of the money under Paragraph 10Z2. It is not necessary for an account forfeiture notice to be sought if the law enforcement agency decides instead to seek forfeiture of the money by order of a court under sub-paragraph 10Z2(2).

272 Paragraph 10X requires the Secretary of State to make regulations about how an AFN is to be given.

273 Paragraph 10Y sets out the conditions under which an AFN lapses. The AFN lapses if an objection is received; an application for forfeiture is made; or if the AFO is recalled or set aside. Under sub-paragraph 10Y(2), if the AFN lapses due to an objection being made, the relevant AFO will cease 48 hours after the objection. Sub-paragraph 10Y(3) provides that, if within the 48-hour period a senior officer applies to either extend the period of the AFO under Paragraph 10T or to seek forfeiture of the money under Paragraph 10Z2, the AFO will continue to have effect until the relevant time.

274 Paragraph 10Z sets out the procedure for applying for an administrative forfeiture to be set aside. The application must be made before the end of the objection period. It can be made after a longer period if the court is satisfied there are exceptional circumstances. The court must consider whether the money could be forfeited under paragraph 10Z2 (judicial forfeiture). If it is satisfied that the funds could not be forfeited under that paragraph, it must set aside the administrative forfeiture and order the release of that money.

275 Paragraph 10Z1 provides that any money forfeited under an account forfeiture notice must be paid into the Consolidated Fund.

276 Paragraph 10Z2 sets out the procedure for applying to a relevant court for the forfeiture of the money in a frozen account. If the court is satisfied that the money is intended to be used for the purposes of terrorism, consists of the resources of a proscribed organisation or is property earmarked as terrorist property, it may order forfeiture of those monies. Where a court orders forfeiture, the bank or building society with which the monies are held must transfer those funds to an interest bearing account nominated by the enforcement officer.

277 Paragraph 10Z3 provides that, where a court declines to order forfeiture and the law enforcement agency appeals that decision, it may also apply for an extension of the account freezing order pending the appeal.

278 Paragraph 10Z4 provides that any party aggrieved by a forfeiture order or the refusal [to] make such an order, can appeal that order or decision. The time period for the lodging of an appeal is 30 days from the day that the court makes the order or decision. If the appeal is upheld, the court may order the release of the whole or part of the funds. If a forfeiture order is successfully appealed, and the funds are returned to the individual, any interest which accrued during the time that the funds were held by the police shall also be returned to the individual.

279 Paragraph 10Z5 provides that, where an application for forfeiture is made on the basis that an organisation is proscribed and there is subsequently a successful appeal against a refusal to proscribe the organisation, an appeal against the forfeiture order may be brought within 30 days of the deproscription order coming into force.

280 Paragraph 10Z6 provides that any funds forfeited under an order should be paid into the Consolidated Fund.

281 Paragraph 10Z7 provides that if an AFO is made and none of that money is subsequently forfeited, the person by or for whom the account is operated may make an application to court for compensation. Paragraph 10Z7(3) provides that the court, if satisfied that the applicant has suffered loss and the circumstances are exceptional, may order compensation be paid to the applicant. The amount of compensation to be paid is the amount the court thinks reasonable, having regard to the loss suffered and any other relevant circumstances.

282 Paragraph 3 of Schedule 4 to the Criminal Finances Act amends paragraph 19 (general interpretation) of Schedule 1 to ATCSA to make consequential amendments which reflect the definitions used in new Part 4B of Schedule 1 to ATCSA.

Counter-terrorism financial investigators

Section 41: Extension of powers to financial investigators

283 Section 41 inserts into TACT new section 63F, which makes provision for counter-terrorism financial investigators.

284 Sub-section (1) provides that TACT is to be amended as set out in sub-sections (2) to (5).

285 Sub-section (2) inserts a new section 63F (Counter-terrorism financial investigators) into TACT. New section 63F(1) requires the metropolitan police force to provide a system for the accreditation of financial investigators, known as counter-terrorism financial investigators (CTFIs) Section 63F(2) provides that the system of accreditation must include provision for monitoring the performance of CTFIs and the withdrawal of accreditation, in specified circumstances. Sections 63F(3)–(7) provide that a person may be accredited as a CTFI if they are: a member of civilian staff of a police force in England and Wales, or a member of staff of the City of London police or the Police Service of Northern Ireland. A person may be accredited in relation to TACT or ATCSA, or in relation to particular provisions of either of those Acts. The accreditation may be limited to specified purposes. The metropolitan police force is required to make provision for training in financial investigation and the operation of TACT and ATCSA.

286 Sub-section (3) amends Part 1 of Schedule 5 to TACT to allow an appropriate officer (which term is defined in paragraph 5(6)) to apply under paragraph 5 to a Circuit Judge or District Judge for an order requiring a person to produce or to provide access to materials (consisting of or including excluded or special procedure material) in his possession. New sub-paragraph 5(1A) provides that a CTFI may only apply for such an order for the purposes of a terrorist investigation so far as relating to terrorist property. Part 1 of Schedule 5 is also amended to allow CTFIs to apply for an order under paragraph 13 (explanations) requiring any person specified in the order to provide an explanation of any material produced or made available to a counter-terrorism financial investigator under paragraph 5.

287 Sub-section (4) amends Schedule 6 to TACT (which makes provision for financial

information orders) to enable a CTFI to be named in the order and to require a financial institution to which the order applies to provide customer information for the purposes of a terrorist investigation.

288   Sub-section (5) amends Schedule 6A to TACT to enable a CTFI to apply for an account monitoring order for the purposes of a terrorist investigation. It also provides that, where an application for an account monitoring order is made by a CTFI, the description of information specified in that order may be varied by a different CTFI and an application to discharge or vary that order may be made by a different CTFI.

289   Sub-section (6) inserts new paragraph 10(7A) in Schedule 1 to ATCSA which makes provision for the payment of compensation where cash was seized by a CTFI.

Section 42: Offences in relation to counter-terrorism financial investigators

290   Section 42(1) inserts new section 120B into TACT which makes provision for the offences of assaulting, or resisting or wilfully obstructing a CTFI who is exercising a relevant power (the relevant powers are specified in sub-section 120B(5)).

291   Section 120B(3) provides that the offence of assaulting a CTFI carries a sentence on summary conviction in England and Wales of imprisonment for a term not exceeding 51 weeks or a fine, or both; and in Northern Ireland, imprisonment for a term not exceeding 6 months or a fine not exceeding level 5 on the standard scale, or both.

292   Section 120B(4) provides that the offence of resisting or wilfully obstructing a CTFI carries a sentence on summary conviction in England and Wales of imprisonment for a term not exceeding 51 weeks or a fine not exceeding level 3 on the standard scale, or both; and in Northern Ireland, imprisonment for a term not exceeding 1 month or a fine not exceeding level 3 on the standard scale, or both.

293   Section 120B(6) makes provision for a different maximum custodial penalty in England and Wales for such offences committed before the coming into force of section 281(5) of the Criminal Justice Act 2003.

294   Section 42(2) inserts a new Part 4C in Schedule 1 to ATCSA which makes provision for equivalent offences of assaulting or obstructing a CTFI who is exercising a power conferred on them under Schedule 1.

Enforcement in other parts of United Kingdom

Section 43: Cross-border enforcement of criminal orders

295   Section 43 amends TACT to insert a new section 120C which provides for an Order in Council to be made providing for the cross-border enforcement of certain investigatory orders (specified in new section 120C(2)) made under TACT. This allows relevant orders made in one part of the UK to be enforced in another part.

C3   DEVOLUTION

ANNEX C – TERRITORIAL EXTENT AND APPLICATION IN THE UNITED KINGDOM

Provision	Extends to E & W and applies to England?	Extends to E & W and applies to Wales?	Extends and applies to Scotland?	Extends and applies to Northern Ireland?
Part 1: Proceeds of crime – Chapter 1: Investigations				
Sections 1 to 3	Yes	Yes	No	Yes
Sections 4 to 6	No	No	Yes	No
Section 7	Yes	Yes	No	Yes
Section 8	No	No	Yes	No
Section 9	Yes	Yes	Yes	Yes
Part 1: Proceeds of crime – Chapter 2: Money laundering				
Sections 10 to 12	Yes	Yes	Yes	Yes
Part 1: Proceeds of crime – Chapter 3: Civil recovery				
Section 13	Yes	Yes	Yes	Yes
Section 14	Yes	Yes	Yes	Yes
Section 15	Yes	Yes	Yes	Yes
Section 16	Yes	Yes	Yes	Yes
Part 1: Proceeds of crime – Chapter 4: Enforcement powers and related offences				
Section 17	Yes	Yes	No	Yes
Section 18	Yes	Yes	Yes	Yes
Schedule 1	Yes	Yes	No	Yes
Section 19	Yes	Yes	Yes	Yes
Section 20	Yes	Yes	No	Yes
Section 21	Yes	Yes	Yes	Yes
Section 22	Yes	Yes	No	Yes
Section 23	Yes	Yes	No	Yes
Section 24	Yes	Yes	Yes	Yes
Section 25	Yes	Yes	Yes	Yes
Part 1: Proceeds of crime – Chapter 5: Miscellaneous				
Section 26	Yes	Yes	No	No
Section 27	No	No	No	Yes
Section 28	No	No	Yes	No
Section 29	No	No	Yes	No
Section 30	No	No	Yes	No

Provision	Extends to E & W and applies to England?	Extends to E & W and applies to Wales?	Extends and applies to Scotland?	Extends and applies to Northern Ireland?
Section 31	Yes	Yes	No	In part
Section 32	Yes	Yes	Yes	Yes
Section 33	Yes	Yes	Yes	Yes
Section 34	Yes	Yes	In part	In part
Part 2: Terrorist property				
Sections 35 to 42 and Schedule 2	Yes	Yes	Yes	Yes
Schedules 3&4	Yes	Yes	Yes	Yes
Section 43	Yes	Yes	Yes	Yes
Part 3: Corporate offences of failure to prevent facilitation of tax evasion				
Sections 44 to 50	Yes	Yes	Yes	Yes
Sections 51 to 52	Yes	Yes	In part	In part
Part 4: General				
Sections 53–59 and Schedule 5	Yes	Yes	In part	In part

Appendix D
FURTHER READING

UK government publications

- **The Action Plan for anti-money laundering and counter-terrorist finance 2016**: www.gov.uk/government/uploads/system/uploads/attachment_data/file/517992/6-2118-Action_Plan_for_Anti-Money_Laundering__web_.pdf
- **Anti-money laundering guidance for money service businesses**: www.gov.uk/government/publications/anti-money-laundering-guidance-for-money-service-businesses
- **Bribery Act 2010 guidance**: www.gov.uk/government/publications/bribery-act-2010-guidance
- **Money laundering regulations**: www.gov.uk/topic/business-tax/money-laundering-regulations
- **Money laundering supervision for estate agency businesses**: www.gov.uk/guidance/registration-guide-for-estate-agency-businesses
- **The Serious and Organised Crime Strategy 2013**: www.gov.uk/government/uploads/system/uploads/attachment_data/file/248645/Serious_and_Organised_Crime_Strategy.pdf
- **Tackling tax evasion: Government guidance for the corporate offence of failure to prevent the criminal facilitation of tax evasion 2016**: www.gov.uk/government/uploads/system/uploads/attachment_data/file/560120/Tackling_tax_evasion_-_Draft_government_guidance_for_the_corporate_offence_of_failure_to_prevent_the_criminal_facilitation_of_tax_evasion.pdf
- **UK national risk assessment of money laundering and terrorist financing 2015**: www.gov.uk/government/uploads/system/uploads/attachment_data/file/ 468210/UK_NRA_October_2015_final_web.pdf

Other publications and useful websites

- **Bespoke Compliance** (author's blog on CFA 2017)

  www.bespokecompliance.co.uk

- **EU**

  EU Directive 2015/849: eur-lex.europa.eu/legal-content/EN/TXT/?uri=celex%3A32015L0849

- **The Financial Conduct Authority (FCA)**

  A firm's guide to preventing financial crime: www.handbook.fca.org.uk/handbook/document/FC1_FCA_20150427.pdf

- **Joint Money Steering Group (JMLSG)**

  General guidance: www.jmlsg.org.uk/industry-guidance/article/jmlsg-guidance-current

- **OECD**

  OECD tax guidance and forum: www.oecd.org/tax/transparency

- **Sentencing Council**

  Fraud, bribery and money laundering offences – definitive guideline: www.sentencingcouncil.org.uk/wp-content/uploads/Fraud_bribery_and_money_laundering_offences_-_Definitive_guideline.pdf

INDEX